A Wood Called
BOURLON

A Wood Called
BOURLON

THE COVER-UP AFTER CAMBRAI 1917

WILLIAM MOORE

Pen & Sword
MILITARY

First published in 1988 by Leo Cooper Ltd

Published in this format in 2014 by
PEN & SWORD MILITARY
An imprint of
Pen & Sword Books Ltd
47 Church Street
Barnsley, South Yorkshire
S70 2AS

ISBN 978 1 47382 126 2

Printed and bound in England
By CPI Group (UK) Ltd, Croydon, CR0 4YY

Pen & Sword Books Ltd incorporates the Imprints of Aviation, Atlas,
Family History, Fiction, Maritime, Military, Discovery, Politics, History,
Archaeology, Select, Wharncliffe Local History, Wharncliffe True Crime,
Military Classics, Wharncliffe Transport, Leo Cooper, The Praetorian Press,
Remember When, Seaforth Publishing and Frontline Publishing

For a complete list of Pen & Sword titles please contact
PEN & SWORD BOOKS LIMITED
47 Church Street, Barnsley, South Yorkshire, S70 2AS, England
E-mail: enquiries@pen-and-sword.co.uk
Website: www.pen-and-sword.co.uk

Dedicated to the children
of Bourlon

Contents

Introduction

It is rare to come across a man who actually owns a Great War battlefield. The blasted villages and splintered woods associated with names on campaign maps do not seem to warrant title deeds. To me it seemed strange that the same family was in possession of Bourlon Wood after hundreds of years.

I had gone to the Ferme de l'Abbaye while researching another story about the Resistance and did not expect to see a military cemetery at the bottom of the garden. Beyond it lay the Bois, green and shady on a warm summer's morning.

'Canadians,' said the Comte de Francqueville. 'From 1918. A lot of English are buried at Anneux Chapel on the main road, but only a few from the 1917 affair. There were so many corpses then the Germans burnt them. Or so it is said.'

Before the Great War only the guests of the de Francquevilles went shooting in the wood. They used the fine hunting lodge as their headquarters. In 1914 and afterwards for a time the only guns and dogs to be seen were those of German officers off duty. It remained a pleasant retreat behind the lines until 1917 when the war drew closer. Abruptly in November of that year, the Bois was swept from obscurity by a torrent of flame and thunder. After the first great tank attack surged past to reach the gates of Cambrai victory bells were rung in Britain. Mention the battle today and automatically it conjures up visions of primitive armoured monsters lurching over barbed wire and trenches 'to the green fields beyond'. The infantry have been forgotten over the years, yet whole divisions gave their all in attempts to secure the Bourlon massif which dominated the entire sector.

When it had to be given up because the Germans scored a victory at the other end of the Cambrai battlefield, the government wanted to know the facts.

Politicians and generals are naturally suspicious of one another – both invariably think they know best. Government ministers are apt to believe that only they are in touch with the pulse of 'the people'; senior officers incline to the view that every decision concerning the armed forces is made, not on its merits, but with an eye to winning votes. The 'Ruddy Civilians' syndrome is alive and well and flourishing in service messes today, just as the 'Typical Brasshats' line may be heard in political clubs. At the beginning of the Great War and for some time afterwards the High Command was in the ascendant. Sir William Robertson, who had risen from the ranks to become Chief of the Imperial General Staff, the government's senior military adviser, was wont to cut short arguments with 'Well, I've 'eard different'. That wouldn't do after thousands of British troops and more than 100 guns had been captured south of Cambrai. The Staff at the War Office and in France, had to fight an unparalleled rearguard action.

Curiously, when a third party came in search of the truth behind the biggest reverse suffered by Britain on the Western Front since April 1915, government and generals, united against the House of Commons. 'What's it got to do with you?' was the attitude. MPs were not even told on whose authority the victory bells had been rung. Indeed there has never been an official explanation. When I went in search of one I unearthed some fascinating cameos – half-truths in official telegrams . . . a clash between Old Etonian generals . . . fork-tongued utterances at Westminster. And always the trail led back to Bourlon.

Without the aid of Pierre de Francqueville this book would not have been written. Generous with his time, he was not only enthusiastic but highly constructive. No one else could have gleaned so much from the village worthies; no one has such deep knowledge of the Bois. To a warm welcome in her home, Nicole de Francqueville, added encouragement and sought out ancient photographs. At La Folie, just a couple of miles from Bourlon, I had the honour to meet someone who had known the great Bois in 1914 – Pierre's mother, Comtesse Bernard, now in her nineties but with her memory unimpaired. Comte Guy, another of her sons, gave me the benefit of an old soldier's eye for the ground.

There is a heart-warming fund of good will for the British in France. Dr Pierre Briffaut, doyen of Cambrésian historians, went out of his way to be helpful, as did Monsieur Leman, regional Director of Antiquities. In the modest village of Graincourt, Monsieur Mario Cargnelli, the mayor's secretary, did not hesitate to enlighten me on the subject of the catacombs under the church which both sides used during the Great War. Monsieur Jean-Luc Gibot, of Gouzeaucourt, proved to be an expert on the subject. My wife and I were made most welcome at Cambrai's reference library.

In Britain I owe a special debt to Colonel de Burgh of the Badley Library, Royal School of Artillery, and his assistant, Mrs Zana Hunt. I look forward to the day when Colonel 'Paddy', a D-Day and Arnhem veteran, publishes his memoirs.

Once more I enjoyed the excellent modern facilities at the Public Record Office, Kew, and the advice of its research staff. The Reading Room at the Imperial War Museum was fruitful as ever and David Nash unearthed some important material by patient delving. Valuable contributions were also made by my brother-in-law Philip Moyes, the aviation historian, and my old friend Major Tim Thomas, of the Queen's Own Hussars.

Others whom I must thank include Lieutenant-Colonel Sir Julian Paget Bt, of the *Guards Magazine*, and Lieutenant-Colonel Sir John Johnston, another Guardsman, who kindly gave me permission to use a facsimile of a letter written by Earl Alexander (then a lieutenant-colonel himself), following the Bourlon battle; Major D. I. A. Mack, RHQ the Royal Highland Fusiliers; Lieutenant Colonel Neil McIntosh, the Green Howards; Lieutenant Colonel Richard Sinnett, Royal Welch Fusiliers; the staff of Leeds Public Library reference department; David Fletcher of the Tank Museum, Bovington; Alex Masterman, re the Royal Guernsey Light Infantry; Douglas Pratt, PRO of Eldridge, Pope, the Dorchester brewers, and Terry Champion and Paul Haley of *Soldier* magazine who gave me sound advice and assistance on photographic matters.

Through the good offices of the Venerable F. W. Harvey, Archdeacon of London, I contacted Mr C. A. Wratten, Secretary of the Central Council of Church Bellringers, who supplied essential evidence on the matter of the victory peals in 1917.

One final word of thanks – to my wife, for her enthusiasm and suggestions during the search for material and for typing and preparing the manuscript.

Alderholt, Dorset

CHAPTER ONE
Malbrouk s'en va . . .

Officers near the General watched him closely, switching their gaze to the ridge and back again. He was studying it intensely. Ugly memories came crowding back to survivors of previous Flanders battles. If ordered to attack there could be no holding back, but it would be a bloody business.

The General seemed unaware of his audience. His practised eye took in the slope rising gradually to the sun-dappled oaks under which there was much surreptitious movement. He studied the thatched cottages on the flanks, the freshly-turned earth around the batteries. To his left lay the city with its magazines, munitions and hospitals; the enemy would want for nothing.

'Gentlemen!'

The telescope was tapped into its case, reins were gathered, spurs applied and the cavalcade jogged and squelched over fields still soft after the rain. Orders put life into the waiting columns. Fifes and drums struck up 'The Grenadiers' March' and the redcoats turned their backs on the great Bois de Bourlon. If Monsieur de Villars had hoped they might risk an assault he was disappointed. There would be no battle of Cambrai that summer. 'Malbrouk' went off to besiege the fortress of Bouchain, seven miles away, leaving the enemy to make of it what they would.

Marshal de Villars was too good a soldier to have counted on a rash onslaught. He must have known the Allies[1] would hesitate to spend lives as freely as at Malplaquet two years earlier. Marlborough himself had called the climax to the 1709 campaign a 'very bloody battle'[2] and Villars had written to his sovereign: 'If it please God to give your Majesty's enemies another such victory they are ruined.'

The Dutch infantry, in particular, had suffered appalling casualties on the approaches to the Bois de la Lanière. Cannon balls from flanking guns had ripped through whole ranks of the redoubtable Blue Guards, whose bodies choked the ditches. Holland after Malplaquet was like Scotland after Flodden. The Dutch apart, the Allies had recovered from the shock of their 'victory', and, by exchanging shattered battalions with the garrisons of the Flanders fortresses, placed an army of 90,000 men in the field. By the time it reached Cambrai it had already stolen a march on Villars.

To repel any attempt to invade France a line of earthworks had been thrown up from the Channel to the Ardennes. From west to east it was covered by the Canche, the little Gy stream, the Scarpe and the Sensée and ran via the fortresses of Montreuil, Hesdin and Arras to Maubeuge on the Sambre. Not permanently occupied, the trenches could be manned whenever a threat arose, such as when Marlborough appeared west of Arras and set his dragoons cutting acres of hazel and willow to make fascines to fill the double ditch protecting the lines. The French made ready but overnight he had slipped away to the east and, unopposed, crossed the Sensée and the earthworks at Arleux. Marlborough's tailor had used the words Ne Plus Ultra to describe the magnificent new scarlet campaign coat he had made.[3] Villars had mockingly used the same phrase to describe the entrenchments – but the joke had rebounded. The forced labour of thousands of peasants, the flooding of grazing land on likely approaches, the building of dams and bastions had been brought to nought. By the time Villars caught up with 'Old Corporal John' (Marlborough was then 61) the Allies were moving on Cambrai. No sooner had he barred their route at Bourlon than they were off again, bound for the Scheldt.

The Marshal gave his orders. Drums rolled. The regiments of Picardy, Navarre, Rousillon formed ranks and, colours flying, led the army from the ridge after their tormentors. Through the great wood they went, past the ancient wayside cross on the road to Fontaine Notre Dame, while the artillery was dragged down to the Roman highway linking Bapaume and Cambrai, the iron tyres of the unsprung waggons grinding the rutted surface. Marshal de Villars[4] had spent more than 40 of his 58 years making war and had seen it all before, but he mounted his horse with the optimism of a born Gascon. After all, at Malplaquet he had nearly lost a leg.

Peeping from the windows of the red brick château below the hill, the ladies shed a tear or two as their martial visitors took their leave. The uniforms were so splendid, the young men so handsome. Village girls, more wary of the soldiery, kept a discreet distance as the brave show passed. Not until the last camp follower vanished did the ploughboys and cowherds come out of hiding. Not everyone wants to go for a soldier.

Only the echoes of cannon roused the roe deer in the deep glades of Bourlon that summer. Old men hearing the distant rumble recalled events thirty-four years earlier when the King had besieged Cambrai. The Sun King had come in person to attach the city to France for good and all. There had been a surfeit of cannon fire then around the walls. Young folk did not know how lucky they were. A pitched battle on the line occupied by *Monsieur le Maréchal* and Bourlon village would have gone up in flames. As for the wood, well, a musket ball cannot do much harm to an oak but the sawyers would have had trouble with metal fragments for years afterwards.

Bourlon Wood covers 600 acres, a fragment of the great forest which in Roman days flourished between the Scheldt, the Somme and the North Sea. Its survival as a natural feature is probably due to its rugged contours. Drive past it today and it looks kempt and regular. Aerial photographs give away no secrets. In fact there is nothing consistent about the interior. The ground tilts like a misshapen soup plate towards the route nationale and is seamed with deep gullies, studded with outcrops and patches of marsh. Early inhabitants of the area found the Artois plain much more attractive and it abounds with Gallo-Roman remains. They shunned the gloomy groves tumbling over the broken edge of the plateau; spoke fearfully of the mysterious stream which flows from a spring in the centre of the Bois and scurries down a ravine until it disappears in a jumble of rocks to take some subterranean path to the distant river. They wondered what manner of thing it was that, after heavy rain, uttered hoarse, enraged bellows from a crevice in the rocks.[5] The unknown lurked in the twilight under the dripping leaves and the ancients kept away. Mediaeval citizens made haste between the wayside calvaries.

Some four miles from the eastern edge of the trees as they stand today lies Cambrai, its famous Beffroi and the clochers of St Géry and Notre Dame cathedral readily identifiable. The slopes of Bourlon have provided a grandstand view of history on the march. From them watchers saw Roman Cameracum give way to the halls

3

of a Frankish king; Charlemagne building a stronghold on the banks of the Scheldt; the Normans sacking the city in the 10th century.

Afterwards power passed into the hands of bishops as haughty as any secular prince. Cambrai prospered and the communities in Cambrésis with it. Villages took root, among them Bourlon, in the north-western lee of the wood, and Fontaine Notre Dame on the other side at the gates of Cambrai. In the Middle Ages the track joining them became the subject of a road improvement scheme. The contractors were sound engineers and tons of rubble were pounded into the foundations. Depressions and gullies were crossed by causeways with embankments 20 feet high in places. Deep ditches were dug to drain off the heavy winter rains.

It might be a stiff two-mile climb from Fontaine to Bourlon château but it could be done by a horse and cart. Pack mules, the usual mode of transport in rural areas, were not essential.

At the end of the 17th century the castle belonged to one Jean de Barbaize and it was from him that Jean-Baptiste de Francqueville bought it. The Francquevilles were prosperous *magistrats* – law officers and government officials – who served in the old provincial *parlement* of Flanders. They originated in Douai, only sixteen miles from Bourlon, and, though traditionally functionaries, there was an artistic streak in the family. The works of classical sculptor Pierre de Francqueville, friend of Henry IV, may be seen today in Florence, in Windsor Great Park and at Kew.

By the time Jean-Baptiste bought the lordship of Bourlon the city of Cambrai and its environs had become definitively part of France. Until it capitulated to Louis XIV in 1677 it had endured an uneasy independence as a 'neutral' city of the Holy Roman Empire, its protection allegedly assured by treaties between the German princes to the north and east and the French to the south.

It had also been part of the Spanish Netherlands – hence the timbered Maison Espagnole which houses the modern tourist office – and a French protectorate under Henry IV.

Whatever its fortunes Cambrai and its environs remained staunchly Catholic. Among many religious houses was an abbey on the edge of Bourlon Wood. Tucked away behind the oaks and elms, the village went comparatively unscathed during the wars. Timber from the Bois went to build men o' war for the King's navy.

Then as now the villages of Cambrésis were much of a

muchness, sited a few miles apart generally in folds in the gently rolling landscape. Streets tended to be wide with houses detached or in small groups with sizeable gardens. Farms with high walls opened onto the thoroughfares. Old buildings were made of the soft dull white stone called marne which the Spaniards found so useful. Nearly every commune had its château, some quite elegant, like the red brick mansion built by the Cardevaques of Havrincourt in 1693. At the heart of the villages stood the churches – considerably larger than their average counterparts in England – often placed below a spur so their spires resembled the hats of so many witches peeping over the landscape.

Came 1789 and in Cambrai the Revolutionary Tribunal moved into the College of Jesuits. Soon bands of *sans culottes* were heading for the châteaux, but at Bourlon the birds had flown. The *parlement* of Flanders had done frequent business with the *parlement* of Artois. The Comte de Francqueville had become friendly with a celebrated Arras lawyer, Maximilien Robespierre, and it is believed that it was he who sent a warning.[6] The Francquevilles survived The Terror. Bourlon oak went to build ships for Napoleon.

During the Franco-Prussian War battles were fought near Cambrai – at Bapaume, St Quentin and Le Cateau. In late January, 1871, the Prussians were at Caudry on the Le Cateau–Cambrai road, at Rumilly just south of the city and at Marcoing on the other side of the river. French troops[7] were being evacuated by train to the fortresses of Lille, Douai and Valenciennes when news arrived of an armistice. On 29 January the campaign in Northern France was over.

Had Jean-Baptiste returned from the grave towards the end of the last century he would have had difficulty in recognizing the old white stone castle he had bought. It was almost hidden by two massive new wings, a testimony to affluence rather than taste. The house was furnished with fine pieces, the grounds boasted modern stables and outhouses. An avenue of beeches ran for half a mile from the gates to a spur where huge limes, planted before Napoleon's day, made a majestic entrance to the wood. Deep in the heart of the forest was a chalet used by shooting parties.

If some thought the modernized château ugly, it did not appear so in the eyes of Ludovic de Francqueville. To him everything about Bourlon was beautiful; his home, *his* village and *le Bois*. Born the year after Waterloo, Ludovic devoted himself to managing his property and looking after the interests of the Bourloniens. He was a diminutive man, generous and autocratic. 'Who is the swine who did not vote for me?' he bellowed at a public meeting on the one occasion when he was not unanimously re-elected Mayor of the Commune.

If he had any other passion it was horses and he travelled to Ireland frequently to buy bloodstock, never failing to be astonished that no one there spoke French. He was an accomplished coachman and daily drove up the avenue to the wood where all the private roads were maintained to a standard equalling the old public highway to Fontaine. The ladies of Bourlon Château could be sure of a smooth journey when they made a favourite excursion to the 'Carrefour Madame', the junction in the middle of the forest.

Occasionally the Francqueville carriages crossed the route nationale to enter the red brick gothic gateway to another wood, as level as Bourlon was rugged. A few minutes' trot brought them to the gravelled forecourt of La Folie, a charming creeper-covered house, the home of Ludovic's bachelor brother Emil. The façade of the building looked across a meadow to a lake fished by grey-blue herons. The aspect was delightful, the mosquitoes voracious. They were a constant source of irritation to Ludovic's son, Roger-Alexandre, who inherited the La Folie estate. In 1908, on his father's death, Comte Roger became Lord of Bourlon as well.

In the years before 1914 Cambrai lost its old fortifications, retaining only the massive citadel; ramparts were levelled and ditches filled to make boulevards. The town had more than 20,000 inhabitants and a goods station as well as a passenger terminal testified to its expansion. Weaving fine cloth was still a basic industry but there were soap works, bleachers and dyers, sausage manufacturers and confectioners. As for sugar beet factories, the countryside was studded with them. Most important for a town 70 miles from the North Sea were the docks. A canal which linked the Scheldt with the Somme at St Quentin skirted Cambrai's south-western boundary. It was a major commercial waterway, some sixty feet wide and holding about seven feet of water.

In 1907 a complementary canal was begun north of Cambrai at Arleux, where Marlborough had crossed the Ne Plus Ultra lines not quite 200 years earlier. Intended to link the Sensée in Flanders with the Oise at Noyon, it came within five miles of the St Quentin Canal. Designed to take 300-ton barges, the Canal du Nord was to have a surface width of 120 feet and contain about eight feet of water. Its length – 58 miles. By 1914 most of the digging had been done and monstrous chalky spoil heaps rose at intervals along the sides. One of them stood only a mile from Havrincourt where the cutting, through a spur, was 90 feet deep.

Lock houses had been built, machinery installed and the bed and walls of the canal lined with brick up to a level of six feet or so; but it was still dry in the summer of 1914.

People travelled miles to marvel at this fine piece of engineering, witness to a thriving economy, augury of good times ahead. Confidence abounded. Had not Bleriot, a Cambrésian, been the first aeronaut to conquer the Channel?

In contrast to his father, Roger was a man of the city. He was tall and slim where Ludovic had been diminutive; imposing and aloof where his father had been at ease with people; and he was sternly religious. Having served briefly as a regular officer, he left the army to run his estates and succeeded his father as Mayor of Bourlon.

The commune's 2,000 inhabitants either worked on the land, in service, or in a tile factory on the northern edge of the wood. There were four shoeing smiths – and a brewery. About twenty people were permanently employed at the château and others worked at the 'Château Black', a fine house on the edge of the wood owned by a family of English origin.

A single-line railway from Cambrai ran via Fontaine over the ridge to Bourlon station just outside the village and then north to Marquion. It did good business.

By all accounts Bourlon was a busy, cheerful place where 'Monsieur Bernard', Comte Roger's son, was more popular than his father. The people set to with a will to decorate the village when he brought back his bride in 1914. Twenty-year-old Anne de la Forest d'Armaille, from the Niévre, was just beginning to find her way around when war was declared.[8]

French planners envisaged a short, sharp clash between great armies. Almost all able-bodied men were immediately mobilized. Bernard de Francqueville, then 34, was among the first to go – and one of the first to return. Wounded in the shoulder in Belgium, he

7

had taken one look at the primitive arrangements for evacuating casualties, made his way to the nearest railway station and bought a ticket home. It was only 10 August. Comte Bernard had no doubts about the likelihood of the enemy reaching Cambrai and insisted on taking his wife to her family south of Paris. They left by car with two suitcases. Out of a sense of duty Comte Roger, then 62, remained behind with his wife and his brother-in-law, the Abbé de Mun. A great deal had happened in a very short time.

Men of the 1st Infantry,[9] senior regiment of France, left their barracks in Cambrai on 5 August and crammed into railway coaches on which someone had chalked '*Train de plaisir pour Berlin*'. Reservists began to arrive from Verdun to join the 162nd Regiment. In the middle of the month watchers counted fifteen train-loads of British troops steaming slowly through the town and at least some soldiers of the Royal Sussex Regiment made a gift of their brass shoulder plates to admirers. Troopers in khaki were at the cavalry barracks by the 16th.

'They have a fine appearance with their flat caps, their puttees, gleaming buttons and their spotless uniforms,' wrote an onlooker. 'They don't speak our language but their gestures are most expressive. Passing their hands across their necks, they indicate they are going to cut the enemy's throats and the crowd cheers.'

Shabby French reservists, promenading off duty with wives and children clinging to their arms, made a poor showing by comparison.

Gradually a more serious mood replaced the festival atmosphere. Europe was waking from a peace that had lasted 40 years and the city fathers were not prepared to deal with the sudden upheaval: a handbell was rung from an open window of the Town Hall when they had important news to announce.

On 23 August the rumble of cannon could be heard and the next day drew nearer. The British had fought at Mons. Refugees appeared. On the 25th the military hospital was evacuated and the trains ceased to run. More wounded straggled in and the colleges of Notre Dame and Fénelon were turned into casualty clearing stations. As in the darkest period of the Franco-Prussian War the statue of Our Lady was carried in through the streets, the clergy, led by Archbishop Chollet, chanting the litanies of saints, and the crowds repeating the last phrases. As Cambrai was no longer a fortress the garrison left the citadel but, having locked the ponderous double gates, could find no one willing to hold the keys.

Old men recalled summary executions carried out in 1870 after *francs-tireurs* ambushed Prussian troops. The mayor issued a notice calling in all firearms – suitably labelled so they could be reclaimed if the enemy did not arrive.

On the 26th the first Germans entered Cambrai – a wounded officer brought in on a cart with his orderly. The crowd were keen to lynch them but a wary councillor pointed out that, like French soldiers, they had only been doing their duty. Rifle fire could be heard in the suburbs.

Abbé Emile Delval,[10] a teacher at Notre Dame College, who wore a Red Cross armband in his new role as a nursing assistant, found his first task was to persuade a retired schoolmistress that this was no time to go shopping: she had been pulling on her gloves as she left her home with basket and parasol.

A regiment of Territorials from Mayenne and the Sarthe opposed the enemy outside Cambrai and brief, fierce clashes occurred as detachments fell back through the streets. The Germans had to use a field-gun to subdue one strongpoint. When the fighting died down the town council waved white handkerchiefs from the windows of the Hotel de Ville. From their vantage point they watched enemy troops looting tobacconists, which the Germans seemed to regard as fair game. Other shops were spared, with the exception of the grandly-named 'France Lumière' which was robbed of all its flash lamps.

During the afternoon the mayor decamped and at 7.30 his colleagues were sitting in the dimly-lit council chamber when the door flew open and a German officer entered, flanked by armed soldiers. Cambrai received its first order from the new masters: 'Turn up the lights!'

In the days following, artillery continued to groan and the flow of wounded increased, many of them in khaki. A farmer reported a furious battle at Caudry, five miles from Cambrai, where he had seen hundreds of British and German dead, marking the stand of General Smith-Dorrien's British II Corps at Le Cateau on 26 August.

Whatever their nationality, all bodies brought in had been robbed, Abbé Delval noted. He also recorded that the number of deaths in the make-shift hospitals was becoming an embarrassment. Coffins were reserved for officers only. Men were wrapped in groundsheets or blankets, the French being buried on one side of the graveyard, Germans on the other. Beyond the cemetery walls tramped a succession of weary, dusty German columns.

A German officer riding at the head of an infantry company pulled up in the street one morning and politely asked Abbé Delval the road to Fontaine. Instinctively he pointed the way, realizing with surprise that 'It was the first time I had voluntarily helped the enemy'. The officer saluted and led his men up the straight road past Bourlon Wood.

CHAPTER TWO

Secret Tumbrils

For 19-year-old Léonce Carrez, who had been excused military service on health grounds, war came to Bourlon the day retreating Territorials began to limp down the route nationale from Cambrai.[1]

The Carrez family worked fields running down to the main road and a weary French officer requisitioned a horse and cart with Léonce's father as driver. It was needed to carry the equipment of exhausted troops and Léonce saw the pile of haversacks grow higher as it passed into the distance. There was no knowing whether he would ever see his father again and that evening the Curé called to offer comfort to the family.

Next day their alarm increased: they watched helmets and lance pennants bobbing in file above the stack yard's high wall. Uhlans! Monsieur Carrez, however, returned unscathed with his cart and resumed muck-spreading duties. As Léonce wielded his fork he saw column after column of Germans emerge from Fontaine and tramp along the RN 29 towards Bapaume. Dragoons and uhlans patrolled their flanks. For a time they were billeted on the farms, helping themselves to anything they needed. When they moved on *'nach Paris'*, other troops, service units and administrative officers took their place. They looked set for a long stay. On 11 October all males aged between 16 and 20 were ordered to assemble in the square at Bourlon. Léonce went into hiding.

The young men were told they must spend a few days collecting the dead around Bapaume. Weeks passed before they were heard of again – in Germany, engaged in war work. Soon a monthly roll call was instituted and the Bourloniens had to report to the neighbouring village of Sains-les-Marquion where the fathers of 'refractaires' like Léonce shouted, 'Gone away before the war' when their names were called.

There was a grain of truth in what Monsieur Carrez said. Léonce had spent three years at Berthonval agricultural college. If Carrez père felt uncomfortable it was because the assembly was always attended by the interpreter from the newly-established Kommandantur, Reserve Lieutenant Mayer. Mayer, in civilian life a veterinary surgeon in Hamburg, was billeted at the Carrez farm.

The wildest rumours flew about Cambrai in the first weeks of the war, one of the most persistent being that an army of Japanese had disembarked at Toulon to aid France. Abbé Delval was tired of hearing it.

Yes, he believed the Germans had looted the personal effects of the 162nd Regiment, left for safe-keeping at Madame Gillet's school in the Rue Vaucelette. He had spoken to eye-witnesses.

Yes, he accepted the invaders had destroyed Bonavis farm as a reprisal, though he doubted whether a French patrol had fired on a convoy there.

No, he did not believe they had threatened to burn Bourlon Wood and that Monsieur de Francqueville had bought them off for two million francs. Apart from the great difficulty of destroying a veritable forest one had to appreciate the character of Monsieur de Francqueville.

The German officers occupying part of Bourlon château had no doubts of their 'hosts'' attitude: they were treated with cold disdain.

Outward signs of occupation spread. By the end of September a rash of notices threatened the death penalty for anyone firing on German forces and the destruction of the house from which a shot came. Thousands of spades and all stocks of horseshoes were commandeered. Telephones were requisitioned, bicycles had to be surrendered. The council ran out of funds to pay its employees.

Allied planes made their first raid and hit a military fuel dump, killing twenty Germans; but some bombs fell wide and there were three civilian casualties. People were shocked to think they could die at the hands of their own side.

Most wounded of the early battles having been evacuated, Cambrai's schools re-opened for classes. At 10.30 on 19 December the city bells, silenced by order of the Germans, began to peal. Abbé Delval: 'Everyone lifted his head; no doubt about it, it was the sound of our bells. My pupils thought the French had arrived and the little ones began to cheer with all their might.'

People hurried into the streets and found German soldier shouting: *'Hoch!'* The military governor had ordered the bells to be rung to celebrate a great victory on the Eastern Front. 'They were rung in Berlin today,' he explained. Many of Delval's pupils burst into tears when the truth was known.

The same day orders were issued restricting the sowing of beet – according to rumour because it competed with German production – and directing farmers to grow cereals and potatoes instead. A census of horses, carts and carriages was called for and the owners were ordered to assemble in specified squares and streets in the city on 28 December. Details were recorded and the Germans helped themselves to the best animals and vehicles.

Spy mania obsessed the enemy. Notre Dame College officials had trouble explaining away a wireless aerial left over from an experimental apparatus they no longer possessed. When the suggestion was made that the Comte de Francqueville had a set – probably a disgruntled villager wanting to settle an old score – the château was searched from top to bottom. Nothing was found but on 13 February Monsieur was accused of spying and driven off to solitary confinement in Valenciennes. Madame de Francqueville and her brother had to leave the château.

More arrests followed, Abbé Blas of Fontaine for warning his parishioners from the pulpit not to let their names go on the Germans' interminable lists; the Curé of Anneux as an accomplice of Comte Roger. Unable to explain away a bicycle and an ancient pistol without any ammunition, he was thrown into the citadel. The Curé of Cantaing was another victim.

Abbé Delval heard that the Germans had dug a trench around Bourlon château in their search for a cable – somewhat illogically if it was a wireless they were seeking. They had taken over the whole place as a headquarters.

It was not the best of times for the Francquevilles. Bernard had returned to the front and, about the time his father was arrested, was wounded again, this time in the thigh.

Reserve Lieutenant Mayer, who remained at the Carrez farm, tightened his grip on the *seigneurie* of Bourlon and missed little. Léonce Carrez was the first *réfractaire* to be caught, after sneaking into the main farmhouse from his usual hiding place in a loft. German soldiers arrived and went straight upstairs to the room where he was sitting. Local gendarmes picked up another offender soon afterwards. For failing to register with the Germans Elysée Delsaux was gaoled for a month by a civilian court in Cambrai, but Léonce was marched before a board of officers at the château. Caught by 'front line' soldiers, he was considered subject to military law and awarded three months' 'cells' in Germany, which meant solitary confinement. With a sergeant on one side, a soldier on the other, he went by carriage up the great beech avenue and through the wood to Cambrai. That night he was on a train to the Fatherland.

Léonce's three months lasted more than a year. Having served the gaol sentence in a civilian prison in Bonn, he was transferred to an internment camp at Holzminden, near Hanover, where thousands of foreigners and prisoners-of-war were held. Today his description of an ill-fitting maroon uniform with a yellow stripe down the trouser legs and a brassard displaying 'F' for French has a sickening and familiar ring. Léonce was finally repatriated after pleading ill-health to visiting doctors. One of these, opening the young man's mouth by gripping his nose and chin as if he were a horse, declared, 'You have good teeth – you can work'. But a Swiss in the party overruled him. By the summer of 1916 Léonce was back in Bourlon weighing little more than six stone. A few days later he was given an identity card at the Kommandantur and told he would be found something useful to do. Jobs were allotted by Herr Mayer, still resident at the Carrez farm. In the local patois he told Léonce philosophically

'C'est la guerre pour mi,
C'est la guerre pour ti,
C'est la guerre pour tous les gins.'

Mayer was right. The war spared no one. Even Cambrai's notables turned up at Holzminden, hostages for the town's failure to pay fines levied for non-co-operation. With the death penalty hanging over them, Monsieur Olivier, manufacturer of the famous *'bêtises'* (local bonbons) and Monsieur Gaudechot[2] of the ceramics firm were not required to wear uniform and ate superior rations. Léonce had been happy to receive rotten potatoes they threw out.

Gates which closed behind some opened for others, among them

Comte Roger, who had also been held as a hostage. Through the Red Cross he returned to France via Switzerland and joined his wife at their Paris home. Because of her poor health she had been allowed to travel south, also via Switzerland, soon after his detention.

Monsieur learned that his son had recovered from his second wound and was serving on the staff of the 72nd Division at Verdun.

The harvest at Bourlon had been normal in 1914, mediocre in 1915 and, due to the shortage of draught horses to work the land, poor in 1916. Women reaped the fields under German surveillance. They made secret pockets in their skirts and filled them whenever their soldier supervisors were distracted. This was achieved by arrangement with the engineer of the steam locomotive powering the threshing machine who occasionally let in the clutch too quickly and unseated the drive belt.

Contraband corn was ground in coffee mills. The women stole good German sacks to make clothes and once even went on strike. Mayer responded by locking them up in a barn for a night.

Life became harder. The official ration was inadequate and villagers lived off their vegetable gardens and raised rabbits.

The new occupants of the château were a puzzle to the local people, though no one doubted their importance: the German Crown Prince had once paid a visit. Twenty-four-year old Germaine Laude, her sister Pauline, and a dozen local girls could vouch for that.[3] They had to report daily for cleaning duties and some had actually seen the Kaiser's heir.

Germaine had no reason to like Germans. Her husband, mobilized in August, 1914, had been taken prisoner at Verdun. Her brother, Henri Coguillon, 17, had been one of the youngsters who reported to the square on 11 October. He was also in Germany . . . they believed. There was no means of corresponding, only rare news through the *mairie*.

Germaine watched the Germans systematically clear the château of furniture. When she asked why they were rolling up two fine Gobelin tapestries they replied, 'Removing them for safety'.

As the year wore on forced labour *'kommandos'* were set to work on defences well behind the front line. Whole pine woods were cut down for dug-out props, though Bourlon's oaks and elms were spared.

Prodigious amounts of concrete reinforced with old railway lines went into the blockhouses which dotted the fields on the Flesquières spur on the other side of the Bapaume road. Five squat monstrosities, stout enough to withstand hits from the biggest shells, were built in La Folie wood which hid a munitions dump. A bunker with three-feet-thick walls was set into the farmhouse which had once been Bourlon Abbey.[4] It was approached by the ancient vaulted crypt and overlooked most of the village. A massive structure was built just within the fringe of the wood looking west over the Bapaume road. Observers reached two steel observation hatches by iron ladders set in shafts in the walls. Nearby were two smaller pill boxes but there was no major effort to fortify the entire ridge.

The Germans did not seriously believe their opponents would ever get that far. In the spring of 1917 they withdrew from the salient which remained to them after the Somme fighting and settled down to let the Allies dash themselves against the prepared defences.

Their security obsession grew. Civilians needed passes to be out after dusk and travel between villages became almost impossible. Roads used by troops had to be avoided. Germaine Laude sneaked across the fields to attend her grandfather's funeral at Sauchy. Great secrecy attended other burials. After the German withdrawal Bourlon was only five miles from the front line. Supply carts gathered in the village each evening and it was said that they came back from the trenches full of corpses which were hidden in barns and later buried in the depths of the wood. The nightly procession of tumbrils struck dread into the hearts of the village children.

To Edmonde Foulon,[5] almost five when war broke out, the distant noise of battle was like the roar of the sea to a child of the coast. She was too young to know in 1915 that the rumbling from Artois was the death knell of thousands of her countrymen advancing up the hostile slopes of Vimy Ridge. In the summer of 1916 she was unaware that the growing storm that rattled the school windows was the echo of Haig's slow march on Bapaume. But she knew the war was drawing nearer. Grown-ups would go out to look at its smoke from the high ground above the château. Furthermore the Germans had removed the church steeple so that the British observers would not know where to locate Bourlon.

The children were baffled by the destruction of the steeple; no use trying to explain to them the niceties of scientific gunnery which required even devout French sappers to bend[4] the golden Madonna on Albert's basilica, so reducing its value as an aiming point.

In April, 1917, the British struck from Arras only 16 miles distant and Mayer gave his last orders as Lord of Bourlon. Gathered in the square, the villagers were given an hour to pack their belongings and then, pushing wheelbarrows and carrying knapsacks, they formed a column which set off through the wood to Cambrai. Some found accommodation in neighbouring villages, others in the city. The Foulons moved into a house in the Rue St Ladre along with Madame's parents.

For the first time in hundreds of years there were no children in Bourlon; not a word of French was spoken. The four smithies were under new management. There were no Coguillons in the carpenter's workshop where father had followed son for generations and where even Germaine and her sister had helped to make coffins for the village worthies.

That the commune retained its identity was largely thanks to the clergy. When their parishioners marched off, old Abbé Daquin and Monsieur Roch, his curate, went with them. So did the nuns who ran the school. The *bonnes soeurs* immediately re-opened classes in a building at the goods station in Cambrai, then realized that railways were legitimate targets for bombers. It was as well they found new premises in the Rue Vaucelette. Not long after they moved an ammunition truck blew up, killing a number of civilians, including two elderly Bourloniens called Obled. Little Edmonde Foulon was in the living-room when a stray bomb in the backyard fatally wounded her 87-year-old grandfather. Death from the air was not the only thing that took its toll. Her young brother died of fever.

Despite occasional incidents the presence of civilians in Cambrai inhibited the Allies and enemy soldiers packed the town barracks. The ancient Rue des Liniers where the officers were housed 'had the appearance of a students' quarter'.[5] Conversations were carried on across the street – which is fairly wide – and there were nightly sing-songs.

For the civilian population the main problem was finding enough to eat. Food was distributed by the municipal authorities from the warehouse of a grain merchant. Under a system based on coupons, entitlements were according to age. Basic rations were bread, cereals, potatoes, lard, swedes and Jerusalem artichokes. An inferior product known as 'American bacon' was distributed by the International Red Cross.

Bourlon itself was in a forbidden zone but Germaine Laude made one return journey with an uncle, travelling across country. She noticed her home had been partly destroyed – probably by a shell.

Evacuated countrywomen had to work in the fields around Cambrai while the men worked in the *kommandos*. Léonce Carrez belonged to a group digging trenches near Rumilly on slopes overlooking the St Quentin Canal where 'we did as little as possible'. On the morning of 20 November he was travelling to work with his gang when an enormous sound wave seemed to engulf the countryside and 'the sky over Havrincourt glowed like a brazier'.

The Battle of Cambrai had begun. The brazier had been simmering for weeks.

CHAPTER THREE
Dinner Guests

The sternest critics of Sir Douglas Haig would hardly accuse him of being unable to read a map. When on Sunday, 16 September, 1917,[1] the Commander-in-Chief of the British Expeditionary Force was presented with the details of a highly original plan to breach the hitherto remarkably durable German lines, his eyes quickly took in the dominant features. Pointing to a green patch on the squared and numbered sheet spread before him, he said that if he did adopt the proposal the big wood must be a priority objective.

'I'll send Davidson[2] to Albert to discuss matters with your staff,' he told General Sir Julian Byng, commanding the Third Army. Brigadier General John Davidson was head of the Operations Section at GHQ in the little Pas de Calais town of Montreuil sur Mer. The Staff had seen lots of generals carrying lots of plans that year. Officers who spent fourteen hours a day at their desks found it hard to forget them. Even as they took the air on the ramparts their minds were full of charts and lists, barrage tables and zero hours. An infinite variety of coloured lines gave jaunty and plausible precision to 'objectives' which defied recognition in the desolate landscape miles to the north-east. 'Up there' the bright chinagraph-pencil optimism melted into the unrelieved squalor of smoking crater fields.

And yet, despite its forbidding walls and citadel, Montreuil was intended to be a peaceful place. In the 9th century a devout local chieftain gave shelter to dispossessed monks from war-torn Brittany and built them a monastery. The isolated outcrop in the

THE WESTERN FRONT 1917 – ALLIED OFFENSIVES UP TO MID NOV

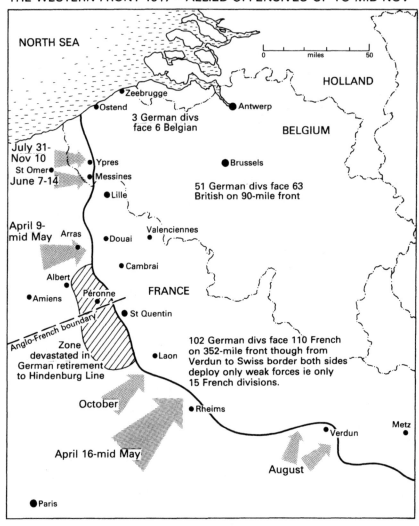

NORTH SEA

HOLLAND

0   miles   50

●Zeebrugge

●Ostend

●Antwerp

3 German divs
face 6 Belgian

BELGIUM

July 31-
Nov 10

St Omer● ●Ypres

June 7-14   ■●Messines

●Brussels

51 German divs face 63
British on 90-mile front

●Lille

April 9-
mid May   Arras

●Douai

Valenciennes
●

●Cambrai

Albert
●

Amiens● ●Péronne

FRANCE

●St Quentin

Anglo-French boundary

Zone
devastated in
German retirement
to Hindenburg Line

●Laon

102 German divs face 110 French
on 352-mile front though from
Verdun to Swiss border both sides
deploy only weak forces ie only
15 French divisions.

October

●Rheims

April 16-mid May

●Verdun

Metz
●

August

●Paris

marshes bordering the River Canche must have seemed an ideal spot for prayer, meditation and repentance. Its residents could not entirely forget worldly cares as the Channel was only a few miles away, a highway for marauding Norsemen. Later the monks were given the relics of Saulve, Bishop of Amiens, who had evangelized the region two centuries earlier and the monastery took his name. Unhappily Montreuil did not remain a haven, being regularly besieged and sacked over the centuries, but its earliest residents and Haig's staff did have some things in common. Both were subject to discipline, sworn to obedience and required to have faith, though, in their search for a sign, the monks were luckier than the acolytes of the military order. Saulve had already obtained admission to the Calendar of Saints. In 1917 devotees of 'G', 'A' and 'Q'[3] branches were still waiting for miracles. Would Davidson discover the answer to their prayers in the classified document container locked in General Byng's car speeding back to Albert?

Despite its description, there was nothing grand about the 'château' of Beaurepaire but much that represented sound bourgeois commonsense and turn-of-the-century commercial stability. If it had any peculiarities it was that the front was almost identical to the back – as if the architect had either run out of ideas or was so pleased with the façade that he duplicated it. A few kilometres from Montreuil and just outside the hamlet of St Nicolas, it fitted the requirements laid down when Haig sought a personal residence soon after becoming Commander-in-Chief. It had central heating and its small wooded park was surrounded by a high wall.

The owner obligingly agreed to move out to Le Tréport for the duration and in February, 1916, Haig's military household took over her comparatively modest country home. Hardly a day passed without the gleaming boots of the influential and the famous treading the black and white chequered tiles of Madame Behaghel's hall. Many got to know the sweeping staircase to the bedrooms on the first floor, awaking next morning to gaze across the windswept Picardy plain stretching towards the distant battlefields or watch planes circling the adjacent airfield.

On 16 September Sir Edward Carson, Minister without Portfolio in the War Cabinet,[4] had taken his leave on the steps of the house. First Lord of the Admiralty until July, 1917, he was in a position to bring Haig up to date on the fight against the unrestricted U-boat warfare campaign which had opened at the beginning of the year. The Commander-in-Chief had found him a relaxing guest after his previous visitor, the Minister of Munitions. With his agile and probing mind, Winston Churchill had been an exhausting companion.[5]

Churchill put out of mind, Carson gone, Byng dealt with, Haig prepared to receive Mr Asquith, who had been Prime Minister until replaced by Lloyd George the previous December.[6]

'Squiff' was to dine that evening and spend a few days in France. Haig admired his intellect and was amused by his ability to remain lucid even 'in his cups'. The Field-Marshal would be sure to bring out the 1840 brandy.[7] Asquith was in favour of powerful attacks on the Western Front, so his visit was well timed.

The Great War was three-quarters of the way through its third tumultuous year. Nations which had embarked on hostilities confident and exuberant found themselves reeling, dazed, along uncertain, treacherous paths.

Russia was collapsing but the Western Front still stretched unbroken from the Channel to the Swiss border. In terms of ground the positions were little changed from those taken up at the end of 1914. Limited advances had been made by the Entente armies in their attempts to free occupied territory but nothing decisive achieved. Bigger guns and better equipment had been countered by deeper dugouts and more lines of trenches behind thicker belts of barbed wire. Furious persistence in attack was met by resolution in defence. Early in June, 1917, Haig made another attempt to end the stalemate. The British exploded nineteen mines tunnelled under Messines Ridge and captured the heights which had given the Germans excellent observation over the 'back area'. This enabled the Field-Marshal to embark on a campaign in which he had great faith.

On 31 July the Third Battle of Ypres opened with the object of piercing the German line and clearing the Belgian coast. Originally it was to have involved an amphibious landing below Ostend and the gaudy map tracings at Montreuil extended as far as the Dutch frontier.

In retrospect Haig's hopes for the campaign seem 'super-optimistic and too far-reaching, even fantastic' but, as the Official Historian, Sir James Edmonds, states: 'A Commander-in-Chief usually has some quite distant objective in mind'.[8]

While Haig made enthusiastic preparations, some members of the Government expressed misgivings. If the combined Allied armies had been unable to beat the Germans thus far, Lloyd George wanted to know how the British could do it single-handed?

As the French had only a minor role in the operation, it was a good question. Haig, however, felt that he was in a strong position to handle the astute Prime Minister. Earlier that year Lloyd George had put his faith in French military leadership. He had gone so far as to try to subordinate Haig to General Robert Nivelle,[9] who had superseded General Joffre at the end of 1916. Moreover, in the spring, to suit French requirements, the British had loyally attacked a week before them, scoring an appreciable success at Arras, whereas the much-vaunted 'Nivelle Offensive' had foundered in the Champagne. French morale plummeted and there were mutinies and acts of indiscipline. Lloyd George had backed the wrong horse and in effect the Soldier was in a position to say: 'What did I tell you? You actually wanted to place us under them and now look at the mess they're in.' The Politician, not normally lost for words, could only hold his tongue.

Among Haig's reasons for choosing the Ypres Sector for his cherished attack was its proximity to the U-boat bases and the need to thwart a campaign which, according to Sir John Jellicoe, then First Sea Lord, could lead to disaster. He also wished to draw enemy attention from the shaken French army and to retain the initiative. In any case, Haig believed that 'even if my attacks do not gain ground, as I hope and expect, we ought still to persevere in attacking the Germans in France. Only by this means can we win; and we must encourage the French to keep fighting.'[10]

The offensive was prepared lavishly but blatantly, no attempt being made to achieve surprise. On 31 July gains were measured in hundreds of yards and in some places not even the first objectives were captured. It rained and, the complex Flanders drainage system having been wrecked by heavy shells, rising water began to find its own channels. After costly fighting and insignificant advances in vile conditions during August, there was a pause while preparations were made for a fresh assault in September. The weather improved but the drainage system did not. On the night of 19 September, while the Commander-in-Chief was dining with Lord Derby, the Secretary of State for War,[11] a fine drizzle turned to rain. Troops completing their approach march were soaked.

The attack, launched the next day on a front of about eight miles, led to the capture of nearly all the limited objectives of the

Second Army, commanded by Sir Herbert Plumer[12] in which two of the six assault divisions were Australian. The Fifth Army, under Sir Hubert Gough,[13] which attacked alongside the Second, did not achieve as much.

Haig considered the Battle of the Menin Road Ridge a success, though the price paid by his two armies in the period 20–25 September was 20,255 officers and men. The British machine-gun companies, especially, 'had a large percentage of losses and of killed'.[14]

The number of German dead found in captured positions and intelligence reports of falling enemy morale greatly encouraged the British Commander-in-Chief. At Montreuil the question was: 'Will the enemy crack?' Nearer the front line the view was not so rosy.

Captain Edmund Blunden of the 11th Royal Sussex, looking towards Gheluvelt from the splintered groves of 'Shrewsbury Forest': 'Never (to our judgment) had such shelling fallen upon us. For what reason? The Germans had clearly no idea of letting the British advance any further along the Menin Road . . . guns of all calibres poured their fury into our small area. It was one continuous din and impact.'[15]

There was no longer a comprehensive trench system. A sea of shell holes provided doubtful shelter for the infantry outposts. The late September sun lit the cracked concrete of captured pill-boxes in which small groups sought refuge from the crunching salvoes. The dead of both sides lay everywhere.

When Byng produced his alternative plan, GHQ was still looking forward to an Indian summer and prospects for his proposed operation faded. Sir Douglas thought the enemy might retreat after further heavy attacks at Ypres and determined to hold formations in reserve to pursue them instead of releasing them for an offensive elsewhere. There was talk of cavalry thrusting towards Roulers, a railway depot about seven miles behind the German lines. Such enthusiasm was not shared by the two Army Commanders concerned. Quite independently, in outlining their proposals for further limited advances, both Plumer and Gough expressed serious doubts about opportunities for 'exploitation'.[16]

On the morning of 2 October they were called to a conference at Cassel, where the Second Army had its headquarters and Sir Douglas retained the use of a house. In attendance was Lieutenant-General Sir Launcelot Kiggell, his Chief Staff

Officer,[17] Davidson and Brigadier-General John Charteris, head of the GHQ Intelligence Branch. Other sections were also represented. Backed by this array of advisers, Haig 'pointed out how favourable the situation was'.[18] Plumer and Gough put their cases, but the Commander-in-Chief was determined to convince them he was right. He reminded them that the Germans had missed a golden opportunity during the First Battle of Ypres in the late autumn of 1914 when a final push might have broken the exhausted British line. There would be no question in this case of a lack of resources – fresh divisions would be brought from other sectors and alternative operations under consideration would be abandoned.[19]

Charteris repeated his assessment of German morale – steadily sinking. Many divisions had lost heavily and there had been a drop in efficiency.

Sir Douglas, in buoyant mood, left for lunch content that both Plumer and Gough accepted his views. At Blendecques, near St Omer, where he had another residence, his guests that night were Lord Robert Cecil, Under-Secretary of State for Foreign Affairs and Minister of Blockade, and Lord Edmund Talbot, who had been visiting neutral Switzerland. The scions of the ancient houses of Salisbury and Shrewsbury added to his knowledge of the 'bigger picture'. On their return to London they would be able to reflect the optimism at GHQ.

The Third Battle of Ypres was dominated by the big gun; the preliminary bombardment was estimated to have cost £22,000,000.[20] Tanks were tried – despite the misgivings and warnings of the Tank Corps – but could no more cope with the soft ground than the infantry. They were easy targets for enemy gunners. A new German chemical shell containing 'mustard gas' added a further hazard. Evaporating slowly from shell holes[21] and debris, the liquid contaminated clothing, caused severe blistering and, because of its persistent nature, remained a menace for days. It may well have been a critical element in the battle, for although the British masks gave adequate protection to the lungs, its other injurious properties were high. The Allies had no similar blister agent with which to retaliate and it was many months before they produced one.

Without such novel aids, the British were reduced to basic tactics. Unable to make any dramatic advance while the enemy held the dominating Passchendaele-Gheluvelt ridge, they simply deluged it with shells (applied in various permutations) hoping to silence the opposing artillery and destroy the entanglements. At zero hour the bombardment was lifted to more distant targets and the infantry left their holes and advanced on those occupied by the enemy.

Massed British machine-guns thickened the hurricane, lashing the area to be captured, and a 'creeping barrage' of bursting shrapnel scourged the ground immediately ahead of the attackers.

During the shell storm the Germans remained under cover. At the last moment, when they heard the tell-tale mass of machine-guns joining in,[22] they scrambled out of their concrete bunkers and set up automatic weapons in craters.

If the British did capture their objective they worked frantically to prepare for the inevitable counter-attacks. After a limited advance they could count on the protection of their bigger guns while the field artillery was being dragged forward. The situation normally stabilized after the counter-attacks subsided and the whole process began again.

It was a method requiring mountains of munitions and hordes of men. In theory the supply problem was not great because the battle was fought on the doorstep of the British base area. Unlimited issues of ammunition were not enough, however. To be effective the explosive had to be delivered at the right time and place – and in the right quantities. Even then there was no guarantee of achieving the required destruction.

Despite wet weather, three massive blows were ordered in quick succession, on the 4th, 9th and 12th of October. Ground was gained in the first but at a conference in Cassel the same day Plumer glumly observed that in his opinion only the advanced troops of the enemy defensive formations had been encountered. By contrast Charteris was of the opinion that German reserves were being consumed.[23]

On the 9th the British barrage was noticeably weak, though a limited advance was made at heavy cost.

As far as the 12th was concerned the enemy recorded that they were hardly troubled by counter-battery fire and had not been so for three days. Plumer, playing the senior role in the offensive by this time, had turned down a plea by Gough to cancel operations because of rain but was forced to call a halt at the end of the day. The attack lurched forward, then stuck in the mud.

The great battering train was disintegrating – men, horses and guns. As the agonizing expansion of the Salient continued, so did the devastated zone across which the 18-pounders had to be dragged. Plank roads were laid and disappeared. Vital gun platforms, laboriously built of timber and road metal, tilted and sank under the recoil of weapons.[24]

In addition, the enemy on higher drier ground made good shooting against the exposed British positions. In the three months following the opening of the offensive the Second Army alone required 820 18-pounders to make up losses from all causes. Many heavier pieces also needed replacing.[25] Even when guns were operating normally British 'shells lost their splinter effect in the loose and water-soaked earth'.[26]

Major-General Charles Harington, Chief Staff Officer of the Second Army: 'The very soft nature of the ground apparently affected the detonation of percussion shells to such an extent that prisoners have on several occasions remarked on the harmlessness of the bursts, or the failure to detonate.'[27]

The same 'stifling' effect applied to German shells but they were crashing on troops trying to advance across the open, where blast alone could hurl a soldier into a waterlogged crater. Moreover mustard gas rounds did not rely on splinters or shock waves for their effect, but spread the corrosive oily agent in the impact area. Tainted earth could be a menace for days and burst of Yellow Cross[28] were especially dangerous around battery positions.

Without artillery supremacy – which, despite superhuman efforts, the British gunners never achieved – the essential element of success was lacking. The failure on 12 October was almost inevitable.

After nightfall there was the usual surge of activity. Trains of mules and limbers made their way 'up the line' with water[29] and ammunition and strings of ambulances jolted over the roads to the rear. Shells continued to pound the ruins of Poelcapelle brewery, still in enemy hands. A mutual chord of sympathy had been struck during daylight in this sector. The 7th Buffs recorded: 'Both the Germans and ourselves were able to attend the wounded by flying a white or Red Cross flag, white handkerchief or rag. The enemy never fired on a wounded man.'[30]

Sir Douglas Haig dined that night with Sir John Simon who had been Attorney General and Home Secretary in the Asquith Government and was seeking a post where he could be of use.

Haig found him 'charming and able' and arranged for him to be attached to the headquarters of the Royal Flying Corps where he held the rank of major.

The next day the Second and Fifth Army Commanders met Haig at Cassel. He seemed surprised to learn that the mud had become so bad that light engines on the narrow gauge railways had sunk to half-way up their boilers, while the tracks themselves had vanished. Gough and Plumer were relieved to learn that no more attacks were contemplated for ten days[31] and the Commander-in-Chief had decided to implement plans for an alternative assault on the German lines covering Cambrai. Two days later Haig studied the details with Byng. Orders were given for four infantry divisions to begin training for a combined operation with the entire Tank Corps.[32]

Lord Esher arrived from Paris that night and brought Haig up to date with the French political scene. A man of many talents (he had organized Queen Victoria's funeral, Edward VII's Coronation and suggested the establishment of a general staff for the Army), he had worked closely with Sir Douglas on the creation of the Territorial Force.[33]

The Commander-in-Chief was disgusted to learn that the French were planning to release 300,000 servicemen for civil employment. Little wonder they were pressing him to take over more of their line.

Though Haig had decided to reorganize for the next stage in the Battle of Ypres the Germans had no intention of just sitting back and waiting. British working parties struggling to improve communications were under constant bombardment. A shortage of labour was made up by the infantry who supplied porters for the pioneers – the latter being considered construction experts – before taking their chances in the line.

'The relief was completed by 8.45 pm. During the night the enemy shelled the Battalion's sector heavily with gas shells and 4.5 in . . . Jerk Trench, between Stirling Castle and Jerk House, was smashed up.

'As soon as it was light on the 19th shells again swept the Battalion's sector, while from Polderhoek Château violent machine-gun fire swept the trenches. No one dared move – all lay 'doggo' as long as daylight lasted. But once darkness had fallen all ranks worked with feverish haste in repairing the battered trenches.'

The day's casualties for the 6th Duke of Cornwall's Light Infantry (raised from Kitchener volunteers) were twelve dead and seventeen wounded.

After being relieved, they were employed in carrying baulks of timber for the Royal Engineers building 'Plumer's Drive South' in Sanctuary Wood.[34]

The HE content of bombardments drowned the softer burst of the gas shells – including Blue Cross[35] which caused sneezing and could prevent a man adjusting his respirator, making him vulnerable to lethal fumes. If they did nothing else, the gas attacks forced the troops to wear uncomfortable and restricting masks when they were also expected to work or fight.

Gas was also used to good effect by the French at this time. On the 22nd they employed it extensively in a surprise attack on the Laffaux Salient in the Champagne and within a fortnight forced the Germans to pull back still further from the Chemin des Dames where Nivelle had come to grief in the spring.

Two days later it was the turn of the Austro-German forces to use gas missiles at Caporetto to spearhead an offensive which drove the Italian Armies headlong from the Isonzo river north of Trieste. The same day at Ypres the Fifth Army[36] made a minor attack and on the 26th the final struggle for Passchendaele began.

The charred ankle-high ruins were stormed by the Canadian Corps on the 6th and were considered to have been secured by 10 November. That day columns of horsemen began to fill the roads north of Montreuil and head eastwards. With them went their impedimenta, pack animals, limbers, batteries of 13-pounders with teams of six horses to each gun. The clatter of hundreds of hoofs, the clink of chains, the snorts and occasional neighs brought peasants to their doors. It was a magnificent sight even in the rain. The Cavalry Corps was on the march.

Just what was so beguiling about the cavalry? In truth very little except a desire to justify its existence. It still suffered from an inferiority complex born in the Boer War when its performance had fallen well below expectations. Field-Marshal Lord Roberts had even ordered the discarding of the lance and sword on active service once he took over supreme command in South Africa. Infantry had been mounted in large numbers.

Witnesses before the Royal Commission inquiring into the Army's readiness for the Boer War fell into two schools as far as the cavalry was concerned. One wanted 'men mounted with rifles

. . . who can shoot'.[37] The other, in the words of Lieutenant-Colonel Douglas Haig, believed that 'cavalry can do everything that mounted infantry can do and other duties in addition; all money available for mounted troops should be spent on cavalry'. If infantry were to be mobile, he would prefer to see them 'in motors'.

This prophetic glance was followed by other predictions:

'Artillery seems only likely to be really effective against raw troops . . .

'Cavalry will have a larger sphere of action in future wars', and

'We must expect to see it employed on a larger scale than formerly.'

In the end the lance and sword were retained, though troopers were also armed with the standard infantry rifle. The solution might have pleased George, Duke of Cambridge, who had opposed change during more than 30 years as Commander-in-Chief of the British Army.[38] His Royal Highness had been instrumental in getting Haig admitted to Staff College after he had failed the examination. Patronage had also played a large part in obtaining the entry of the Hon Julian Hedworth George Byng, seventh son of the Earl of Strafford and grandson of a Waterloo general. His sponsor for a commission in the 10th Hussars had been the Prince of Wales – later King Edward VII. For Staff College he was among 'specially selected' candidates. Like Haig, Byng had a good record in South Africa, where he had commanded the tough volunteer South African Light Horse. In the pre-1914 cavalry argument he had sided with the shooters rather than the stabbers and jabbers.

At the beginning of the war both the Germans and the French had fielded ten cavalry divisions. By 1917 most enemy formations had been sent east or dismounted. The French retained their cavalry corps, though without the breastplates and plumes which had brightened the 1914 scene. Fully re-equipped, they waited . . . and waited. Meanwhile the British arme blanche in France had expanded to five divisions, including some regiments from the Indian Cavalry Corps of 1915,[39] sometimes referred to as the Iron Rations – to be used only in an emergency.

As even their traditional scouting role had been assumed by aircraft in the first weeks of the war the value of hussars, dragoons and lancers had been questioned in high places and King George V, in a chat with Haig at Buckingham Palace in June, 1916, had expressed the view that the cavalry might be reduced to save maintenance costs. Sir Douglas said this would be 'unwise'. To reap the fruits of any success the Army would need the mobility of the mounted arm. Yet, more than a year later, the cavalry had still achieved nothing on horseback, their occasional employment resulting only in heavy loss to men and animals. Each regiment had been given twelve lightweight Hotchkiss automatics and there was also an extra independent Vickers machine-gun squadron per division. Still no one knew how best to use them.

For three years fighting had been confined to a strip of devastated land. Lines of earthworks studded with concrete emplacements and protected by barbed wire had regularly been blown sky-high by the most powerful explosives known to man, but every time, when the dust settled, it revealed they had fallen to ground in a different pattern impassable by horses.

On 31 October, as the struggle for Passchendaele raged, Haig read an appreciation of the general situation written at the request of the War Council by Lord French (Sir John had been ennobled), Commander of the Home Forces. The tone suggests French may have had the help of his friend Winston Churchill:

'Up to a very short time ago Sir Douglas Haig's own utterances in public; his statements to people who interviewed him; his secret messages to the War Cabinet; and his assurances to the troops under his command, all expressed the firm conviction which had complete possession of his mind that he could break the enemy's line in such a manner as to pour large bodies of cavalry through the gap he had made and compel a great German retreat. As a matter of fact, masses of cavalry were actually brought up to points close behind the trenches, in this hope and expectation.'[40]

The Commander-in-Chief had lunched that day with Mr Jimmy Thomas, Labour MP and General Secretary of the National Union of Railwaymen, whom he classed as a 'broad minded patriot'.[41] He took a less appreciative view of Lord French, whose comments he considered to have been inspired by jealousy and disappointment. Haig may have derived some satisfaction from the knowledge that events were in train which would enable the cavalry to fulfil its destiny. General Byng would see to that.

CHAPTER FOUR
A Malicious Dwarf

Byng must have had great expectations when he was authorized to launch an assault which could change the face of the Western Front. In three years of active service he had not put a foot wrong. Having commanded a brigade, a division and, in May 1915, the Cavalry Corps, he had been sent hurriedly to Gallipoli to replace the commander held responsible for the Suvla Bay fiasco – a landing that fizzled out for want of drive. Even today one wonders just who was responsible for sending out Lieutenant-General Sir Frederick William Stopford[1] to a merciless, hostile shore. He had retired as GOC London District before the war and was more at home in the tricky world of Society, Ceremonial and the Season.

Exit the ageing Master of Ceremonies, enter the bold Hussar; though, once on the spot, Byng did not show any desire to rush headlong against the enemy despite the urgings of the Commander-in-Chief, Sir Ian Hamilton.[2] He saw the need for more ammunition, more guns, and, when opinions on quitting the Dardanelles were canvassed, he supported the withdrawal party.

The Turks were completely deceived. Early in 1916 the only British on the Peninsular were either occupying cemeteries or rotting under the prickly scrub in the silent ravines. These stifling gullies were found to be carpeted with bleached bones in 1919.

On his return to France Byng spent three months commanding XVII Corps on the lower slopes of Vimy Ridge which he came to know well. In May he took over the Canadian Corps in Flanders just before it was blasted from the summit of Mount Sorrel, a grandiosely-named hummock near Hill 60. With the aid of a brigade of 6-inch howitzers rushed up by Haig,[3] he quickly retook it.

Command of the Canadian Corps called for diplomacy as well as leadership – Dominion politicians were no less interested than those of the Mother Country in the fate of potential voters. As far as 'imperial' generals went, Byng was the genuine article. Apart from service with 'colonials' in South Africa, his wife had strong Canadian connections. Furthermore, the King-Emperor knew him well enough to call him by his nickname on informal occasions. 'Bungo' – his older brothers had been 'Byngo' and 'Bango' at Eton – was undoubtedly an asset to his new command. Royal influence could get things done when normal channels were obstructive.

Under Byng the Canadians saw action on the Somme in September when they helped to secure the Thiepval Ridge.[4] On the 15th, when tanks were used for the first time in warfare, six machines were attached to the corps, all of which were quickly put out of action from one cause or another.

The general experience of the Canadian divisions on the Somme was similar to that of their British and other Dominion counterparts. Success was measured in yards at a high cost and the reasons for seizing ground were often obscure. Afterwards Byng, concerned at the heavy losses, 'ordered his staff and each division to make detailed studies of every aspect of the offensive battle and to analyse the recent actions fought by the Corps'.[5]

The lessons learned were applied the following year when the Corps, covering the left wing of the Arras offensive, captured Vimy Ridge in operations lasting from 9 to 12 April. On the first day patrols of the Canadian Light Horse managed to get forward about noon but were driven back. A mounted division was brought up too late.

Some sixty tanks had been spread along the front at Arras, but again conditions were unfavourable. After a promising start the battle degenerated into another slogging match.

There was some criticism of Byng for not making more of his opportunities on 9 April and it was said he stuck too rigidly to the time-table he had laid down. Nevertheless he had secured the left flank of the attack and, in any case, ultimately the responsibility lay with the Army Commander.

No matter. The Canadians were the heroes of the hour and Byng's star shone bright. When Sir Edmund Allenby was transferred to the Middle East Byng was selected to replace him at the head of the Third Army.

There were five British armies in the British Expeditionary Force in 1917, each commanded by a full general whose word was law for hundreds of thousands of men (the strength of the BEF was around 1,700,000). To control his multitudes he employed a large staff, frequently housed in a château in a central location well behind the lines. In other châteaux lived the lesser staffs of the lieutenant-generals commanding the corps which made up the Army. Army and corps headquarters tended to be static, some occupying the same spot for months or even years.[6]

The number of corps an army contained was related to its length of front and its task. Gough's Fifth Army (originally constituted as the Reserve Army for the Somme offensive) was probably the most travelled of the headquarters involved, having been transferred to Flanders in 1917 to take over what had been part of the Second Army area. It began the battle with four corps under command and finished with one. When things began to go wrong the responsibility for the operation was gradually shifted back to Plumer and the Second Army.

A corps could be made up of a number of divisions but two or three were generally found to be the most a staff could handle with comfort.

Headquarters at all levels were obsessed with boundaries. Montreuil ordained those for the various armies, which allotted them to corps, which drew them up for divisions, which allocated them to brigades, which marked them carefully on the maps issued to battalions.

At the end of the chain of command Lance-Corporal Atkins was responsible for a length of trench or a shellhole with a limited field of fire.

Unexciting though boundaries may sound, they were of crucial importance. In positional warfare everyone needed to know who was responsible for what. An attack delivered against the junction of two formations was likely to have the effect of a lever thrust between two stones. There had to be no doubt as to who controlled vital bridges. When a river bisected a front, the same commander needed to be in charge of both banks. The rules were quite firm – and logical

When Byng took command of the Third Army it was holding a 32-mile stretch of front running from just north of Arras to a point about five miles north of the industrial suburbs of St Quentin, then in German hands. There the British linked up with the French, who would have preferred them to extend their front still further south. To the British it seemed that their line was always being extended. To their allies it appeared that they could afford to do so.

In July, 1917, General Fayolle drew up a small table in one of his famous notebooks.[7] According to this the Germans on the Western Front were deployed as follows:

Opposite the Belgian Army three German divisions faced six on a front of say 23 miles;

Opposite the British Army 51 divisions faced 63 on a front of say 90 miles;

Opposite the French Army 102 faced 110 on a front of some 352 miles.

A Portuguese and an American division were also available.

On this count 156 German divisions faced 181 Allied on a front of 462 miles. In August, after a meeting with Pétain, Fayolle revised this to give a total of 148 enemy divisions in the West. By October the British assessment of the German total strength was 145 with 82 in Russia, nine on the Danube and two in Macedonia.[8]

Fayolle dwelt on the fact that the British, whose numbers then equalled those of the French, held only a sixth of the line, but the comparison was false.

If the French appeared to be shouldering the greater burden, it was also true that much of their front was quiet. There *were* active sectors but from east of Verdun to Switzerland they deployed only fifteen divisions. The opposing sides had come to a tacit understanding that to mount an attack in the region was impractical – surprise unlikely, transport lacking and the terrain unsuitable.

By comparison the British front at Ypres was shrouded in smoke and flame as the guns continued to redistribute the mud on the Gheluvelt ridge; elsewhere sudden claps of thunder marked the application of the raiding policy insisted on by bellicose commanders. Only on Byng's front was there a semblance of calm. German units shattered in Flanders were sent to the 'sanatorium' in the south to recuperate and absorb reinforcements. They could do this confident that they were sheltered by the strongest entrenched position in the West.

The German withdrawal to the Hindenburg Line in March, 1917, was one of the shrewdest strategic strokes of the Great War. Not only did it wreck Allied plans but it unsettled the British and French high command psychologically.

Was the retirement the first of the fruits of victory – a sign of a weakening of the Kaiser's resolve – or was it some devilish Hun plot? The new line had been dug to form a chord across the salient held by the enemy at the end of the Somme operations in November, 1916. Had the Germans fallen back to a shorter line to conserve manpower because of the heavy casualties they had suffered? It was tempting to think so.

The glowing communiqués issued for public consumption during the summer and autumn had stressed the huge losses inflicted on the enemy. War correspondents were fond of quoting young warriors who talked grimly of 'killing lots of Boches' and 'we made them pay'.

No doubt the rhetoric was intended as consolation for thousands of bereaved families. To justify the enormous sacrifice, the generals pointed to the territory abandoned by the Germans. The retirement *had* to be regarded as an Allied victory. It would have been too painful to conclude that by occupying his carefully-prepared positions the enemy – who used the code-name Alberich for the operation, possibly after the malicious dwarf in Wagner's Nibelung Saga[9] – was making himself even more at home, that he was preparing for a long stay. Yet to the trained eye there could be no doubt about his intentions. Aerial reconnaissance, ground patrols and the reports of spies showed that the Hindenburg system was built to last.

The German High Command intended to construct field fortifications from the Belgian coast to a point on the Moselle but priority was given to the section between Arras and Soissons on the Aisne.

The *Siegfriedstellung*[10] relied on defence in depth for its security. Attackers were to be enmeshed in crossfire from a complex of trenches and strongpoints. It would not be enough to over-run and clear one line or two lines. In earlier years opponents had 'dug in', sometimes 50 yards apart, but the gap had steadily widened. The sentries and listening posts of the Hindenburg system were five or six hundred yards in advance of the first major defences and the area in between was dotted with machine-gun nests, often of reinforced concrete.

The main line of resistance was dug into the reverse slopes of contours. More than 100 years earlier the Duke of Wellington had regularly marshalled his redcoats behind ridges so that when the enemy appeared they were (a) surprised; (b) riddled with volleys or cannon fire; (c) driven back by shock action.

Arguments about the siting of trenches lasted as long as the war itself, but the reverse slope school held that if a position was dug about 500 yards from a crest, so that an attacker would not be 'on it' immediately he appeared, it was highly effective. Not everyone agreed and as late as November, 1916, the Royal Naval Division found itself on the Somme trying to hold trenches 'planned by a short-sighted fool and destroyed by a watchful enemy'.[11]

Observers concealed in concrete bunkers overlooking the Hindenburg system were ready to direct shells on troops trying to cross the ridges to get at trenches dug where the British 18-pounders would have no field of fire.

From the air the barbed-wire entanglements appeared impregnable, four belts some 50 feet deep and three feet high with 20 feet between them. Aerial photographs showed them laid out geometrically, broad arrow heads projecting to funnel advancing infantry into 'killing grounds' beaten by machine-guns. The trenches themselves were up to 12 feet wide at the top, a serious obstacle for the 1917 Mark IV tank which was generally capable of spanning only ten feet. The whole complex was honeycombed with underground headquarters, signals installations, aid posts, ammunition stores and barracks.

'The dug-outs were all designed to a pattern; the stairways, supports and all timber used having been turned out by the saw-mills in replica by the thousand . . . They represented the first successful application of mass production to the construction of dug-outs.'[12]

Ventilation shafts enabled whole companies to shelter 25 or 30 feet below ground. Shored-up tunnels, six feet high and four feet wide, led to the firing line and connected nests of pill boxes. All were lit by electric light.

Before the Hindenburg position lay a devastated zone from which the fitter inhabitants had been evacuated, the 'useless mouths' left at collecting points. Allied troops had been forced to rebuild roads as they crossed it. The rubble of demolished houses was very useful for this purpose but no villages meant no billets.

Behind the custom-built defences facing the Third Army there were natural obstructions including the unfinished and dry Canal du Nord. A monstrous furrow in the chalky soil marked its path from a point about eight miles behind the German front to a wrecked bridge where it entered British lines near the forest of Havrincourt. The deserted spoil heaps provided ready made observation posts and fire positions.

The Canal du Nord's 'twin' was in full use. From the junction of the Sensée with the Scheldt, about 16 miles behind enemy lines, it ran south without entering Allied territory, forming a 60-foot-wide moat in front of Cambrai. Strongpoints had been built into the villages between the canals.

With its waterways and streams, its hedges of barbed wire standing stiffly in waving acres of rank grass, its open spaces covered by hidden machine-guns, all ranges known and noted, the Hindenburg system did not invite an attack.

In the only assault made on it up to autumn 1917, it had taken ten days to capture one obliterated village. The fighting at Bullecourt south of Arras had resulted in severe losses to the 2nd Australian Division and the 62nd (West Riding) Division. It had given the Aussies a complex about tanks which, used in small numbers, had either arrived late or been put out of action so quickly they had served only as aiming points for the opposing machine-guns.

After their gruelling experience at Ypres, a battle which was only slowly drawing to a close, why did the British want to attack yet again that year? The Americans might be taking an inordinately long time to arrive but they were on their way, albeit short of essential equipment such as gas masks and artillery. Why not wait until they were fully trained and assembled in divisions before trying to drive the Germans out of France? Why not husband all resources, rest the weary, repair the worn and remain on the defensive? Let the Germans do the attacking for a change. Why not let their troops charge the Allied strongpoints? Plenty were being built. Near Hermies on the Third Army front positions with 30 feet of cover were burrowed into the chalk. In another type of dug-out 'the team of a single machine-gun could shelter from the heaviest bombardment, and bring its gun into action in the time it took two men to run up a ladder.'[13]

No one doubted that the Germans would attack in the West in the spring of 1918. Intelligence sources calculated they could transfer two divisions a month from Russia. Returned prisoners of war were being re-distributed. The enemy was gaining strength, so why did the British Commander-in-Chief, having tried in vain all summer and autumn to inflict a mortal blow, think he could deliver one in the winter?

What about the need to bolster French morale? The French themselves had done that, first by replacing Nivelle with Pétain, who had tackled the root cause of the mutinies, and secondly by administering two sharp defeats on the enemy. Fayolle had been appointed to command the *Groupe d'Armées du Centre* (GAC) on 2 May, a fortnight after the fiasco on the Chemin des Dames. Under his control limited attacks at Verdun in the summer had regained many disputed spots which were household names – including the Mort Homme, Point 304. Yet in the second half of 1917, for the first time in the war, the French actually lost fewer men than the British.[14]

When calamity befell the Italian Army at Caporetto on 24 October, Pétain felt strong enough to agree immediately to send three divisions to its aid. The British High Command hesitated. By 9 November 'all the Italian armies stood in good order behind the Piave'.[15]

Were the reasons political? To this the answer must be 'yes' – if Sir Douglas Haig may be regarded as a politician, a description which would certainly have horrified him. But what else had he become, if only through sheer force of circumstances? According to the *Concise Oxford English Dictionary* a politician is 'one skilled in politics, statesman; one interested or engaged in politics, esp. as a profession; one who makes a trade of politics'.

No one could say Haig indulged in party affairs but he had a shrewd eye for who really counted in both the Conservative and Liberal hierarchies. And he handled with consummate skill the statesmen, ministers in and out of office, newspaper proprietors and journalists, all the *gros personnages* who trekked to France to be entertained and informed at one of the châteaux at his disposal. He also had a special relationship with General Sir William Robertson,[16] who, as Chief of the Imperial General Staff, was principal military adviser to the government – what else but a quasi-political post?

Both Haig and Robertson insisted that the war could be won only by defeating the German army on the Western Front and that operations elsewhere were mere distractions. There were very good arguments to support their case, especially if the outcome of the world conflict had to be seen in terms of Victory as opposed to Peace. Both urged that every available man should be sent to swell the armies in France; but in furtherance of this aim Robertson lost the impartiality required of the CIGS. Haig's private papers make it clear that he had become the dominant partner in the duo. The fact that as a field-marshal he was a step above Robertson, a full general, is sometimes overlooked. 'Wullie' was one of the old school. He had been troop sergeant-major in the 16th Lancers the year Haig was commissioned into the 7th Hussars. Respect for rank was ingrained. He had little time for anyone outside the Army, so might have been encouraged to learn that more than 50 years after his death in 1933 it would still be possible to hear the phrase 'bloody civvies' in some officers' messes.

A major plank in the platform of the 'War must be won in the West' party was the argument that the torrent of shells and constant battering of the enemy lines throughout 1916 and 1917 was wasting away the German field army and destroying its morale. In discussing Allied strategy with the War Policy Committee before the opening of the Third Battle of Ypres, Haig had quoted a report made by an American relief worker who had left Belgium in the spring of 1917:

'The morale of the German troops is bad; they realize that they are beaten, but live in hopes that something will turn up to save them from disaster.

'There has lately been noticeable deterioration in the uniform and equipment of the German troops; the latter no longer present a smart appearance.'[17]

In late September Lloyd George was told while visiting Haig's headquarters: 'The considerable wastage imposed on the enemy by a continued offensive may be expected to leave at the end of the year but a small balance, if any, of the 500,000 men in the reserves he now has available.'

Brigadier-General Charteris's intelligence report claimed that of the total number of German divisions (in the East and West) 135 had suffered severe defeats that year and 'that number will be increased in the next few weeks'.[18]

GHQ radiated optimism; GHQ required that the amateur strategists in Whitehall should trust them. Talk of reinforcing the Italian front was airily dismissed. Then the thunderclap burst in the gloomy valleys of the Julian Alps and the Italian armies began to stream to the rear. The demoralized Germans had found half a dozen divisions to spearhead the Austrian attack. Consternation!

As far as Lloyd George was concerned the tables had been turned. In April and May he had eaten humble pie. The collapse of the Nivelle offensive had shown his faith to have been misplaced, his judgment in error. Now it was Haig's turn to have to face unpleasant facts. At Ypres the planned breakthrough had not occurred and, bitter thought, the amount of ground captured was no greater than that taken by Nivelle. Worse, the British had paid even more dearly for their gains. The U-boat bases on the coast remained operational but the war at sea was being won by the Royal Navy; the convoy system was proving highly successful. As for the slaughter of the enemy in Flanders, it had not prevented him taking a fearful toll of British lives. Robertson and Haig were crying out for more men to make up the losses.

With Haig the situation was no longer simply a matter of doubtful judgment. All the influential figures who in the previous months had left Montreuil enchanted and returned to London to report the Commander-in-Chief's calm assurance, his certainty, his methodical destruction of the Prussian military machine would be recalling their visits. They would be remembering their briefing, the forecasts . . . trying to recall what they had told their friends, in confidence no doubt, on their return home. Despite the impeccable manners, the frank soldierly exposition of the strategy and the 1840 brandy, it looked as though they had been 'taken in'. Sir Douglas's credibility was at stake.

Haig's position was not unlike that of a stage impressario whose backers begin to mutter about seeing a return on their investment. The long-running Ypres show was drawing to a close without showing much of a profit and it was no good blaming everything on the weather. One had to allow for that with open-air theatre. It wasn't excuses Haig needed but a new star turn.

This was not a novel situation for the Commander-in-Chief. He had been in a similar quandary the previous year at the end of the four-and-a-half month performance on the Somme. No expense had been spared but the result had been disappointing. Then, just as the curtain was coming down on a flop, the Fifth Army put on a dazzling finale. It had been preparing yet another assault when rain set in and it looked as though the attack would have to be cancelled. On 8 November, while Gough pondered the question, Sir Launcelot Kiggell called in sombre mood. He spoke of a conference of Allied commanders to be held on the 15th. There were rumours that the politicians were seeking a replacement for Haig. It was even being suggested that a solution to the war could be found in some other theatre of operations. Gough did not like the sound of this. He believed passionately that the Germans would have to be beaten on the Western Front:

'A change in the strategy which had so far guided the British and Allied Councils might have far-reaching and disastrous consequences, but if the power of the British Army could be demonstrated, and if it were possible for the Fifth Army to win some success before the date of the conference, the Chief's position in retaining the right policy would be materially strengthened.'[19]

Kiggell reappeared at Gough's HQ two days later, taking an even gloomier view of the situation because of the state of the ground and troops. To attack or not to attack? It was made clear that the decision was Gough's. After the weather improved he decided to go ahead. The battle opened in fog at 5.40 on the morning of the 13th. The ruins of St Pierre Divion, Beaucourt and Beaumont Hamel (which gave its name to the battle) were captured, along with 7,000 prisoners. Fighting continued for some days, but the British kept most of their gains. Haig was delighted and sent Gough a telegram of congratulations which struck a significant chord.

'Remembering Kiggell's words, I knew that Sir Douglas Haig's message was no formal courtesy but a deeply-felt congratulation. For my part I was glad to know that the result of the battle was not confined to the very severe defeat we had inflicted on the enemy.'[20]

Haig left for the crucial conference at the French GHQ at Chantilly, full of confidence. At lunch he sat next to General Joffre and received his congratulations. At a banquet in Paris that evening he was placed between Asquith and Lloyd George.

The main conclusion reached by the conference, attended by Russian, Italian, French and British representatives, was that the prime theatre of operations would remain the Western Front.

Haig had seen the Battle of Beaumont Hamel as a fitting end to the fighting in 1916. He could not expect Gough to pull a rabbit out of the hat in the autumn of 1917 – he seemed to have lost his touch – but Byng! There would be all sorts of oohs and aahs when the curtain went up and the tanks and aeroplanes roared into the extravaganza's opening number. He'd surprise them all yet!

CHAPTER FIVE

Enter 'Uncle' Harper

The Long Bar of the Trocadero was crowded – there was no shortage of drink during the Great War. It was a favourite rendezvous for officers – officers stationed in London, officers on leave, coming or going, or simply officers who had come to town to see Chu Chin Chow. The message was: drink and be merry for tomorrow you could be taking part in the next Push which is going to be done by the Byng Boys, the Third Army. They say they've been saving the tanks for a show sometime in the middle of November.

Lieutenant Hill,[1] Lewis gun officer of the 7th Royal Sussex, could hardly believe his ears. Everyone was talking about what was going to happen next in France – where and when. As his own battalion was training in the Third Army rear area he pricked up his ears. On leaving them at the end of October he understood that his 'crowd' were merely practising a new method of attack (the British Army constantly expected to be going forward). The troops were not even allowed to discuss the methods in their billets in case civilians picked up something – instruction had to be given in the open on the training area. Now it seemed that either all had been revealed or the Trocadero had a direct line to the War Office. Young Hill would have plenty to tell the CO when he returned to his unit.

Lieutenant-Colonel George Impey[2] listened with astonishment when Hill rejoined the battalion far behind the line at the attractive village of Vieil-Hesdin on the Canche, the same river that flowed down to Montreuil, 17 miles away, where all secrets were kept.

Unlike the barman at 'The Troc', the colonel knew nothing.[3] Up to the first week in November he had been using two-wheeled stretchers and wheelbarrows to represent tanks in training schemes. Could someone have been pulling Hill's leg? Was it all part of an elaborate ruse?

If Impey passed on young Hill's information it did not get far up the chain of command. Under the rigorous security which applied to 'Operation GY', the code name for the Cambrai operation, it should have caused a sensation. Never had precautions been so strict. Assault formations were kept well in the rear while arrangements were completed. Due to take place three weeks after Haig gave authority for the attack, the speed and skill with which it was mounted demonstrate staff work at its best. If it was the talk of the Trocadero, it was definitely 'hush hush' in France. As far as security went the planners were actually assisted by the fact that final deployment would be in the area devastated by the enemy in his spring withdrawal. There were no civilians to indulge in idle chatter – nowhere for spies to hide. Yet this isolation was hard on the troops.

The majority of British soldiers had grown accustomed, when out of the line, to living among the local population, using the amenities of towns. Facing the Hindenburg Line they were the only inhabitants of large tracts of unrelieved desolation. The Germans had meticulously removed all roofs and billets had to be either improvised or recreated in the shape of tented camps or huts. 'Tommy', a gregarious, friendly soul, 'missed vaguely the sights of village life, the gallant old men and the women setting about their endless toil, the clatter of the farm, the children who watched the falling in for a parade, and came in the afternoon to listen to the band. More definite was the loss of the shops . . . the warmth and comfort of the estaminet'.[4]

The military police considered that units in the 'Teuton-made veldt' – note the echo of the Boer War – had greater disciplinary problems than those in the populous regions to the north.[5]

To put some colour into the drab existence of the PBI,[6] divisional 'A' staffs showed some basic understanding and a certain originality. Under the first heading must come the two truck-loads of beer – 90 barrels in all – railed every day from a brewery in Amiens to the 36th (Ulster) Division, holding a wide front facing the Hindenburg Line north of Gouzeaucourt.

Another enterprise was a soft drinks factory on the banks of the

Canal du Nord. Bottles labelled 'Boyne Water' were sold at a penny or twopence a time (proceeds to buy comforts for the troops). A brazen attempt to extend the trade to the nearby 16th Irish Division caused uproar. A group of irate Southerners set off to have a few words with the Orangemen and several hundred impartial troops had to be turned out to hold the peace.[7]

The Ulstermen and the 20th Division on its right were holding the attack frontage and made extensive preparations to receive the additional assault troops at the last minute. Before they arrived more than 500,000 shells for 18-pounders alone had to be unloaded at railheads, brought forward and hidden. Trains steaming up stealthily by night were subject to a variety of delays and might be several hours late. Hundreds of bored infantrymen hung about the sidings trying to keep warm. One staff officer who sent lorries for his labourers only when he had work for them was remembered with gratitude long after many others had been forgotten.[8]

The abuse of troops who, unbeknown to them, were also going to take part in the battle, had become commonplace, but it was no less pernicious for that. The work force laboured under the impression they were preparing the ground for a large-scale raid which, hopefully, someone else would carry out. The Ulstermen looked with foreboding at the German positions on Spoil Bank, a mountain of chalky earth from the canal cutting.

Two years had passed since the 'Bloody Hand' of Ulster sign had appeared in France. In October, 1915, its mood was confident and optimistic. The infantry had been well schooled before the war in the Ulster Volunteer Force (a Protestant private army dedicated to oppose the imposition of Home Rule on Ireland). They were highly motivated and perhaps for this reason had been given one of the hardest tasks when the great battle opened on the Somme on 1 July, 1916. They came within an ace of capturing the stronghold of Thiepval before being driven back with the loss of 5,500 men. Ulster was appalled at the sacrifice. It was even muttered that the British Government was taking cynical consolation in the fact that it would not have so many battle-hardened unionists to deal with after the war.

The casualties were replaced mainly from the 36th Division's own reserve battalions and it later fought successfully at Messines and at Ypres, but the fervour and the unquestioning faith in the high command had gone.

The pressures behind the Cambrai plan were to some extent born of professional frustration. The Tank Corps, in particular, wanted to extract itself from the slough of Ypres. Confidence in the clumsy machines was fading fast in high places. With one or two exceptions its operations had been disappointing. Its title had been changed from Heavy Branch, The Machine Gun Corps, in July, 1917 – it was not entirely impossible it could be changed back. Could it be relegated to the status of high-grade trench stores to be drawn by generals facing specific problems? Haig himself, though by no means opposed to the new weapon, saw it chiefly as 'an adjunct to the infantry attack'.[9]

A new arm without influential friends was vulnerable, as a contemporary example showed. After Loos the four companies of Royal Engineers who released the chlorine gas cloud had been expanded into a brigade, but the teething problems experienced in their first battle had dampened the Staff's enthusiasm for it. By 1917 its power was dissipated, and some twenty units were scattered the length and breadth of the front line. Divisional commanders used them as they saw fit, if at all, some being strongly opposed to cloud gas operations. To avoid a similar fate the Tank Corps needed a resounding success and an excuse to launch an operation which might decide its future.

Lieutenant-Colonel J. F. C. Fuller, Chief Staff Officer of the Corps,[10] thought he saw this change only a few days after the Ypres offensive opened. All the fears that had been expressed about the incompatibility of tanks and deep mud were being realized. Certain there could be only one outcome on such alien terrain, he had been considering alternatives. On 4 August an outline for one of these was produced. In a preface to it Fuller declared that from the tank point of view the Ypres battle was already dead and, with chilling foresight, the infantry operation 'comatose'. To carry on without regard to the conditions would not only wear out machines and reduce the number of trained crews, but repeated failure would have a demoralizing effect on the troops working with the tanks. He proposed an operation 'to restore British prestige and strike a theatrical blow against Germany before the winter.'

'Restore British prestige' was a curious statement. Memories of the Messines success were still fresh and the hideous shadows over Ypres had only begun to lengthen. Fuller may have assumed that the weather would force Haig to reduce the scale of the attack (a logical conclusion for a lieutenant-colonel not privy to the secrets of high command) and thereby lose face.

He first suggested a limited operation to capture St Quentin, which would undoubtedly prove a 'theatrical' blow if successful. The French Third Army under General Humbert had lost heavily attacking in the sector two days before the Nivelle Offensive opened. The town was protected by the Hindenburg system and only a few yards of forward trench were captured. Though the ground had not been wrecked by shell fire (one reason for Humbert's repulse was his lack of heavy artillery), there were other snags. St Quentin lay at the junction of the Franco-British line. Operations would require the participation of both Allies. Brigadier-General Hugh Elles, the Royal Engineer officer commanding the Tank Corps,[11] may not have been as brilliant as his lieutenant but he immediately saw this as a complication. A joint venture was unlikely to go down well with Montreuil which would look more favourably on a solely British achievement. The French were supposed to be dispirited. It was not a good proposition. Elles himself had already put forward a plan for a limited thrust by the First Army from Festubert towards Lille – the ground was considered suitable for tanks – but it had been turned down.[12] He thought Fuller's suggestion of a raid on the enemy position hemmed in by the canals in front of Cambrai was much more viable. Elles raised it with the GHQ Operations Branch, but Davidson, heavily involved in preparing the Menin Road Ridge battle, could do little more than show polite interest – which at least was something.

Elles also had certain responsibilities at Ypres but found time to discuss his plan with a subordinate who had useful connections. Colonel John Hardress Lloyd, who had captained the English polo team in America in 1911 (though he was an Irishman), made an approach to another devotee of the sport, Sir Julian Byng. Hardress Lloyd was a tough customer who had gone to France with the 4th Dragoon Guards in 1914 and later commanded the 1st Inniskilling Fusiliers at Gallipoli. Byng listened carefully.

In the meantime another frustrated regular soldier was pressing for a similar plan but for a different reason. Brigadier-General Hugh Tudor, commanding the artillery of the 9th (Scottish) Division, was one of the pioneers of scientific artillery work. Instead of one gun firing 'overs' and 'shorts' to establish the range of a target and make the information available to neighbouring

47

batteries, he urged the use of accurate maps and survey methods. This required the calibration of each barrel and a study of its peculiarities plus the consideration of atmospheric conditions. It meant that by mathematical means the artillery could spring its own surprise, almost impossible under the traditional system of 'registering' targets.

Tudor wanted to use 'predicted' fire to neutralize the enemy batteries at Cambrai so that tanks, unhindered, could flatten paths through the dense entanglements. The 9th Division was holding that particular sector of the front in the summer of 1917 and Tudor envisaged a thunderbolt from the blue opening the way for infantry and cavalry to roll up the enemy line northwards.

His ideas were sympathetically received by Brigadier-General Hugo de Pree, Chief Staff Officer of IV Corps, in which the 9th was serving. De Pree was also a gunner.[13]

The plan went before Lieutenant-General Sir Charles Woollcombe, the Corps Commander.[14] Realizing that Ypres would have priority for men and material, he scaled it down to a straightforward *coup de main* to seize a stretch of the Hindenburg system and destroy the supporting batteries.

The scheme went to Byng, who was more enthusiastic. The Tank Corps was asked to take a closer look at the projected scene of operations. By the time it did so Tudor had departed, along with the 9th Division, to fight at Ypres (the Scots remained there until mid-October) but he had made an impression. Elles himself reconnoitred and went away satisfied with the ground conditions. He thought that not only could the enemy lines be ruptured but a gap could be exploited.

The enthusiasm of the younger men – Elles was 37, Fuller 39, Tudor and De Pree 46 – fired Sir Julian's imagination. He saw the possiblity of 'passing' the Cavalry Corps through a broken front to ride round behind Cambrai to play havoc with the German communications.

On the ground the sudden torrent of shells on carefully predicted targets – waves of tanks – fast-trotting columns of horsemen – above them squadrons of aeroplanes. A number of officers, including Fuller, expected much from low-level attacks. There would, of course, be an important role for the infantry.

Of sixty-two infantry divisions under Haig's command in autumn, 1917, fifty-one are listed by the Official Historian as having taken part in the Third Battle of Ypres by 10 November (the date it was theoretically 'closed down', though it squelched on for weeks afterwards). Forty-one were British, four Canadian, five Australian and one New Zealand. Most of the others had been involved in at least one major offensive that year, at Arras or Messines, or in some brief, bloody and frantic side-show such as the enemy surprise attack on the 1st and 32nd Divisions on the Belgian coast in mid-July.

With divisions being shuttled from one corps to another, decimated, then made up again, the basic training of the infantry in general was barely adequate. The very description of some divisions had become misleading. Units in the original 1914 BEF consisted of regulars and regular reservists in which officers and NCOs knew each other and their men thoroughly. Territorial formations, if less expert in drill and weapons handling, had enjoyed a certain cohesion for much the same reason. The Kitchener volunteer units were formed of high-quality recruits. By winter, 1917, with rare exceptions, all the valuable common bonds had been stretched to the point where their grip was often nominal. Even before the Somme, regular and 'K' brigades had been exchanged in a few divisions. All the Territorial units outwardly retained their structure but reinforcements were no longer exclusively from their own recruiting areas.

The description of a division as Regular, 'K' or 'Territorial' referred to its origin, not necessarily its actual personnel. The introduction of conscription in May, 1916,[15] meant that the composition of units became even more diverse. With improved technology, the value of a formation depended increasingly on management and training. Tradition and custom alone could not be relied on to overcome shortcomings, and regimental eccentricities cut no ice with the Kaiser's machine-gunners. One khaki warrior looked very much like another to the men behind the 1908 German Maxim.[16]

The availability of 'fresh' divisions for the Cambrai offensive was limited. In the event the task of training with tanks fell to the 6th (Regular), the 51st and 62nd (Territorial), and the 12th and 20th (New Army) – the 20th having to send battalions from its reserve brigade as it was still holding the line. To exploit the attack the 29th, a regular division, was to be brought to a high state of physical fitness.

Ten training days were allotted to each division due to fight with tanks. In simple terms this meant battalions spent only two days with real Mark IVs. Brief as it was, this period enabled the infantry to rid themselves of some of the fears that had arisen once they knew tanks were to be employed on a large scale, for example the fate of anyone lying disabled on the battlefield. The solution: 'Small parties of men were detailed to accompany each tank [clearly not the advance tanks] for the purpose of removing any such wounded lying in its path'.[17] Tank Corps instructions for combined operations were simple but needed rehearsing. The machines were to operate in waves of groups of three. To help them cross wide trenches bundles of brushwood ten feet wide with a diameter of about four and a half feet had been produced by a Chinese labour company. Tanks pulling in opposite directions had been used to tighten the chains binding the fascines. A device enabled the massive faggots to be dropped from the snout of the tank without any of the crew having to emerge.

On Z-Day Tank No. 1 of a battle group would advance 100 yards ahead of its companions, crush the enemy's wire, then, without attempting to cross the front trench, turn left and roar along the parapet blasting the garrison with its forward machine-gun and the weapons in its starboard sponson. Tank No. 2 used the gap made by the leader, dropped its bundle to help it cross the front trench, then also turned left to take the defence in the rear. Tank No. 3 passed over No. 2's fascine and then 'cast'[18] its own into the support trench, crawled over and attacked the defenders. The infantry would follow the second and third machines. Sections of Mark IVs were to rally later (No. 1 using its fascine as required).

The relief at getting rid of one and three quarter tons of brushwood was tempered with the need for every crossing place to be marked with a red and yellow flag [19] placed at least 'three paces' to one side of the dropping point. If machines were under fire tank commanders had permission to throw out their flags. The infantry were warned to look for them and stick them in parapets as a guide to following sections.

Tank Corps battle drill required foot soldiers to stay close to their allotted Mark IV except when the machine was ploughing through entanglements and they were in danger of being dragged by trailing strands. Platoons (around 35 men) were to advance in sections of single files, easily deployed and quickly passed through the two-feet-wide lanes cut in the wire.

The commanders of four of the specially-trained assault divisions accepted the advice of the Tank Corps 'Training Note' issued by Third Army headquarters on 30 October. Major-General George Montague Harper,[20] of the 51st, a tall man of 'extremely strong views', did not. Though only 49 when war broke out, he had a fine head of white hair (but a black moustache) which is perhaps why some contemporaries called him 'Uncle'. Harper was a Royal Engineer who had seen action in South Africa and served as an instructor at the Staff College where he worked under Colonel 'Wully' Robertson and then Henry Wilson, the next commandant. He must have impressed his seniors because by 1911 he was Deputy Director of Military Operations. Came 1914 and he joined the general stampede of officers afraid of missing what was expected to be a short war. He went to France as Chief Operations Officer at GHQ. It was during this period he featured in one of Sir William Robertson's rare jokes. Being asked by a visiting politician the meaning of the label 'O.A.' on an office door, 'Wully' replied: 'Old 'Arper'.

Harper had assumed command of the Highland Division in 1915 and was proud of its record. It had successfully held High Wood on the Somme and been 'over the top' on Z Day at Beaumont Hamel, Arras and Third Ypres.

During a liaison visit before the Arras attack Major E. L. Spears had been impressed by Harper's use of models and a dummy battlefield to train his men. The General had told him: 'The time had come . . . when soldiers should use their brain again.' Spears commented: 'This principle he certainly applied.'[21]

Harper's inspired contribution to the Battle of Cambrai took the form of varying the tank drill so the machines attached to the 51st Division turned right, the opposite direction to everyone else. This in itself was not vitally important. However, 'Uncle' also insisted that his infantry should advance in waves, not files, and 'avoid casualties from fire directed at the tanks by never coming within one hundred yards of the machines'.[22] His decision was not entirely arbitrary. On previous occasions disabled tanks had been deluged with fire to the peril of anyone near them. Nor was 'Old 'Arper' unsympathetic to all things mechanical. He had ridden a large bicycle to and from the War Office.[23] There are indications, however, that he was not the most progressive of military thinkers – 'When on the staff of General Headquarters he had resisted the development of machine guns'.[24]

As Harper had expressed the view that the whole Cambrai plan was 'a fantastic and most unmilitary scheme'[25] it is hard to understand why he was given a key role at the head of a division which had already been thrust into the heart of the furnace three times within a year. 'Old 'Arper' was not entirely unco-operative. Near the date of the attack Highlanders on reconnaissance were allowed to wear trousers instead of the kilt to avoid being identified by the enemy.[26]

CHAPTER SIX

Low Fliers From Down Under

A German flight leader signalled with a gloved hand to his pilots. Below him four mud-coloured biplanes were flying westward at 10,000 feet. Somewhere under the haze was St Quentin. He cocked his guns and put the Albatros into a shallow dive. The others followed suit.

Caught up in a flurry of hurtling planes, black crosses and violent thuds, Second-Lieutenant Dick Howard was at 6,000 feet before he was able to pull his De Havilland 5 into a right-hand rising turn and fire two short bursts at an enemy machine 100 yards away. Then two more opponents forced him to break off. As quickly as it had flared up the encounter was over. The Germans droned off east and the drab biplanes reformed and continued their flight home. It was just after noon on 16 November.

At lunch the mess of 68 (Australian) Squadron, Royal Flying Corps, was full of excitement. They had gone looking for trouble and found it. Mechanics having found sundry holes in Howard's plane and a bullet in an engine cylinder, it was trundled off to a repair depot for immediate attention. Every plane was going to be needed in the days ahead.

The Squadron, the second offered to the Air Board by the Dominion government, had been formed in Egypt in 1916 from men of an existing squadron and volunteers from the Australian Light Horse. In September, 1917, after training in England, it joined III Brigade RFC – the air element of the Third Army. The DH 5s were destined for 'close support' and 68 Squadron's aircraft were fitted with racks for 25-lb bombs. Low-flying training with

THE PLAN

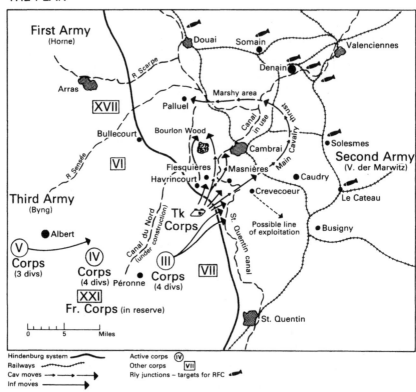

First Army
(Horne)

Arras

XVII

Bullecourt

R Scarpe

Douai

Somain

Valenciennes

Denain

Marshy area

Palluel

Bourlon Wood

Canal in use

Main Cavalry thrust

Cambrai

Solesmes

Second Army
(V. der Marwitz)

R Sensée

VI

Flesquières

Havrincourt

Masnières

Caudry

Third Army
(Byng)

Crevecoeur

Le Cateau

Albert

Tk
Corps

Canal du Nord
(under construction)

Possible line
of exploitation

Busigny

V
Corps
(3 divs)

IV
Corps
(4 divs) Péronne

III
Corps
(4 divs)

St. Quentin canal

VII

XXI
Fr. Corps (in reserve)

St. Quentin

0   5   Miles

Hindenburg system

Railways

Cav moves

Inf moves

Active corps (IV)

Other corps VII

Rly junctions – targets for RFC

none-too-reliable engines was a hazardous business. Second-Lieutenant Harry Taylor was lucky to emerge unscathed from a haystack after his 'rotary' cut out after take-off.[1]

The Squadron joined a growing armada. Byng could count on 289 machines in the expanded RFC brigade of which 134 were single-seat fighters. The enemy was believed to have about seventy planes of all sorts facing the Third Army, including a single squadron of a dozen Albatros scouts – Jagdstaffel 5.

Two flights of DH 4 day-bombers belonging to 49 Squadron arrived from England on 12 November as reinforcements and more 'heavies' were lent by the First Army or came from GHQ resources. They were to be available to Byng as long as he needed them. Rail and road junctions behind the enemy lines were ringed on target maps – a policy similar to the 'interdiction' bombing applied in France in 1944 to isolate the Normandy bridgehead.

Byng's fliers faced a familiar problem. They had to avoid raising suspicions by undue activity while at the same time preventing enemy observation planes from detecting the build-up on the ground. To mislead the enemy, large sweeps[2] were carried out over distant areas but over Cambrésis the British found an unexpected ally. Though fair for the time of year 'morning after morning dawned with a thick ground mist which hung about all day'.[3] Under this clammy shroud hundreds of thousands of yards of camouflage netting was erected. During daylight all movement was controlled. Where the enemy could look directly over the British lines individuals were allowed to cross the open only at 100-yard intervals. Working parties were restricted to ten men who had to use selected communication trenches to approach the firing line. No one was allowed into this first zone without a pass.

In the second, which enemy balloon observers could sweep with their binoculars, marching parties were limited to a strength of thirty-two (about a platoon) and horsemen to groups of sixteen. All were ordered to keep in single file to the side of roads, using trees as cover where available.

In the rear zone, exposed to air reconnaissance, no unit larger than a company was permitted to move by daylight, and if two were on the march there had to be an interval of at least 200 yards between them.

By night empty vehicles increased the deception by carrying lights if they were moving out of the line, to give the impression the Third Army's front was being thinned to send reinforcements to Ypres. All incoming traffic was blacked out.

The persistent mists dulled the senses of the German observers hidden in the ruins of Havrincourt, mechanically lifting their field glasses to examine the sprawling woodland opposite, across the shallow valley. They made notes to hand over to their reliefs but failed to record a remarkable vanishing trick. A road which had been visible one day had disappeared the following morning, hidden by a two-mile stretch of bushes, branches and netting.[4]

The men of the German 54th Division had seen enough of woods of a different sort in Flanders where they put up a stout fight before yielding the village of Westhoek in August. Survivors of that hurricane were glad of the calm of Cambrésis. Perhaps they did not want to believe the silent landscape could hold such terrors as they had experienced; but it was wishful thinking. By the second week of November a maze of light railways was operating in Havrincourt Wood. Behind the camouflage screen men were feverishly marking out gun positions, digging communication posts, building howitzer platforms, erecting and hiding shelters for infantry, selecting 'lying-up' positions for tanks. In other woods and other ruined villages the story was the same. In the meantime, miles away beyond Arras and Albert, the men who would occupy these positions were training. Behind locked doors models of the terrain were studied by a select few. To allay rumours, the story was put about that the Tank Corps was to open a joint training centre near Albert. Troops, who put two and two together when a water obstacle was included in their training schedule, were encouraged in their belief that they were preparing for operations in Italy where all battles seemed to be fought on rivers. The appearance of Brass Hats to watch them was accepted as a necessary evil.

On the 13th Sir Douglas saw the 6th Buffs and 7th East Surreys rehearse an attack on a trench system marked out with tapes. The next day, accompanied by Kiggell, he watched a demonstration put on by the 29th Division. He attended more sessions on the 15th and also found time to write to the War Office concerning problems arising from the Italian situation. Incongruously, in view of impending events, he mentioned the BEF's need of rest and training.

An important conference was held on the 16th when Byng's final plan was unfolded to the Corps Commanders involved.[5] The Commander-in-Chief went over it and then returned to his

56

quarters to entertain Mr Austen Chamberlain[6] to dinner. Sir Douglas seems to have acted as a magnet for the 'great' unemployed. Chamberlain had felt obliged to resign as Secretary of State for India that year after a Royal Commission criticized the mounting of the campaign against the Turks in Mesopotamia which resulted in the capture of thousands of British and Indian soldiers at Kut el Amara. He was yet another visitor whom Haig found 'charming and able' and was rewarded with a tour of the offices at headquarters.[7]

Far from the orderly life of the château and the urbane conversation of the dinner table, other men were shouldering heavy packs and blundering out of badly-lit ruins into the shadowy streets of Péronne on the upper Somme. Arriving that morning after a roundabout train journey, battalions of infantry had been hustled into makeshift shelters with orders to stay out of sight. They had smoked, eaten their haversack rations and watched the light fade, then at dusk emerged to form platoons and companies. The old walls echoed to the sound of marching troops. Péronne had seen many armies during the centuries – only 47 years earlier its ramparts had defied the Prussian batteries, though not for long. On a chill night in January, 1871, the invaders brought up heavy French guns captured at Amiens and set the houses and the ancient church of St Jean ablaze.[8] More systematic destruction had been inflicted on Péronne by the sons and grandsons of the old adversary before they retreated to the Hindenburg Line.

The villages to the north of Péronne had also been wrecked, but five miles along the Cambrai road one of them swallowed up an entire column under the spell of a magician on a bicycle who knew the secrets of the ruins. Another long wait began.

The next night, after the new arrivals moved on, there would be more to take their place. By the 17th four infantry divisions had passed through Péronne and vanished into the wasteland. The cavalry had arrived three days earlier, completing its last two marches by night.

'No one quite seems to know what we are doing here,' wrote a young officer, 'but rumour has it that great events will take place.'[9]

Considerable energy had been expended on providing water for the growing concentration of men and beasts. An old sugar beet factory behind the line had been adapted to slake the thirst of 2,000 horses an hour. One hundred and fifty tons of oats and a similar weight of hay were hidden close to the front.

Any lingering doubts the incoming troops might have had about

57

the extent of the coming attack were dispelled by the sight of RAMC personnel taking up position. The men of a London Field Ambulance, who had hoped to spend the winter in a camp just outside Bapaume on the edge of the old Somme battlefield, had been resigned for some time to a change of scenery. As their quarters were close to the main road 'there were plenty of opportunity to see things. Innumerable stories of tanks and dummy tanks filled the air.'[10]

On the order to move they summarily despatched the stock of a small poultry farm set up in anticipation of the festive season. Christmas dinner was eaten on 14 November. There was no room for ducks and geese in the old German dug-out under the battered château of Louverval.

'The woods behind the village had been cut down and the great hulks of trees lay prone . . . already overgrown with brambles . . . through this fallen wood our reserve trenches now ran. In the village itself the houses were in ruins, though in the gardens marigolds reflected something of former glories.'[11]

How long could the luck of the assembling host hold? As the concentration was nearing completion a train loaded with tanks ran into a lorry and was derailed at a crossing just behind Havrincourt Wood. Discovery seemed inevitable, but the tanks managed to crawl off the flatcars under their own power and by morning they were under cover.[12] At almost the last moment there was another major alarm, involving the infantry.

To reach one particular outpost on the edge of Havrincourt Wood a man had to squeeze along a narrow trench which opened off the front line and wound its way under the barbed wire to a sandbagged emplacement in no-man's-land. Each night this sap-head was manned by a section of soldiers who took it in turn to watch and listen and doze on the first step. Just before dawn on 18 November a peaceful vigil ended in ear-splitting crashes, vivid flashes and gusts of acrid smoke. When the rain of shells lifted slight, shadowy figures slid heavily over the parapet into the midst of the dazed garrison.

'Jasus, it's Jerry!'

Some time later when the uproar died down a British patrol crept cautiously up the débris-filled communication trench. They reported that five men and a sergeant of the 1st Royal Irish Fusiliers were missing, seized under cover of a 'box' barrage which had isolated the post. At the same time, miles to the south, a raid on a much larger scale had netted forty soldiers from the Lancashire battalions of the 55th Division, but their loss, from a formation only indirectly involved in the pending attack, was not considered as potentially dangerous as the capture of the Irishmen.

Would the Germans be able to extract anything from their prisoners? The Fusiliers had been in the area for weeks and were well aware that batteries were crammed almost wheel to wheel along the camouflaged rides running through the tangled undergrowth, that piles of road metal had been dumped behind the lines, and that fatigue parties had been employed endlessly to unload ammunition trains at the rail heads. A sustained bombardment of Havrincourt Wood would wreak havoc.

At Third Army headquarters the rest of the 18th passed with mounting tension. At 2.30 the same afternoon an order was issued giving the 20th as 'Z Day'. That night the Tank Corps completed its preliminary assembly; its entire strength of 476 machines was on the spot. Of these 378 were classed as 'fighting tanks', destined to operate in the van with the assault troops, the remainder being used for supply, radio and other duties. The next move they were due to make would take them into battle positions.

Despite the anxieties, the enemy remained inactive. At mid-morning on the 19th the signal went out – Zero Hour would be at 6.20 am, an hour before sunrise.

On the very day that Zero Hour was divulged, a last-minute attempt was made to finalize French involvement in the battle. Haig had informed Pétain on 1 November of his intention to attack at Cambrai. The French Commander-in-Chief promptly offered to provide three infantry and two cavalry divisions[13] to push south through any gap made. This was not exactly what Sir Douglas had in mind. He had hoped his allies would take over some of his line, thus making British troops available as a reserve. According to the Official Historian, the Field-Marshal 'saw that the task of the Third Army would be made no easier by the presence of French troops massing behind the right flank of the attack'.[14] Precisely why is not explained.

Hesitation over the offer of substantial reinforcements, particularly infantry, was a strange response from generals concerned at the shortage of men. The plan that emerged from the seeds sown in August called for an attack by the centre of the Third Army involving only two corps to begin with – IV under

Woollcombe and III under Sir William Pulteney.[15] Aided by tanks, Woollcombe was to carry the Hindenburg defences with his right wing, the 62nd and 51st Divisions, then bring his left wing (56th and 36th Divisions) into play, striking north along the enemy trenches. His corps was to pivot on the left and overrun the Bapaume–Cambrai road, the 62nd Division thrusting towards Bourlon and the 51st between the wood and Cambrai.

On the right of IV Corps, three of Pulteney's divisions (6th, 20th and 12th) were to break through the Hindenburg front and support systems to allow the 29th Division to pass through their positions, cross the canal and capture the last line of defences (generally called the Beaurevoir Line) covering Cambrai.

Once the canal crossings had been secured by III Corps, three cavalry divisions were to cross to the east bank and destroy the enemy communications as they rode behind the town to head north. There they were to make contact with the 1st Cavalry Division thrusting between Bourlon Wood and the western suburbs of Cambrai, to complete a pincer movement.

The main objectives were to be attained within 48 hours by which time strong German reserves could be expected on the scene.

The rest of Byng's army was committed to holding the line while behind Bapaume he retained a corps of three divisions, the commanders of which were warned secretly that they might be called on to exploit success in the battle.

By Western Front standards the numbers involved were small. Two armies with seven corps had opened the proceedings on 31 July and up to six corps had been engaged on quite narrow fronts in later battles at Ypres, plus the French First Army under General Anthoine, which had fought alongside the British on the seaward flank.

Clearly there was a potential role for the troops offered by Pétain and on the 19th Haig and Byng met their commander, General Degoutte,[16] at Albert.

Also present was Lieutenant-General Sir Thomas D'Oyly Snow,[17] whose VII Corps, on the extreme right of Byng's front, joined hands with the French. His troops had only a minor role in the 'Operation GY' but the previous day Haig had written to Pétain suggesting they might advance with Degoutte's corps, under the overall command of the Frenchman. If this was a rather unsubtle attempt to prepare for a shortening of the British line it

60

failed. Degoutte, possibly sensing political implications, declined the proposal. All that resulted was an instruction to Byng to make arrangements for the French to advance from any bridgehead established over the St Quentin canal south of Cambrai.

This was ridiculously short notice but the staff of the Third Army were even more startled to learn that Degoutte's troop trains were due to arrive at Péronne early the next day. Arrangements to receive, feed and billet the French were hurriedly improvised. Inconvenient though this unexpected development may have been for the 'A' staff on the eve of battle, the location of the French could hardly have been better. From Péronne they could advance if required up the routes taken earlier by the British assault troops. But why had they appeared in such a casual way to take part in an operation otherwise meticulously planned at tactical and logistic levels? Did the British ever intend to employ the French seriously? Of all the conferences held during the planning of the Cambrai offensive, few give rise to as many unanswered questions as that held with the French Corps Commander at Albert that day. Certainly Degoutte was no one's fool. Clemençeau was to say of him six months later: 'He looks like a fat little Chinese cook but he knows his business and keeps calm.'[18]

The ability to keep calm was a virtue to be envied as the minutes to Zero Hour ticked away. At the highest level the generals wondered if the prisoners taken on the 18th had given anything away. At the lowest a man's thoughts were concentrated on whether he would survive the coming ordeal, whether the Brass Hats had really found a solution this time, and, of supreme importance, when he would be allowed a cigarette. All smoking was banned as the troops marched to their assembly positions on the night of the 19th. Once they reached the end of the route taped out by the sappers the infantry were ordered to rest, but still no smoking. Many lay in the open on dank, chill ground. Tea and a rum ration were issued to as many as possible but time dragged in the mist-wreathed fields. Men wrapped blankets round their shoulders but these quickly became soaked with dew. Shadowy figures began to strip the camouflage from the hidden guns and tanks. Cold metal ran with condensation.

On Hubert Road in Havrincourt Wood the 18-pounders stood almost wheel to wheel, their limbers ranged behind them. Some tanks, fascines hoisted, edged forward in low gear. From the

'Tankodrome' at the south-eastern edge of the wood they crept along the rides at around a mile an hour until they were within 1,000 yards of the enemy outpost line. On the far right of the attack sector cover was sparse and Dessart Wood, about four miles to the rear, had been occupied by a hundred Mark IVs. A much longer trek faced these machines.[19]

As on a normal night, occasional harassing fire from the British guns provoked answering bursts of machine-gun bullets. Then, about one o'clock, salvoes of heavy German shells burst on Oxford Valley, a sunken road running from Havrincourt into the wood and bisecting Hubert Road.

According to Brigadier-General Austin Anderson, commanding the 62nd Division's artillery[20]: 'The Boche showed great uneasiness and fired very heavily during the night, though fortunately not on any vital places. We listened . . . in great suspense (divisional HQ was about a mile from the edge of the wood) and watched the flashes of the shells bursting apparently very near our line of guns, but one could get no information . . . for no telephones[21] were allowed until the moment of attack . . . At 5.45 am there was a particularly furious burst of firing which died down at a few minutes before six and was succeeded by dead silence.'

A 49-year-old veteran of two North-West Frontier campaigns, Anderson wondered 'if the Boche' had some 'infernal surprise for us.'

The stillness was broken at ten minutes past six by the tanks. Engines which had been ticking over were put into low gear and the machines rumbled forward, vibrating exhausts belching clouds of fumes. The time for concealment was past and they made up ground to be in position at Zero Hour. Flights of low-flying planes caused long lines of horses tethered in the rear to plunge and roll their eyes. The cavalry divisions had marched to their assembly areas after midnight, off-saddled and picketed their mounts. Liaison parties were already up with the infantry and there was nothing more to be done. Officers 'waited eagerly for dawn and the chance of action at last'.[22]

CHAPTER SEVEN
Frustration at Flesquières

In the village of Sailly, well behind the German lines it was business as usual. Soldiers were finishing breakfast, heading for their bunks if they had been on guard all night, stamping warmth into their feet as they assembled for fatigues on the uneven pavé. At precisely 7.20, their clocks being an hour ahead of the Allies, pillars of flame and smoke erupted in their midst, buildings collapsed, roofs flew into fragments. Choking fumes billowed from yawning craters.

All known resting battalions had been pinpointed by assiduous R.E. surveyors and the larger calibres among the 1,003 guns supporting the attack concentrated on their destruction. Sailly's 'entitlement' in this torrent of devastation was to be twenty-five rounds from each of two 9.2 inch guns. Every five minutes, with a blinding flash and a roar, they sent their 380lb missiles hurtling into the sky. The barrels recoiled on specially constructed railway mountings, cranes swung the next rounds towards the breach and the gunners of the 442nd Siege Battery[1] pressed their hands over their ears.

When Sailly had been duly chastised, they would turn their attention elsewhere. No. 1 gun was to pulverise another village while No. 2 sent fifty shells into the barracks at Cambrai.

There were some sixty 8-inch and 9.2-inch pieces, evenly divided,[2] in Byng's arsenal plus 140 of the latest 6-inch howitzers. The 'super-heavies' consisted of eight 12-inch and three 15-inch weapons, the latter firing a shell weighing 1,450 lbs. Nothing was being left to chance.

CAMBRAI - THE ASSAULT THAT MADE HISTORY 20 NOV 1917.

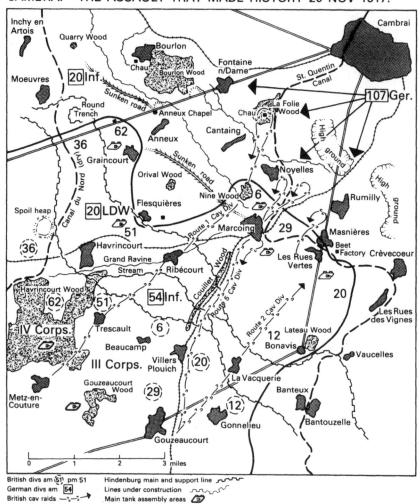

British divs am (51) pm 51   Hindenburg main and support line

German divs am 54   Lines under construction

British cav raids   Main tank assembly areas

Sand pits   Areas reached by tanks

Rly line

A dark red, man-made glow mocked the feeble dawn. British observers watched 'showers of SOS rockets of all colours'[3] soar out of the boiling clouds over the Hindenburg system, unheeded signals for help. The German artillery had been overwhelmed.

'Our men, some with rifles slung, advanced leisurely across no-man's-land at the same speed as the tanks, as if at a rehearsal. A very curious impression was given to those watching the attack from the rear by numbers of men stopping to light cigarettes.'[4]

Smokers in the little groups trudging behind the Mark IVs were seen clearly by a Sopwith Camel pilot flying low overhead.[5] The casual Tommy, rifle on his shoulder, Woodbine in mouth, strolling over the tumbled enemy sandbags, was the classic picture the propagandists and popular press had been trying to project since trench warfare began. Cynical old hands shook themselves and wondered if it was really happening, but dishevelled prisoners were already stumbling to the rear.

Senior staff officers checked their watches as the bombardment began. There were 48 hours to go before great decisions would have to be made.

By midday on 20 November, 1917, the Tank Corps had proved its case: given suitable ground it could break defences hitherto held to be impregnable. A considerable part of the six-mile frontage under attack had fallen into British hands and casualties, by comparison with previous offensives, had been insignificant. After five hours of battle the staff of one field dressing station, equipped to receive a gory flood, was nonplussed to record only a trickle of walking wounded.[6] The tanks had 'gone over' with panache. Showing a fine sense of history Brigadier-General Hugh Elles had taken his place in the first wave of 'H' Battalion in a machine flying a large brown, red and green flag.[7] He might have chosen Harvester, Harrier or Huntress from the sections involved but instead selected a Mark IV male perversely called Hilda.[8]

So, unless you happened to be on the wrong side, it was just bully for the tanks. Bully too for the artillery. The theory of predicted fire had also come of age; the sudden storm of explosive stunned the defenders and paralysed their batteries. Only a few random shells were reported in response.

There was yet another successful development to record. Despite bad visibility, made worse when the smoke of the barrage was trapped under low clouds, the Royal Flying Corps took to the air. A few kilometres east of Cambrai, at Estourmel just off the Le

Cateau road, the commander of the solitary fighter squadron in the German Second Army area told his irate superiors it would be 'madness' to attempt to fly in such conditions. Nevertheless, under threat of court martial, he ordered the twelve Albatros pilots of Jagdstaffel 5 into their cockpits.[9] They were listening to the distant rumble of battle when anti-aircraft guns on the approach to the field barked a warning and three biplanes roared low over the grass to drop small bombs. A couple of German fighters managed to take off but part of their work was done for them. After two of the Sopwith Camels, from No. 3 Squadron RFC, vanished into the mist the noise of their engines was cut short by loud explosions as they crashed into trees. The third member of the flight was shot down and killed.

According to the tactics of the day the ground attack squadrons had been trained to fly in formation, but the adverse conditions made this impossible. Where it was tried flyers kicked rudders and worked 'joy-sticks' frantically to avoid colliding with their companions. Wisely the Australians of 68 Squadron worked in pairs. The first six pilots set out soon after 7 am and for more than an hour bombed troops and shot up roads before returning to the Advanced Landing Ground (ALG) at Bapaume to re-stock with ammunition and to refuel. Ground fire had been fierce and Captain John Bell, the Flight Commander, flying jacket blood-stained and torn, nursed his tattered DH 4 back over the lines only with difficulty. He managed a forced landing and was dragged almost unconscious from the fuselage which dripped petrol from the punctured fuel tank. His rescuers hurried him to a casualty clearing station where he was found to have a bullet in the chest.[10] By that time the next flight of six aircraft was on its way to the combat area.

One pair, Captain Gordon Campbell Wilson and Lieutenant W. A. Taylor, were skimming over the German trenches with guns chattering when Taylor's machine was brought down and went careering over shell-pocked ground until both wings parted spectacularly from the fuselage. Clambering out under the startled gaze of a trench full of enemy soldiers, Taylor could hardly have been accused of not having 'done his bit' and no one would have blamed him for giving in. The Australian was not the surrendering sort, however, and the only hand he raised had a pistol in it. As he opened fire his companion, who was circling the spot, swooped down and sprayed the enemy with his Vickers. They regarded this behaviour as unreasonable and bullets hummed angrily around

66

Taylor as he scrambled away. Luckily for him he ran into some British soldiers who had pushed too far ahead of their unit and were doing their best to rejoin it. Arming himself with a dead German's rifle, the pilot took his place in the little firing line as it fell back by stages. On reaching safety Taylor left his new-found friends and set off, intent on reaching the ALG. He had covered some distance when he saw a DH 4 standing unattended in a field! He climbed into the cockpit and attempted to start up, but it was no good. The engine remained obdurate and he eventually got a lift back to base to await the issue of another aircraft.

On that 20 November a pilot's life was simple, exciting and, all too often, short. Many RFC fliers lost their bearings in the fog and, light-weight machines being able to operate from level grass strips, some even landed to check their positions. One pilot[11] was sitting in his Camel in a field by the side of a road studying a map when a marching column of men in field-grey appeared. He went bumping over the turf and took off with hot metal singing around him.

The absence of suitable ground-to-air radio equipment forced a certain simplicity on the air operations. Specific targets were assigned for attention soon after zero hour and for the first 45 minutes planes flew missions over the whole of the Third Army Front to confuse the enemy as to the direction of the attack. Afterwards, using the ALG to replenish and refuel, pilots carried out general raids on communications and points of resistance. Among positions selected for special air attacks in the early phase were woods known to conceal artillery and machine-guns – and Flesquières.

Two heights dominate the 'bare and monotonous plateau'[12] on the western approaches to Cambrai. North of the route nationale, Bourlon Hill rises deceptively steeply from the edge of the road, a glacis running up to the western fringe of the wood. Two and a half miles away across a shallow valley Flesquières squats on a ridge which points a crooked finger at the city.

Separated by shallow depressions which drain the downland into the Escaut and the canal, other ridges reach out for the town in a south-easterly direction but fall short and merge into the rolling plain. Flesquières was well supplied with cellars in which the men of the 84th (von Manstein) Infantry Regiment could take cover. (The title came from a corps commander of Franco-Prussian War fame.) All civilians had been evacuated.

Fourteen batteries were deployed in and around Flesquières,

five of them equipped with 77mm field guns. Some detachments were specially trained to destroy tanks. When the 54th Division fought on the Aisne in the spring it had taken a heavy toll of the clumsy French St Chamonds.[13]

At 7 am on the 20th the batteries were firing on their SOS lines when four biplanes swept out of the murk.[14] A bomb exploded in the middle of a gun-pit and the troops scattered as bullets ripped up the earth around them. One group stuck in the door of a cottage and was riddled. Horse-drawn transport bolted. Three-quarters of an hour later a pilot who had flown clear of the area to deal with a Vickers stoppage flew back but could detect no sign of life. Men and animals lay around the emplacements and a limber had been abandoned but there were no gun flashes. Occasional clusters of shells left dust drifting over the village. British bombardments were scheduled to end at 9.25 am, shortly before the 51st Division attacked.

'Uncle' Harper's home-brewed tank tactics were severely tested. In the initial assault on the Hindenburg front they had worked to some extent and the Highlanders had penetrated well inside the enemy's battle zone.

On the lower slopes of the Flesquières spur, towards Ribécourt, numerous machine guns were in action. A lance-corporal of the 1st/5th Seaforths went out with a small patrol and shot one gunner with his revolver. A tank which came up drove other teams into a deep dug-out and the Highlander bounded after them, killed a German who tried to resist at the bottom of the stairs, and chased out the rest. Three officers and thirty men were taken prisoner and five Maxims captured. The dug-out had been a battalion headquarters. Lance-Corporal Robert Macbeath[15] had shown what could be achieved in close co-operation with tanks. Where this was lacking, stiff fighting with grenades and bayonet ensued.

Any delay was calculated to damage the chance of success but failure to get on in the centre was bound to have repercussions on the wings. From the German point of view Flesquières was an ideal blocking position.

Though the gun-pits had appeared deserted to the pilot who flew over just before 8 am, the 77s had not been abandoned but withdrawn to open positions on the reverse slope where the detachments waited for whatever might come out of the mist. In the trenches in front of the village and in the houses sentries were on the alert to call men from dug-outs and cellars to their battle posts. About 9.30 they gave the alarm. Already the enemy had begun to adapt to circumstances. At an early stage 'many riflemen and machine-gunners saw their opportunity to take cover until the foremost tanks had passed and then to open fire upon the approaching platoons'.[16]

Even so, Harper's tactics can hardly be blamed for the fate of the first wave of tanks which rolled over the ridge. The 77s knocked them out before they could reach the entanglements. Some burned furiously. As precious hours slipped by, some Mark IVs successfully forced paths through the thick wire barriers but it became clear that the distance between the machines and their followers was too great for practical co-operation. As Fuller coldly put it afterwards, the tank loss 'would have mattered little had the infantry been close up, but, being some distance off, directly the tanks were knocked out, the German machine-gunners, ensconced in the ruins of the houses, came to life.'[17]

There was no want of effort by the Highlanders, who eventually fought their way into the first line in front of the village; but, try as they might, they could not establish themselves in the next. The twin trenches lay in the form of an irregular rope ladder thrown at random before Flesquières, the rungs representing the communicating links dug between them. An abundance of dug-outs enabled the defenders to appear where least expected. Whenever tanks gained the upper hand the Scots seemed to be absent. A handful of machines fought their way into the village but by the time supporting troops arrived they had begun to withdraw and the infantry fell back with them. Scraps of khaki kilt apron and strands of tartan cloth marked the hasty passage of Gordons, Black Watch, Seaforths and Argylls through gaps in the wire. The weather deteriorated – 'During the afternoon rain fell heavily.'

Given that Flesquières ridge was a tough nut to crack, the evidence still points to a fault in the 51st Division's battle drill. All the divisions involved had to fight their way through the Hindenburg system – some German troops panicked at the sight of the mass of tanks but many determined islets of resistance held out. The low British casualty returns for the day reflect the correct application by most formations of the new tactics, imperfect though they were, rather than feeble opposition.

The 62nd Division on the left of the 51st had a fierce struggle to take Havrincourt where the enemy fought back from the grounds of the château and in the streets. Sometimes the Mark IVs were ahead of the infantry, sometimes the troops were in advance of the tanks but there was a rough and ready cohesion and the platoons and armour stuck close to each other. A stream of bullets zipping from an unlovely trench-cum-quarry known as the Boggart Hole in Oxford Valley was quenched when 'the tanks literally fell on it'.[18]

Germans in the upper storeys of houses were silenced either by the 6-pounders of Mark IV males or subjected to concentrated automatic fire before riflemen stormed in. The King's Own Yorkshire Light Infantry[19] did not wait for armoured assistance but relied on their own efforts to clear Etna and Vesuvius, two massive craters blown by the enemy during their spring retirement and subsequently fortified. Château and park eventually fell to a joint effort.

By 10.30 am the first field batteries were trotting through Havrincourt into the fields beyond. Specially trained detachments turned captured 5.9s and .77s on their former owners to conserve British shells. Graincourt, on the approaches to Bourlon, became the target for many of them. The church was a prominent aiming point. When the village fell in the afternoon to the 'Dukes', it was discovered the enemy had been using old underground workings as headquarters, liberally furnished and electrically lit. Three enemy pioneers found concealed in the vault housing the petrol generator were told they would have to remain on duty and found it politic to lead their captors to various demolition charges.

The early success at Havrincourt paid handsome dividends. Two hours after zero hour, as arranged, the 36th Division mortared the Spoil Heap for four minutes with 'thermit' bombs. The Germans fled and the 10th Inniskillings charged and took seventy prisoners. From the top of the mound Lewis gunners could cover the advance of the troops engaged on the unenviable task of working their way north along the labyrinth of deep trenches. No tanks had been allotted so the Boyne Water merchants adopted tactics used by the Canadians at Vimy. Specially-picked heavyweights, of which the formation still possessed a few, led the way firing Lewis guns from the right hip, the weight being taken by a sling over the left shoulder.

The Lewis was 'heavy and clumsy but its tremendous moral effect in such broad trenches . . . can readily be imagined'.[20] Each of the flat circular drums contained forty-seven rounds. As long as the supply lasted the gunner could hose the trenches ahead of the bombing parties.

The wide trenches in the Hindenburg system sometimes trapped tanks – infantry came on a ditched Mark IV being vigorously bombed by Germans who, in their turn, were penned in a sandbag redoubt by its crew, defending it from the outside with a couple of Lewis guns – but they also enabled the Ulstermen to move freely. Advancing sections of the Inniskillings kept their eyes on a bobbing flag at the head of the lead platoon.[21] Single soldiers stopped off at each dug-out entrance until parties arrived to extract occupants. Bringing up the rear was a man with a bundle of notice boards. Each cleared dug-out was marked 'Mopped'.

Prisoners were found to belong to the 20th Landwëhr Division, not previously known to be in the area, having arrived only two days earlier. In peacetime the Landwëhr was formed from men who had finished their compulsory service with both the colours and the reserve. Its value had deteriorated as the war progressed and the 20th was being used as a stop gap in a supposed quiet sector until a stronger formation replaced it. The British anticipated its relief by five days.

The identification of the low-grade division was passed back quickly to the Commander-in-Chief's advanced operations centre. Bavincourt, just off the main Doullens–Arras road, was within a dozen miles of Byng's main HQ at Albert and despatch riders were able to shuttle between both places across the eerie wilderness of deserted trenches and crowded graveyards of the old Somme battlefield. Translated into symbols on the large situation maps, their messages were encouraging, even exciting. The weeks of anxiety were over. Imponderables had become fact. Gunners really could blast a target without weeks of hit and miss. The troops said the British barrage had been excellent. 'I could have stroked it as it rolled along in front of me'.[22]

Exultant at the success of the tanks, some Tommies had been seen throwing their helmets in the air and catching them; Germans waiting to surrender thought they were drunk.[23]

Broad paths had been cut through the barbed wire. Progress which had been measured in tens of yards at Ypres was by the mile.

Any doubts about the 29th Division's marching ability had disappeared. Its men had covered six miles in full kit and reached their assembly places in ample time. Before it was known for certain that the Hindenburg Line had been breached a bugler sounded the signal to advance.[24] After bitter fighting, a bridgehead had been established as planned between Marcoing and Masnières. Brigadier-General Cuthbert Fuller,[25] Chief Staff Officer of III Corps, was concerned about reports of two fresh German divisions around Cambrai and questioned the advisability of pressing on over the canal. His caution was swept aside in the euphoria at Third Army headquarters: it was only 11.30. Major-General Vaughan, Byng's chief staff officer,[26] pointed out first of all that the reports were not confirmed, and in any case, if they were, then vigorous action might involve the divisions in 'the débâcle'. He told the Cavalry Corps the new arrivals might be included 'in the rout which appeared to have set in'.[27]

Vaughan did not wish to miss a single opportunity and at the time Fuller contacted him all was going well. Every division in III Corps had captured fortified villages or key points without heavy loss. The 6th had carried Ribécourt, the 20th La Vacquerie and the 12th had taken Lateau Wood and reached the spur overlooking the St Quentin Canal. Only one thing marred the overall picture – the stubborn salient at Flesquières.

In a world which demands instant communication it may be hard to understand why the problem was not solved by a few terse radio messages, but such equipment as did exist was in its infancy. The men on the spot had to rely mainly on mounted despatch riders, signalling lamps, 'runners' scrambling hundreds of yards on foot, pigeons and field telephones. In static positions lines could be buried or run along the sides of trenches. During an advance they were vulnerable. Behind the front fascines had created havoc with overhead cables on the eve of the assault. Scores of ground wires had been chewed up by tank tracks. The sapper linesmen doggedly repaired them.

The Flesquières problem had been identified by midday when either of the flanking divisions could have cut off the defenders. But Major-General Walter Braithwaite[28] had his eyes on the Bapaume–Cambrai road and Bourlon Ridge. His Yorkshire battalions were making good progress and around one o'clock he suggested to Harper that the Highland Division should move troops through the 62nd Division area to take Flesquières in the rear. Even though Scottish reserves were available 'no action was taken'.[29]

General 'Tom' Marden[30] tried to organize a joint turning movement with units of his own 6th Division and the Scots. One of his brigade commanders 'did not regard the conditions as favourable'.[31]

More signals, messages and discussion followed. Everyone agreed the answer to the problem was to attack Flesquières from the rear; no one actually did anything. Minds conditioned to the plodding, painstaking pace of positional warfare were unable to move into higher gear. The Scottish battalions received all assistance short of actual help.

CHAPTER EIGHT

Sabres out at La Folie

Like small versions of Newcastle and Gateshead, the towns of Les Rues Vertes and Masnières are linked by bridges across the St Quentin Canal. In 1917 only one of these, made of iron, could bear much weight. About noon machines of 'F' Battalion, the Tank Corps, clattered towards this crossing at their best downhill speed of 50 yards a minute. They managed to avoid a group of liberated civilians singing the Marseillaise and accepted the gift of two milking cows which they sent to the rear. The animals had belonged to the German town major who was doubtless helping to direct fire from houses on the far bank. Flying Fox II attempted the crossing with the world's first 'panzer grenadiers' clinging to its hull – bombers of the 11th Rifle Brigade. Like a fat man falling through a deck-chair the tank dropped abruptly and became wedged between the ends of the bridge. The Riflemen scrambled for safety, the crew followed them and the startled enemy fired too high to do any damage.

As if outraged at the indignity inflicted on one of its species, Feu de Ciel II rumbled up the street and blew out all the windows of the houses across the canal with its 6-pounders. Other frustrated Mark IVs prowled the banks.[1] Infantry began to cross by a lock gate south of the town. Everyone waited eagerly for the first lancers and hussars to arrive.

To place thousands of horsemen in the field without having them blown to pieces by the German guns was a remarkable achievement. One war correspondent became quite lyrical:

'They streamed past at a quick trot, and the noise of all the horses' hoofs was a strange rushing sound. The rain slashed down on their steel helmets, and all their capes were glistening, and the mud was flung up to the horses' flanks, and as, in long columns, they went up and down the rolling country and cantered up a steep track making a wide curve round two great mine craters . . . it was a wonderful picture to see and remember.'[2]

The vision did not last. By noon only one brigade of the 1st Cavalry Division had crossed the old British front line into captured territory. There it halted while scouts sought a way ahead free from Germans. The rest of the division tailed back some five miles. Battle traffic crowded the roads. Everyone wanted to know the cause of the hold-up.

About 11 am General Harper had phoned IV Corps to say that Flesquières was in his possession, the road forward fit for horses. Off went the 2nd Cavalry Brigade from its lines near Havrincourt. Then a liaison officer with the Highlanders reported 'considerable doubt'[3] about the situation. In Grand Ravine a fork in the road led to Ribécourt and the 4th Dragoon Guards, in the lead, set off to reconnoitre. Germans were said to be holding out in the village. The rear of the column 'waited under cover of Havrincourt Wood for two hours and a half of precious time until at 2 pm the way through Ribécourt was found to be open after all!'[4]

Momentum had hardly been broken as it had never built up. The 1st Cavalry Division was supposed to be the tip of the IV Corps scythe, sweeping in front of Cambrai on the other side of the canal while the blade ripped through the villages and woods to the west of it. Once the obstacles had been cleared regiments were to gallop round behind Bourlon Wood. This bold conception faded with the evening light. A single squadron of the 5th Dragoon Guards crossed the canal but was unable to penetrate uncut wire swept by bullets. The 4th galloped towards Bourlon Ridge, looming dark through gusting drizzle, but trenches at Cantaing barred the way. Two troops, perhaps fifty men, managed to get into La Folie Wood, using their swords on a group of Germans encountered on the way. Enemy headquarters staff fought back from the château windows. The Dragoons seized a handful of prisoners but then reserves, coming up hot-foot from Cambrai, drove them off. They rode back with their squadron leader draped lifeless over the saddle of his charger.

During this foray the bulk of the division waited under cover where it 'remained saddled up and ready for action all the rest of the day and night'.[5]

Standing by the heads of their horses in the chill rain, the troopers could hear the 29th Division trying to extend its bridgehead so that the rest of the Cavalry Corps could cross the canal and ride round Cambrai. There was much speculation about how the other divisions would fare.

Lieutenant-General Kavanagh planned to use crossings less than two miles apart. Two brigades of the 5th Cavalry Division accompanied by the GOC, Major-General Macandrew, moved on Marcoing up one valley; the third, comprising three Canadian regiments, headed for Les Rues Vertes up another. The 2nd Division followed along the same routes but its GOC, Major-General Greenly, rode with the Les Rues Vertes column.

Macandrew was determined on mounted action but by the time he was on the scene the advanced squadrons of the 7th Dragoon Guards were fighting on foot. One had galloped over the bridge at Marcoing but been forced to dismount and join the infantry battle. Shortly before 3 pm a second rode to Noyelles, a mile and a half to the north, cutting down some Germans in the main street before being driven off, having taken twenty-five prisoners. Noyelles had been entered earlier by the infantry but the Germans made 'repeated counter-attacks and our men were in and out on several occasions'.[6] Around 4 pm a frustrated infantry brigadier[7] commandeered a tank and led a company of Lancashire Fusiliers down the main street. The machine crashed through two barricades, flattened a machine gun and the enemy's nerve broke.

At Les Rues Vertes the Canadian cavalry were faced with the spectacle of Flying Fox lying half submerged in the wreckage of the bridge. Undeterred, they explored the banks of the waterway and discovered the 2nd Hampshires filing over a lock gate. With the assistance of local inhabitants another crossing was improvised and the Fort Garry Horse started to cross. This was the sort of bold action Macandrew wanted, but he was still at Marcoing. The man on the spot was Greenly,[8] who had come up with his leading formation. Under a previous arrangement he took charge of the Canadians and went into conference with their commander, Brigadier-General the Right Honourable John Seely,[9] who had been Secretary of War in 1914 until he resigned over the Curragh Incident.[10] Seely had won the DSO while serving with the Imperial Yeomanry in the Boer War but was not a professional soldier. The infantry Brigadier at Marcoing and his Brigade-Major were brought into the deliberations. As it happened, the BM was a cavalry officer and, in his opinion, 'It was not practicable for any considerable force of cavalry to pass over the marshy approaches' or use the improvised crossing. Greenly, at 42, was one of the most experienced cavalrymen in the BEF and since 1914 he had been a frequent participant in the misfortunes of the mounted arm. He 'felt constrained to agree'.[11] The Fort Garry Horse were halted, but 'B' Squadron had disappeared. The idea of a further advance was discarded and the Brigade Major passed unnamed into the Official History, condemned for not having been aware of the existence of an alternative bridge to the south-east indicated by map co-ordinates in the operation order issued by his own division.

Seely was ordered to support the infantry in the bridgehead, at the same time being urged to make sure through the use of patrols that no chance was missed of pushing mounted troops forward. The impetuous 'B' Squadron was left to its fate.

No one was aware that even further to the south, towards Crèvecoeur-sur-Escaut, where the canal makes another sharp bend, crossings were virtually undefended 'until very late in the day'.[12] Aerial photographs of them had been circulated before the attack and the Lucknow Brigade of the 4th Cavalry Division had been specially placed under the orders of III Corps to seize any opportunity which might arise. When, however, in the early afternoon its patrols reported that the infantry had not definitely secured the bridges, it tamely jogged along at the tail of Greenly's division.

It was by these southerly crossings that the French would have come into action had they been required. The abandonment of the Crèvecoeur bridges seems to have been due to panic in the German rear. On the extreme right of the attack an officer led a patrol of the 7th Royal Sussex across the bridge linking the villages of Banteux and Bantouzelle. Houses were deserted along with the trenches covering the crossings. The information was passed back up the chain of command without response.[13] Nothing was done to exploit the situation, to occupy the places or to blow up the bridge. The Sussex dug in on their objective in compliance with orders requiring the 12th Division to form a defensive flank along the Bonavis ridge. Only time would tell whether or not another opportunity had been missed. The failures elsewhere were more evident.

The 55th Division had assisted the main attack by firing

hundreds of gas drums into the Banteux area (from Livens projectors – simple weapons like outsize mortars). As well as a 'Chinese' (dummy) attack, a serious attempt was made to capture a trench near Vendhuille village on the canal. Two strongpoints, one a hill called 'The Knoll' and the other a ruined farm, were defended desperately by the Germans and cost the 164th Brigade, which included the Liverpool Irish, 1st/4th King's Own and the 2nd/5th Lancashire Fusiliers, more than 600 men.[14] No gains were made. This loss, to a division already stretched to its limit, was to have serious consequences. The 55th's costly experience was in sharp contrast to that of the cavalry. When night fell three divisions, complete with lances, sabres, limbers, guns, ambulances and engineers, were spread like Prince of Wales's plumes across the countryside, all dressed up with nowhere to go. The infantry at the canal crossings no longer requiring the support of dismounted units, the Third Army gave permission for Kavanagh to withdraw his troopers as far back as Fins, ten miles behind the front, if he wished. There were better watering facilities there. Around 9 pm columns of jaded horsemen were heading to the rear when a halt was called. Orders had arrived, from Third Army, stating that the cavalry would still have to carry out the original plan the next day. As a return journey could only further tire the horses, carrying about 18 stone on average, all bar one of the brigades camped for the night on the spot they had reached. The Lucknow Brigade managed to trek seven miles back to the morning start line. Taken as a whole, the cavalry's contribution to the day's events had been negligible. Bold moves intended to have important strategic consequences had been reduced to the level of minor tactical adventures and the hardest part of the battle had not yet begun.

One man who saw the problem clearly on the night of the 20th was the Commander-in-Chief. During the planning stage he had emphasized the importance of capturing Bourlon on the first day of an offensive. Only ten days before it was launched he had suggested at a conference that 'specially trained detachments of all arms, lightly equipped . . . under one commander'[15] might be given Bourlon and Marquion (north of Bourlon on the Cambrai–Arras road) as their special objectives.

Byng had responded to these comments – they were not orders – ostensibly by altering his original plan. Under the earlier scheme the list of priorities were:

(i) to break the enemy's line with the aid of tanks;

(ii) send the cavalry through the gap;

(iii) seize Cambrai, Bourlon Wood and the crossings over the Sensée river.

The revised order of priorities was as follows:

The first stage – the breaking of the Hindenburg Line, the capture of the canal crossings and the defences which covered Cambrai on the far side of the canal.

The second stage – the pushing of the cavalry through the gap, the seizing of the Sensée crossings and (the final act in this phase) the capture of Bourlon Wood.

The third stage involved the clearing of Cambrai and the destruction of German forces trapped north-west of the city.

In other words the weight of the attack was still directed to the south; the main role was still allotted to the cavalry. Haig could have saved his breath. Under either plan it must have been apparent to the Operations Branch at Montreuil, if nowhere else, that Byng's objectives were beyond his means. True there were three divisions under V Corps in Third Army reserve, but once they were committed there would be no one left to carry out the routine reliefs of formations simply holding the line, some still weak after their ordeal at Ypres. With such limited resources there was all the more need for care, cunning and economy in plotting the capture of a dominating feature like Bourlon Ridge. In the event arrangements for its seizure were in almost inverse proportion to its importance.

The 62nd Division had been made responsible for seizing this vital objective – but only after overcoming a series of other formidable obstacles. When two brigades had broken into the Hindenburg System, the third was to pass through them, fight for a place in the support line, capture the large village of Graincourt and then Anneux, which was smaller, just south of the Bapaume–Cambrai road.

'After the capture of the village a detachment was to be pushed out to gain possession of the high ground west of Bourlon Wood and join hands with the 1st Cavalry Division which should then be advancing on Bourlon Village from the north-east.'[16]

It was nearly five miles from the third brigade's start line in Havrincourt wood to the Cambrai road. The spur to the west of Bourlon was at least a further mile away. With rifle, 170 rounds of ammunition, respirator, greatcoat (it was November), a pack containing his personal necessities and his iron rations, plus probably a pick, shovel or wire-cutters, steel helmet and perhaps a couple of Mills grenades, the ordinary soldier was carrying more than 60 lbs.[17]

Fully equipped an 11-stone man tipped the scales at 15. With mud clinging to his boots and clothes soaked he was even heavier. No wonder the PBI hated the rain.

To inspire these heavily handicapped warriors to carry out a long march and fight at the end of it called for leadership of a high order. To lead the attack on the Bourlon position Major-General Braithwaite chose Roland Bradford, at 25 Britain's youngest brigadier-general. An outstanding officer, he had won the Victoria Cross[18] while commanding the 9th DLI on the Somme the previous autumn. A great believer in personal contact, he often addressed his men before battle and a fellow officer later recalled seeing him in a dug-out rehearsing a speech and even adjusting the tilt of his cap to give him a jauntier air.[19] From the beginning Bradford saw the need to maintain momentum. He argued that to exploit any success on 20 November his troops needed to be right behind the leading brigades. Braithwaite in part consented though he had some doubts.

'For instance there were the Tanks, which were really to act as the barrage, and we did not know quite how they would perform their task. And there was the non-registration of the Artillery . . . nor did I like being without some sort of reserve.'[20]

Reserves! From the beginning the whole operation hinged on them, or lack of them. All commanders were conscious of the shortage of troops to exploit a success. As a result Harper hung on to his spare brigade at Flesquières, needing men for the next day's fighting. Braithwaite was unwilling to detach troops to help (though he did send some tanks in that direction) because he had his hands full with his own problems. German batteries and machine-guns on Flesquières ridge were firing on the flank of the 62nd Division.

After Bradford, aided by tanks, had begun his drive towards the Bapaume–Cambrai road Braithwaite sent an order forbidding him to advance beyond Graincourt until the situation on the right was cleared up. It had little effect because by nightfall Bradford's 186th Brigade had gone on to capture the sugar beet factory on the RN 29 where the leading troops ambushed an unsuspecting enemy column marching towards Cambrai. Some fifty men were killed by Lewis gun and rifle fire and many more wounded and taken prisoner. Bradford even probed the defences of Anneux, but the two squadrons of the corps cavalry regiment (King Edward's Horse) which had been lent to him were held up by wire and machine guns. Some tanks had gone further forward on their own initiative and shot up enemy-occupied trenches. There were reports that three Mark IVs had explored Bourlon Wood and village and found them unoccupied.[21]

By then it was dark and Bradford's men were too exhausted to take advantage of *that* situation. The 62nd Division's leading troops had covered four and a half miles from the old front line which it claimed was, until the Armistice, the record for an advance *in battle*.[22] Throughout the day its battalions had by-passed opposition already being tackled by neighbouring units, and this had added to the strain. The aggressive tactics paid off and though three officers, including the CO, had been killed leading one 'reserve' battalion forward near Havrincourt Château, the troops had been spared the usual massacre. Indeed total casualties for the Third Army on the 20th were around 4,000 – less than the number of prisoners taken. The front-line soldiers could see for themselves that it had not been a bloody disaster; they had witnessed the captives streaming to the rear. It was a rewarding end to a day of battle which the troops would have appreciated more had they not been due to attack again on the morrow.

Cloud and rain made the night particularly dark. Around the sugar beet factory vivid flashes gave life to darting silhouettes. 'Mopping up' went on until 10 o'clock. Elsewhere bursts of shooting were followed by unnatural silences. Anxious patrols scouted the broken earth for friends. For them there were moments of nerve-tingling excitement. For the great majority the cold, wet unlit world between the two canals was only another tedious, uncomfortable and incomprehensible interlude in the Great War.

An Irish brigade[23] ordered across the Canal du Nord to occupy Havrincourt arrived soaked to the skin and hung about for hours. The last platoon did not find shelter until 3 am. Sappers worked on makeshift bridges and mended tracks wrecked by their own gunners. Exhausted stretcher parties staggered miles to blacked-out dressing stations, motor ambulances not having reached the forward area.[24] From the rear came the menacing bellow of primaeval beasts as huge tractors pulled big guns to new positions. Supplying the 'heavies' through the Havrincourt bottleneck was going to be difficult, so they were concentrated on the left of IV Corps where light railways could feed them and they could cover Bourlon. The wood was beginning to exert its influence.

At 9 o'clock Third Army transferred control of the 2nd Tank Brigade from III to IV Corps. In the initial attack the four infantry divisions committed to creating the cavalry gap south of Cambrai had been allotted 216 Mark IV fighting machines compared with 108 for Woollcombe's force.

The assault had significantly reduced the overall tank strength. Of those working with the Highland Division, twenty-eight had been destroyed by artillery fire but the blackened hulks smouldering on Flesquières ridge were not the only victims of steady nerves and good shooting – sixty-five machines in all had received direct hits. Of the rest 114 had been put out of action by engine trouble, 'ditching' and other causes. Losses had to be made up from the fifty-four fighting tanks, six in each battalion, held in reserve. The thirty-two machines which had used grapnels to rip away barbed wire on cavalry routes were restored to combat duties.[25]

Few soldiers were more weary than the tank crews who fought that day. They had to be dedicated simply to survive in their own environment. Eight men shared a deafening steel box which pitched and jolted on tracks running over unsprung rollers.[26] The most uncomfortable posts were those of the two gearsmen in the rear of the machine, responsible for engaging high or low ratios in the secondary boxes controlling the track speeds. The noise was so great that they received signals from the commander, sitting alongside the driver in front, by hand or coloured electric lights. The longer a tank was in action the more it resembled a mobile oven, with the temperature soaring over 100°F. Vision slits and weapon apertures were too small to permit natural ventilation and fumes accumulated from the 'blow back' of the guns and leaking exhausts.

'In the early days of tank warfare it was noted that after prolonged work inside tanks men complained of headache and faintness.' As 'improved' models appeared, symptoms got worse and included 'giddiness, palpitation, vomiting, mental confusion, unconsciousness, collapse and rise of temperature.'

There was sometimes difficulty 'in getting drivers to understand

and carry out orders promptly . . . the men sitting staring in front of them and merely repeating the orders instead of putting them into execution'.

After being in action some tank crew members exhibited mental depression plus 'drowsiness and an irresistible desire to rest or sleep'.[27]

At Cambrai the Mark IVs had advanced at 6.20 and many of them fought almost non-stop for four hours to break through the Hindenburg trenches. Most were used again later in the day. By dusk many were suffering from mechanical faults.

The 'irresistible desire' had to be kept at bay on the night of the 20th as the tanks gathered, hulls scarred and pitted and smeared with mud. Stores had been dumped at rallying points and, while gunners replenished ammunition racks, their comrades carried out minor repairs. Officers inspected the 'fighting compartments' for damage, wounds were examined and dressed, and drum after drum of a pungent glutinous substance was circulated. The Tank Corps had ordered that all machines 'must be greased up before crews are allowed to rest'.[28]

The survivors of the itinerant squadron of the Fort Garry Horse also rallied that night – in a sunken road in enemy territory. After crossing the canal they had found a way through the wire and, while daylight lasted, attacked enemy parties and even charged an artillery battery. Machine-guns put an end to their foray. Having suffered forty casualties the troopers took their horses into cover. Later Lieutenant Harcus Strachan,[29] who had assumed command after the squadron leader was killed, ordered them to stampede the animals to confuse the enemy. Then he led them back to British lines. Germans who got in the way were 'dispersed'. Three officers and thirty men reached safety, bringing a number of prisoners with them. It was the most dramatic cavalry exploit of the day.

In his journal that night Abbé Delval devoted as much attention to the privations of a pupil just freed from fourteen days in a German gaol as to the battle on his doorstep, though he did begin the entry with a description of 'a sudden rolling cannonade' which hardly diminished until evening.

'The detonations were continual and very strong; doors, glasses, windows, everything danced. Certain explosions, more violent than the others, seemed very close and made one jump. In the distance aeroplanes flew low machine-gunning the ground . . .

'Some young people in the labour gangs who had been taken out to Rumilly by train as usual saw shells exploding in front and behind them. They hastily returned to Cambrai sometimes running in the intervals between bursts, sometimes crawling.

'Some people say the English have advanced as far as Marcoing. Let us wait and hope.'

CHAPTER NINE

Brandenburg Cigars

Sir Douglas Haig and Sir Julian Byng were beginning to pull in diverging directions. At a meeting in Albert on the evening of the 20th the Commander-in-Chief once again emphasized the importance of capturing the Bourlon position, but when the Third Army issued orders its right wing was still being urged to make every effort to burst out of the canal bridgehead the next day. That possibility had already vanished.

The previous afternoon, without being able to lift a hand to help matters, a brigadier-general[1] had watched one of his battalions move steadily up the slopes across the canal towards the last line of trenches protecting Cambrai. They were unoccupied at that moment but he could see dark masses moving downhill towards them. Then mist closed in.[2]

The prize in the race was not quite what it looked. In places the coveted 'Masnières–Beaurevoir Line' was simply a trace – the turf had been removed along with a foot of soil. However, there were numerous shelter dug-outs; it was sited to give the occupants good fields of fire – and it was well protected by barbed wire. All that was required to make it viable was a garrison of experienced soldiers – and it got them.

A week earlier the men of the German 107th Division had turned their backs on the Pripet Marshes and boarded trains which rolled westwards across Poland and gave them a glimpse of their homeland before crossing into Belgium, then France. Advance parties arrived in Cambrai on 18 November and began preparations for the routine relief of the Landwëhr Division.[3]

When the British offensive began the 107th was thrown into action piecemeal and on the afternoon of the 20th one of its units just beat the 1st Border Regiment to the Beaurevoir Line. By the following morning the trace trenches were four or five feet deep, the dug-outs were occupied and machine guns covered gaps in the wire. The defenders looked down apprehensively on the British bridgehead in the kink in the canal between Marcoing and Masnières, where mopping up was still going on.

The prospect facing the 29th Division was not attractive. Before it lay an entrenched ridge behind which stood Rumilly village. A railway ran up the valley towards Cambrai but the enemy occupied the high ground on each side.

Only ten tanks had been officially allocated but thanks to a little private enterprise on the part of a battalion commander, eight more had been 'borrowed'. Originally the 87th Brigade had been warned to prepare a dawn assault but this was seen to be impractical. Zero hour was switched to 11 am, but by the time the 1st King's Own Scottish Borderers and the 2nd South Wales Borderers followed the Mark IVs across fields rising towards the German wire it was almost noon. The artillery not having arrived in strength, the bombardment was 'almost negligible'.[4]

Leaving the shelter of captured ammunition pits, the attackers covered only 200 yards before running into intense machine-gun fire, much of it indirect from positions out of sight on a reverse slope vulnerable only to howitzers or heavy mortars. Armour-piercing bullets penetrated, in some cases, even the 12 mm plate of the Mark IV sponsons. Field guns took on the tanks over open sights. Some turned back streaming dirty grey plumes flecked with orange. Two took direct hits and rolled to a stop. Only a solitary male ploughed on and was lost to view in the drizzle.[5]

The battalions of the 29th Division had not trained specifically with tanks and co-operation was unsure. Gaps opened between men and machines allowing the enemy to repeat the tactics which had been successful at Flesquières. Nevertheless, after covering three-quarters of a mile, scattered groups of dishevelled figures in khaki emerged from the smoke and plunged into the German trenches. One company of the South Wales Borderers which had lost most of its officers reached its objective under the command of its quartermaster-sergeant. Another was led by the only subaltern left standing. Counter-attacks burst upon them and CQMS James Ruffle was last seen using the bayonet to cover the retirement of his men; Second-Lieutenant Franklin Rowlands also fought to the end. By late afternoon the exhausted remnants of the attacking battalions were back where they started. On the right the 20th Division was unable to seize the bridges at Crèvecoeur though they were not fiercely defended.

There was some talk of repeating the assault on Rumilly the following day but after discussing the prospects with tank officers the commander of the 87th Brigade 'deprecated a renewal of the attempt'. He considered that without 'drastic artillery support' he would need thirty-two tanks. With it he might manage with sixteen.

'Neither condition could be complied with; the army cancelled the attack, so exit the cavalry.'[6]

Or so it seemed to the 29th Division, though the Cavalry Corps remained concentrated in Grand Ravine.

Mounted action was certainly the last thing on the minds of the troopers of the 1st Division who were having their first taste of street fighting. Germans had crept back into Noyelles and the 18th Hussars were helping the 2nd Royal Fusiliers to throw them out. A troop of the 9th Lancers brought a Hotchkiss into action from the top of a house and routed a German company which, incredibly, appeared to have halted to eat a midday meal.

It was all part of the effort of IV Corps to carry out the wishes of the Commander-in-Chief that Bourlon should be captured 'at an early hour and as a matter of paramount importance'.[7] The good news was that Flesquières had been evacuated during the night and the Scots had just walked into it. The bad news was that patrols of King Edward's Horse had taken prisoners from the '52nd Brandenburgers'[8] who claimed that they had just arrived from Kovel on the Eastern Front. Under questioning they revealed that at least two other regiments of the 107th Division were in or around Bourlon ridge. The British plan required the 51st Division to press south-east of the wood capturing first Cantaing and then Fontaine Notre Dame and General Harper committed the brigade held back the previous day. Sent forward before tanks had arrived, it was pinned down until they came up. Two Mark IVs, Ben Mychree and Bulawayo II, settled matters by breaking into the centre of Cantaing and setting the church tower ablaze, smoking out a machine-gun nest. Durhams of the 6th Division and the Queen's Bays closed the net and dozens of Germans fled to the shelter of La Folie Wood. The way was open to Fontaine a mile away but Harper ordered his Scots to mark time until Bourlon Wood had been captured by the 62nd Division. Hopes of this were still flourishing in high places and at an early hour the 11th Hussars had arrived near Graincourt – mounted. A squadron trotted towards Anneux, was met with a long burst of fire and galloped back.

Once again Bradford's brigade led the way. Though weary after their exertions the previous day, the men were in good spirits as they waited for the tanks (which were late). A medical officer found boxes of cigars in a dug-out and handed them round. At 10 o'clock shells streamed overhead towards Bourlon village and a white veil hung over Moeuvres where the 36th Division was attacking under cover of a smoke screen. When the tanks appeared whistles shrilled and the Yorkshiremen followed puffing pungent German cheroots.

The battle for Anneux was violent and costly. Enemy riflemen let their opponents enter the hamlet and fired from the upper storeys and attics of houses. Lewis gunners firing from the hip, in the style of the Ulstermen, blasted the windows systematically.[9]

At Anneux Chapel on the main road, just a couple of houses and a religious edifice, the garrison was routed and the defenders of the quarry beyond emerged choking and spluttering with their hands up after being deluged with smoke grenades. Scores of prisoners were taken. After this initial struggle elements of three battalions of the Duke of Wellington's Regiment reorganized along the Bapaume road. In broad terms they held the base of a triangle. The left side was formed by trenches of what had been the Hindenburg Support line, the right by a defended sunken road barring the approach to the wood. At the apex where trench met sunken road stood an iron crucifix. The Dukes were meant to clear the triangle pivoting on their right. Tanks led the move towards the wood but there were none available on the left where the Yorkshiremen were reduced to the tedious business of bombing up the support trench. This required all their attention as many Germans had escaped the preliminary bombardment. The field artillery had been delayed by the Havrincourt bottleneck, the mud being hock-deep in places. Horses were becoming exhausted and one brigade (four batteries) did not reach its battle position until late afternoon. The bombardment did not seriously worry the Germans but merely acted as an alarm signal. The massive bunker hidden in the undergrowth on the western edge of the wood was

88

hardly chipped. From its observation hatches watchers saw the advancing waves go to ground as they approached the sunken road; then a tank rumbled into view and drove parallel to the obstacle firing as it went. Prisoners were hustled back and small detachments of British came on. At the edge of the wood they hesitated, unable to find cover, and after a pause scrambled back the way they had come.

The Dukes reoccupied the sunken road, now littered with bodies and smashed weapons. There were not many cigar-smokers left.

Later the commander of the tank brigade said some machines had entered the wood and he believed that had more infantry been available a further advance could have been made. But Bradford's men had shot their bolt.[10]

He used his reserve battalion, intended to capture the village, to reinforce the others penned in a broad arrowhead position on the left of Bourlon, the tip pointing towards the unattainable iron Christ behind the German lines.

On the left the Inniskillings and Royal Irish Rifles attacking Moeuvres had an equally frustrating experience. Still unsupported by tanks, they too were reduced to the slow process of bombing their way towards the village. Barbed wire had been dragged into the broad trenches and the tactics of the previous day were not as effective. Casualties mounted. The remaining Ulster brigades waited all day on the other side of the canal for the success signal which would enable them to advance between Moeuvres and the Yorkshire battalions outside Bourlon. It never came.

To General Harper the hold-up at Bourlon justified his earlier order halting his troops short of Fontaine. The village might be only two miles or so from Cambrai but to occupy it before the wood had been captured meant exposing the garrison to fire from high ground in the rear – and concentric attacks from the direction of the city. Any satisfaction he derived from his prudent decision vanished the moment he learned that elements of the 154th Brigade were already in Fontaine. Before his message to stand fast had been delivered four tanks had roared down on the village using their six-pounders to destroy field guns en route. Two battalions quickly followed. The 1st/4th Seaforths dug in; the 1st/7th Argylls took up a support position, but they had only a tenuous link with Cantaing. Harper was considering whether to reinforce the

Seaforths in Fontaine, thus putting more troops in peril, or withdraw them and risk incurring the displeasure of the Army Commander, when the matter was resolved for him.

By the evening of the 21st Haig was satisfied that 'no possibility any longer existed of enveloping Cambrai from the south'.[11] On the other hand he understood that only one fresh German division had been identified in the disputed region between the two canals. There were even signs that the enemy was 'considering' pulling back from the sector north of the Third Army penetration. Byng's guns were now able to bombard the approaches to some of these positions and near the village of Pelves, opposite Arras, craters blown in roads were similar to those which had appeared before the withdrawal in the spring. Prisoners taken in the Bullecourt–Quéant sector immediately left of the British bulge complained they had received no rations for 36 hours, presumably because of artillery fire, and a few said they had been 'standing to' for some time 'in anticipation of orders to withdraw'.

With Bourlon in his possession Haig thought it might still be possible to deny the enemy the use of the lines which ran from the important rail junction of Aubigny au Bac, on the Sensée. These fed a narrow-gauge military network supplying the forward areas and the battery positions of the Arras sector. From the ridge his forces would also be able to 'overlook' the causeway at Arleux. As the shell flies the village is about seven miles from the southern slopes of Bourlon. With his supply lines threatened, it could be argued that the enemy would be forced to make a hasty withdrawal from a large area extending from Bourlon to the Scarpe.

To continue the assault on Bourlon meant deepening the bulge and stretching the British divisions still further. More men were needed – but these had just been made available. On the strength of the opening success of the operation Sir William Robertson had found two more divisions for Haig. These had been bound from France for Italy, where the situation was improving. The War Cabinet insisted they would have to be replaced later, but they gave the Commander-in-Chief timely flexibility. The three divisions of V Corps could be brought into the attack; would be, in fact, for Bourlon could not be ignored. The wooded ridge dominated nearly all the ground that had been won since 20 November.

The Field-Marshal decided to concentrate all on the main objective. Up to that point the offensive had been driving along two axes, like clock hands at twenty past one. The minute hand was to be removed. Offensive operations by III Corps were to cease and it would consolidate the positions reached along the St Quentin Canal and the spurs running down to it. Bourlon would be captured by IV Corps once sufficient tanks had been assembled,[12] probably by the 23rd. Until then the divisions involved had to maintain the positions reached, advancing only if an opportunity occurred.

On the other side of the line everyone had confessed frankly to being surprised – Ludendorff at Great General Headquarters, Crown Prince Rupprecht of Bavaria, the Army Group Commander, and General der Kavalerie Georg von der Marwitz. Ludendorff had been 'expecting a continuation of the attacks in Flanders and on the French front' when the blow fell on the Second Army responsible for the Arras–St Quentin sector. By eight in the morning on 20 November he had done his sums and demanded urgent action to switch reserves to the threatened area. The First Quartermaster General summed up the problem neatly:

'The order for a unit to entrain is by no means the same thing as its arrival. It has to march to the entraining stations, where trains have to be ready for it. On the various lines the trains can only follow each other at certain definite intervals . . . and the normal duration of the journey has to be added to all this. So it generally took two or three days for a division, using some thirty trains, to reach its destination. It could seldom be done in less.'[13]

Having made repeated demands for German industry to produce lorries to move troops, Ludendorff felt aggrieved at 'the lack of motor transport'.[14]

Strenuous efforts were made to take advantage of the breathing space afforded by the presence of the 107th Division. Formations holding the line north of the battle area promptly sent their own reserves. Three good line regiments, the 77th, 358th and 364th, went to the aid of the battered Landwëhr division – hence the hot reception given to Bradford's brigade which took prisoners from all of them 'in the vicinity of Anneux and S.W. of Bourlon Wood' on the 21st.[15] The German field commanders showed a willingness to co-operate, to improvise and to form ad hoc units. On the 20th a battery of light anti-aircraft guns mounted on lorries drove at top speed from Cambrai to open fire on the tanks, claiming three victims. It also reported firing on cavalry at Cantaing.[16]

Other AA batteries from the neighbouring Sixth and Fourth

Armies were rushed to the front.[17] Advance parties of reinforcing divisions began to appear in Cambrai.

Abbé Delval, who had not slept very well, learned on the 21st that all young workers were being assembled for removal from the city. He watched the inhabitants of Fontaine and Noyelles trail through the streets pushing wheelbarrows containing their belongings. As he could see himself joining a similar trek if the German decided to evacuate civilians from Cambrai he started to pack a wickerwork trunk, a precaution which threw his housekeeper into despair.

'Things must be serious because the Germans have taken some hostages. Yesterday the Archbishop found his house surrounded by soldiers and Colonel Gloss went to warn him he could no longer leave it. This morning an officer went by car to inform him he was being transferred to the Kommandantur.

'At the same time they arrested Monsieur Demolon, the mayor, and Messrs. Garin, Helot, Morand and Lestoille and took them off to the attics of the Hotel de Ville . . . .

'They say the British have taken Havrincourt, Flesquières and, according to some, Graincourt, Anneux and Marcoing!'

But a more disturbing rumour had reached him – that the British were not pressing their offensive but, having made a surprise attack and taken '14,000 prisoners and a few hundred guns, they are going back to their trenches. . . .

'In any case the Germans are bringing up all the reinforcements they can; yesterday, last night and all day they were passing through on foot or in vehicles; others are arriving this evening.'

The scales were beginning to tilt against the British. Four battalions of West Yorkshires (the 185th Brigade) had relieved Bradford's men during the night. At dawn a barrage of high explosive and gas shells fell on them. Hostile aircraft swept low over the Crucifix, dropping bombs and firing machine-guns. SOS signals soared unseen by the artillery; they were of a new design and more like a rifle grenade than a rocket.

Support companies along the Bapaume road saw the frontline troops falling back in disorder. Following hard on the heels of the barrage, the Germans had inflicted severe casualties. Nearly all the officers of one battalion had fallen. The shaken men were rallied and, reinforced by more West Yorkshires and a company of York and Lancasters, counter-attacked in their turn. By 10 o'clock some of the lost ground was recovered.[18] At this moment on the other side of Bourlon Wood, General Harper's worst fears were realized.

The Scots in Fontaine had made a start on clearing the cellars as soon as it was light but they were weak in number and there were a surprising number of Germans in hiding. A dozen enemy aeroplanes circled over the village and though the HQ staff of the 1st/4th Seaforths lined up in the main street and drove them higher with rifle fire, they continued to swoop from time to time and maintained constant observation. In mid-morning Germans poured out of the trees bordering Bourlon and charged down the hillside while others moved from Cambrai to cut off the village. The main attack came on in five waves at ten-pace intervals with about five paces between individuals.

'A large number of officers directed the advance and the waves kept distinct and in good order and came on steadily regardless of casualties . . . on the left to within bombing distance of our front line.'[19]

Germans emerged from buildings and fired from the church and houses near it. SOS signals for artillery support went unanswered. In the afternoon the woefully thin ranks of the Seaforths withdrew.

Further proof of growing German strength was provided at Moeuvres. The 12th Irish Rifles pushed right through the village, skilfully clearing the dug-outs and houses. They were establishing themselves in a captured trench alongside the cemetery when Germans were seen massing in the distance. This time SOS signals were seen but a company of the Royal Irish Fusiliers trying to come to the rescue were prevented by a machine-gun barrage. The Rifles fell back steadily, covered by Lewis gunners. It took the Germans an hour and forty minutes to drive them out of Moeuvres but in the face of an estimated two battalions no other outcome was possible.[20]

The only success the British could report that night was the capture of Tadpole Copse, a wood which took its name from its outline on the map and straddled a ridge dominating a considerable length of the enemy line[21] west of Moeuvres. The Queen's Westminsters[22] and the London Rifle Brigade[23] made a successful bombing attack, penetrating more than a mile along the enemy trenches. Five batteries of 6-inch howitzers had 'thickened' the supporting field gun barrage.

Earlier in the day Monsignor Chollet and his fellow prisoners in the attics of the Hotel de Ville had heard a particularly violent bombardment. Two heavy batteries were pounding Bourlon Village and five more were systematically raking the wood, back and forth; 60 and 100-lb shells were tearing branches from the fine oaks . . . blowing holes in the carriageways built with such care.

CHAPTER TEN
Etonians and Mongrels

The men of the 40th Division had been incredibly lucky. The last Kitchener division to reach France (in June, 1916), it had held the line, raided the enemy, carried out reliefs and trained, but had missed the Somme, Arras, Messines and Ypres.

Originally the numeral 40 had been given to a formation raised in December, 1914, but this had gone on active service as the 33rd. When the new 40th was raised in September, 1915, the great outburst of patriotic fervour which had filled the ranks of the original 'Service' battalions was spent. There was a serious shortage of volunteers and the War Office had reduced the regulation minimum height to 5 feet 3 inches. Short stocky men were sought to form Bantam battalions.

This would have been all very well if all those forthcoming had been fit, but many of the recruits for the 40th were somewhat suspect: 'unfit to undergo even the training to which they were submitted at home'.[1] One battalion which was given a thorough medical inspection at Aldershot was reduced from 1,000 to 200 men. Finally the divisional commander put it to the authorities that by amalgamating units he could form two brigades from the men already at his disposal but four more battalions would have to be drafted in if the 40th were ever to be able to take the field. These he was given.

Previous 'K' divisions had been raised on a regional basis, such as the 10th Irish, 11th Northern, 12th Eastern, 19th Western – or with regimental connections, like the 14th and 20th Light Divisions.

The 40th was something of a mongrel. As finally mobilized it consisted of a Welsh brigade, the 119th, one with two Scots and two English battalions, the 120th, and a third which was entirely English, the 121st. The 12th Green Howards, composed of craftsmen and artisans from the Middlesbrough area,[2] formed the pioneer battalion.

In the autumn of 1917 the 40th had suffered casualties in many minor actions, particularly south-west of Cambrai, but its units were still fundamentally those which had boarded the troop trains at Woking, Surrey, at the end of May, 1916. Early in November it was billeted around the forest of Lucheux, not far from Doullens, some units in good accommodation, others in 'exceedingly draughty and leaky barns'. Lucheux itself lies at the junction of several valleys and the troops trained on the thickly wooded slopes – 'a welcome relief after the months of trench warfare'.[3] The Welsh played rugby in their spare time and the 12th South Wales Borderers lost by two tries to a dropped goal to the 2nd Battalion which was training only a few miles away up the Arras road. Before there could be a return match the victors vanished mysteriously along with their division.[4] The 12th and the rest of the 40th made the best of their indifferent billets and wondered how long their luck would last.

On the 16th they started to move by route marches, some units covering twelve miles on the 17th, almost double that on the 19th. The booming of guns announced the opening of the new offensive early on the 20th and by the 21st the heads of the columns were close behind the old British front line in the villages of Doignies and Beaumetz les Cambrai, not far from the RN29. The sight of tanks aroused great interest. Few of the 40th had seen them before. None of them had trained with armour.

At 8 am on the morning of the 22nd Major-General John Ponsonby[5] was told that his troops had been placed under command of IV Corps, would relieve the 62nd Division that night and capture Bourlon Wood and village the following day. It was his first battle as a major-general; previously he had commanded a brigade in the Guards Division. Ponsonby's somewhat stern appearance belied his reputation for being popular with the troops and concerned for their welfare; among other things he had introduced one of the first unit newspapers in the Guards Division – a publication called *The Dump*. His involvement in the new attack increased the number of Old Etonians with key roles in the

96

battle. Byng was the senior (until Plumer was sent to Italy three of the BEF's Army Commanders were Old Etonians, the other being Gough). Ponsonby was four years his junior and De Pree, Chief Staff Officer of IV Corps, and Mullens and Greenly of the cavalry were contemporaries. Even at this late stage there were still hopes that the arme blanche would come into its own.

Over the years an impression has grown up that Sir Douglas Haig sat at a desk far behind the lines while others got on with the job at the 'sharp end'. This was certainly not the case at Cambrai. The Commander-in-Chief was constantly out and about. On the 22nd he visited IV Corps headquarters and commented on the need for divisional commanders to keep in close touch with their troops. General Harper and his staff had been four and a half miles behind the start line on the 20th and then moved to Trescault which was about six miles from Fontaine. An advanced report centre was opened at Flesquières but maintaining close control was not a simple matter. Telephone lines were the main channels of communication. Every time a headquarters moved there was a certain amount of interruption and at Cambrai few officers had any real experience of the open warfare conditions which applied during the first heady hours. Used to the minimal advances of previous offensives, senior staffs had lost the art of mobile operations. The passage of so many tanks across the battlefield and the weight of traffic in the congested salient made cable maintenance a nightmare.

Sir Douglas Haig visited Harper during the morning and, after leaving, met Major-General Mullens leading the reassembled 1st Cavalry Division back to Metz and the interminable chore of watering its horses. Mullens expressed his disappointment at being ordered to concentrate in the rear and found the Commander-in-Chief sympathetic. Haig confided to his diary that he would have liked to have ordered Mullens to return, but restrained himself as it would only have caused confusion.[6]

The Chief Staff Officer of the division happened to be a 17th Lancer and a close friend[7] and Sir Douglas borrowed his horse and rode with Mullens and some of his staff to a point where he could view the battlefield, including Flesquières. He was told that many of the wrecked tanks he could see on the ridge had been knocked out by a single German officer operating a gun from a concealed position until he was killed. Haig felt the incident underlined the need for close co-operation between infantry and tanks. From Mullens he gathered that the battle had given the cavalry valuable experience 'and they were all as pleased as possible'.[8]

On his way back to his own HQ, Haig called on Byng at Albert and left satisfied that 'all was in train for a major effort on the morrow'.[9]

Roads laboriously repaired before the offensive were beginning to disintegrate. Their surfaces had been good enough to start with because the divisions holding the front were stretched and the traffic light. When six additional assault formations plus the cavalry crowded on to them they were unable to take the weight.

'Being sunken, it was impossible to widen these mere country lanes, nor was there anything approaching a sufficiency of metal to sustain the huge volume of traffic . . . On the Hermies–Graincourt road there were quite serious blocks in the traffic . . . when a limber broke a pole or a cooker lost a wheel.'[10]

Along these muddy cart tracks plodded the laden platoons of the 40th Division. Transport jostled for a place on the broken pavé of the RN 29, though where it passed through the Hindenburg Line 'there was no recognisable feature at all in the landscape (where) our barrage had done its business, and the sight of that descent towards the canal was one of utter desolation'.[11]

Part of the divisional headquarters spent fifteen hours covering nine miles to reach Havrincourt across the grain of the traffic flow. Two brigade headquarters finally took over from the Yorkshiremen in the labyrinth of underground workings at Graincourt. There seemed to be plenty of room for everyone, and at least it was warm. Above ground there had been a noticeable drop in temperature. Near the sugar factory there was little shelter and after six hours the 13th Green Howards relieved the West Yorkshires in 'a jumbled mass of ruins of a trench system on which much care and energy had been bestowed'.[12]

Between rifts in the clouds a feeble moon occasionally lit the way for the numbed, red-eyed dirty soldiers of the 62nd Division making their way to the rear. More than 1,200 wounded had already begun their journey back but nearly 250 officers and men were known to be dead and almost as many missing, a lot of them lying stiff around the positions retaken by the Germans that morning. Almost asleep on their feet, the infantry struggled through the night against a tide of traffic that grew stronger the closer they got to the Havrincourt bottleneck. One battalion covered seven miles, washed down breakfast with hot tea in shacks in the wood and then tramped another five miles to billets. The PBI of 1917 were not called footsloggers for nothing.

The 40th Division, which up to then had either consolidated or tidied up other people's battlefields, was at last to have one all to itself. In its comparatively well-preserved state (its men had been known to refer to themselves as the Forgotten 40th[13]) the division was a unique survivor of one of the most endangered species on earth. The Brass Hats had meant well by the New Armies, intending to break them in gradually. Then circumstances, political pressures, the need to take the strain off the other Allied armies, had forced the premature use of the raw divisions.

Standing at the door of the slaughterhouse for so long, the 40th's soldiers can have had few illusions about the fate awaiting them. Their senior commanders must have wondered how much, if any, of the original ardour remained. The division's performance promised to make a rewarding study for the disinterested observer.

Certainly there was nothing complicated about the plan the infantry were called on to perform. Two brigades would advance side by side, the 121st to storm the village, the 119th to capture the wood. They would then establish themselves on their final objective, a line running east–west to the north of the village with its right resting on the railway cutting. The 120th Brigade would be held in reserve.

On the right of the 40th the 51st Division, which still had some strong battalions, was preparing another attack on Fontaine. On its left the 36th Division was to renew the struggle for Moeuvres: 'Tanks were to assist the attack for the first time during the operations'.[14]

On the left of the Northern Irish regiments a brigade of the 56th Division was to expand its hold on Tadpole Copse. It was hoped to repeat the bombing success of the previous day. There was talk of an 'advance up the canal' to 'roll up the Hindenburg Support System'.

Unlike the improvised artillery preparation on the 21st the bombardment was carefully organized. Most heavy guns were to cover the 40th Division and included (with those under control of IV Corps) thirty-six of the versatile 60-pounders, twenty-six modern 6-inch and four 8-inch and one 12-inch howitzer. Four

9.2s and a 12-inch howitzer were to lend weight to the guns firing on Moeuvres.

The front and flanks of the various attacks were to be screened by smoke 'and special attention was to be paid . . . to the ground immediately over the (Bourlon) ridge to prevent anti-tank guns from coming into action'. Tasks of divisional machine-gun companies were to be co-ordinated by IV Corps and as many low-flying aircraft as possible were to attack ground targets.

By dint of hard effort ninety-two tanks were made fit for action and divided among the attacking formations. Harper was to get the largest share – forty-eight, Ponsonby thirty-two and the Ulster Division twelve. On paper this was a powerful force, but it was facing an enemy growing in strength. One of the aims of the offensive was to dislocate the railways serving Cambrai. Had these been cut as intended Ludendorff would have had difficulties in concentrating his reserves. As they remained intact, for though the Royal Flying Corps claimed hits on stations damage was insignificant, the enemy was able to respond just as Sir Douglas Haig had foreseen.

German divisions were set in motion from as far away as the Aisne front and batteries, though arriving slowly, took up positions covering the northern slopes of Bourlon Ridge out of sight of the British ground observers. More of the mobile anti-aircraft guns were deployed near Fontaine and, a compliment to the successful activity of the RFC, the Richthofen Circus had arrived from the Ypres sector – Jagstaffeln 4, 6, 10 and 11. British numerical superiority was vanishing along with strategical opportunity though Byng still seriously contemplated the use of the Cavalry Corps.

The position to be attacked formed a shallow arc which began at Moeuvres and curved along the edge of Bourlon Wood to La Folie with its château and grounds within easy reach (via a lock crossing) of the suburbs of Cambrai. To occupy the ridge without carrying the extremities of the enemy line would be simply to make the arc deeper. Recognizing this, the enemy had disputed every foot of the ground at Moeuvres and established the East Prussian 58th Regiment at La Folie. The British, though grasping the need to take Moeuvres, did not pay the same attention to the other flank, south of which lay the boundary between IV and III Corps. As the latter's operations had been 'shut down',[15] the defenders of La Folie, though unaware of it, were in no danger from that direction. Special measures should have been taken to pin down the garrison while Fontaine was attacked, but 'the strength of the opposition was not known to British Intelligence'.[16]

'Int' too was suffering from the stultifying influence of static warfare in which thousands of shells were sometimes expended on a raid resulting in a single prisoner needed for identification purposes. Fluid conditions needed different methods, quicker appreciations, more facts, less optimism. As early as the 21st 'much movement of lorries' was noticed behind the enemy lines south of Cambrai.[17] It was only self-deception to assume automatically that they were evacuating the city. Aerial reconnaissance, though hampered by low cloud, reported increased rail traffic. This was unlikely to be holiday excursions.

A tendency to under-rate enemy powers of improvisation persisted, based on mental images built up before the war. Tourists, in particular, were amused by the emphasis on efficiency in the Kaiser's Germany, its dedication to order and time-tables, its respect for anyone who wore a uniform. Britain roared at Jerome K. Jerome's *Three Men on the Bummel*. It came as something of a surprise after the war to learn that the Germans who had been branded as stupid for firing on the same targets at the same time each night held the 'English' guilty of the same folly. Front-line veterans had more respect for their opponents. A regular officer who served in both wars reckoned ruefully that after a breakthrough a German sergeant-major and a traffic policeman at a cross-roads at noon meant an improvised battle group on the spot at two o'clock. By 23 November the enemy had had three days to get over his initial shock. The German 3rd Guards Division was under orders to relieve the troops in Bourlon Wood.

The assault companies of the 40th Division spent the remaining hours of darkness amid the corpses and wreckage that marked the path of Bradford's advance. Some occupied the sunken road captured by the Dukes. Others settled down in improvised positions around Anneux. There was no time to explain the niceties of armour-infantry co-operation, instruction which seems to have been overlooked at Lucheux, and in most cases the men were too tired to care. They dozed and shivered and listened to a rising wind gusting through the great wood.

Behind the line all was frustration and confusion. Communications were deteriorating rapidly. Army Service Corps drivers, reins in hand, feet frozen, sat waiting for the columns to move.

Near Graincourt tank commanders waited anxiously for the horse-drawn limbers bringing extra fuel and grease up the solitary track through the ruins of Havrincourt. Gradually enough arrived to ensure all infantry units would have some support from Mark IVs and arrangements were made to send on other machines as they were replenished.[18]

'The morning of the 23rd November came in with a blustering north-east wind sending cloud shadows chasing over the undulating ground. An occasional scud of sleet made way for spells of sunshine in which Bourlon Wood to the east glowed in ragged, autumn finery, while Moeuvres church tower stood out above the ruins of the village . . .

'By 9.30 am the forms of tanks making their way up from the south, loomed up more plainly, and the nonchalant manner in which they leant against a brick wall and then moved on leaving a ruin behind them was much appreciated. These tanks which had been out and active for several days . . . certainly added much to the high confidence animating the 13th Green Howards.'[19]

Shortly before zero hour a Welsh soldier wrote: 'It is now daylight and everything is quiet, just a few birds singing now and again.'

As the minutes ticked by flights of British planes appeared. One swooped on the wood and shot a sniper from the top of a tree.[20]

Yellow flashes rippled over the plain as the 18-pounder batteries opened fire. Clusters of heavy shells crumped inside the wood, searching for the cross-roads indicated on the map. Tanks crawled through the waiting infantry and mounted the slopes. The last hands were shaken, the final good lucks muttered. The troops clambered out of the sunken road and, with bayonets fixed or shouldering heavy Lewis guns, set out in the wake of the handful of Mark IVs which had arrived.

The Welsh Brigade's leading battalions headed for the wood while the 121st moved towards Bourlon village. A ground mist[21] gave some cover from view but it was no substitute for the smoke screen which had been planned – and this did not materialize. Had someone in desperation decided preference had to be given to the HE and shrapnel waggons in the ammunition columns trying to negotiate 'the congestion about Havrincourt'? Normal shells were plentiful throughout the day.[22] Whatever the reason, the infantry could be seen clearly as they closed on their objectives.

In some cases the Welsh companies had to cover 1,000 yards down a slope to the main road and then mount an incline to reach the Wood. Shells which fell among them multiplied and formed a barrage. The 19th Royal Welsh Fusiliers and the 12th South Wales Borderers moved steadily through it, crossed an indifferent trench and pushed into the foliage, into the unknown.

Reconnaissance photographs gave little idea of what to expect, though maps of the wood were marked 'saturated with water close to the surface'.[23] The troops were entering a natural arena, the wooded slopes running up to a horseshoe ridge which dominated all within. Secondary growth had invaded neglected clearings where timber had been extracted before the war. At the foot of mature trees hazel and aspen breaks were laced with briars. Young beeches were thick with russet leaves and big oaks, always reluctant to shed their foliage until January, kept the marshy ground in perpetual shade – and provided cover for snipers in the branches.

Other obstacles included two old sandpits, small on the British ordnance survey maps but in reality deep excavations with chine-like cliffs unscaleable by tanks and easily covered by fire. The shooting lodge, which became the 'chalet' to the British, stood like a Norman keep just west of the main south–north track. Its cellars, entered by a winding sheltered path, covered the ground floor area of the building and could hold fifty or sixty men.

The well-maintained roads ran straight for the most part but the causeway principle on which they had been built meant that one man might be at the bottom of a cutting while, 100 yards away, another, almost on the same level, was perched on an embankment. The main fixed defences were the group of pill-boxes at the western end covering the approach from Bapaume. With foresight and more concrete the hill could have been made virtually impregnable. A large dump of barbed wire and pickets found on the outskirts of the wood might well have been assembled with that in mind.

The Lehr Regiment was in the process of relieving the Silesian 52nd when the attack began, so there was no shortage of men to meet it. Tree-top marksmen apart, visibility for both sides was often reduced to about four yards, leaving the advantage with the Germans who could wait in hastily-dug trenches until their opponents blundered on them. The straight paths were ideal avenues for field guns to cover and Maxims to sweep. Nevertheless by 12.30 the Welshmen had fought their way through the wood and were entrenching themselves on the curving ridge at its northern and eastern edges. Though they sank calf-deep in black leaf-mould and their equipment snagged on branches, they charged with rifles up slopes which would have dismayed an unencumbered rambler with a walking-stick. Many a vicious struggle went unseen and unknown in the undergrowth. Little quarter was given in that first inspired surge up the hill. Bayonet, butt and bomb had been used in a desperate mêlée on the Bourlon–Fontaine road and British and German blood had been spilled on the Carrefour Madame; two tanks had been knocked out but others got through and, with their help, the Bantams made it.

The Fusiliers were in sight of the railway line and, thanks to a Mark IV, the Borderers took the factory at the bottom of another steep slope from which the tile clay had been extracted. A party had even reached the final objective – houses on the eastern outskirts of Bourlon. One of the few officers left, Captain J. Symes, who had been with the battalion since its formation at Newport in 1915, was in command.

Urgent but vain attempts were made to contact the 121st Brigade, but if the absence of a smoke-screen had created problems for the Welshmen it had been disastrous for their comrades on the left. The 13th Green Howards and the 20th Middlesex, supported by the 21st, had to move along the left of the wood and cross an almost bare extension of the tree-covered ridge. Over this spur lay the château at the west end of the village. The leading troops were to capture it and swing right into the streets of Bourlon. To get there they had to advance in full view of German observers. Even before zero hour a subaltern had been killed and a 'galling fire from machine guns' met the Green Howards. 'The advance had just begun when young Walton, the Battalion Signalling Officer, was shot through the heart.'[24] Walton had been among thirty-four officers who landed in France with the 13th in June, 1916.

From a distance the havoc wrought by the machine-guns west of Bourlon was not obvious. With companies following tanks and barrage 'the whole show looked more like a field day than very much the real thing'.[25]

To Lieutenant-Colonel Plunkett of the 19th Royal Welsh Fusiliers watching from the right: 'It was rather a nice sight to see the men moving along leisurely as if they were having a day out.'[26]

It was a deceptive picture. The 121st Brigade was moving over ground swept by bullets and pounded by howitzers and field guns firing from positions near Quarry Wood. The leading troops pressed on nevertheless and actually reached a point well west of Bourlon where they took sixty prisoners from dug-outs. These were being taken to the rear when a counter-attack freed them and most of the escorting troops were killed. Shells also knocked out three Mark IVs crossing the spur but three others reached the village.

To an extent the width of the streets and the open spaces, like small village greens, were of help to the tank commanders, but the layout also aided the defenders. Many houses were detached, with gardens; farms opened onto the streets. Nearly all the buildings had cellars and, having been in sole occupation since April, the Germans had enjoyed plenty of opportunity to explore the place. Machine guns could be brought to bear on almost every square inch of ground and the pill-box under the Ferme de l'Abbaye had an outstanding field of vision.

In all, seven tanks penetrated the village and were subjected to violent close-range fire. Parties of the Middlesex and the Green Howards attempted to follow them and unco-ordinated fighting took place on the outskirts. The Green Howards reported one company in the château and its outbuildings with a detachment in the quarry beyond. These exposed positions were 'frequently surrounded by the enemy' and all attempts to push more men over the spur were broken up. The flanking fire from the direction of Quarry Wood and trenches to the west continued relentlessly.

'What orders had been given to the troops on the left I do not know; they appear to have been ordered to wait until the leading battalions of the 40th Division should have gained their respective objectives, but even then no move was made.'[27]

It was not for want of trying.

The 36th Division should have been on the left of the Green Howards, but the two-mile gap between the villages of Bourlon and Moeuvres had become a death trap. This need to attack up the Hindenburg System bedevilled the whole operation. Nor did having to operate on both sides of the Canal help the Ulstermen (though they found the dry bed an excellent place to lay telephone cables).

Two brigades were employed – one to make another assault on Moeuvres, the other to advance more than a mile from the

Bapaume road to Quarry Wood, level with Bourlon village. It was a tall order. In between the start line and the wood lay an isolated strongpoint, Round Trench (though trenches would have been a better description as there was a maze of them). Beyond it lay part of the original Hindenburg Support Line, marked Hobart Trench on British maps, from which counter-attacks had been launched against the West Yorkshires on the morning of the 22nd.

At Moeuvres the infantry were to make a conventional attack but sixteen tanks were attached for the Quarry Wood operation. This was not a generous allotment, particularly as there was no time for reconnaissance. The brigade headquarters concerned, the 107th, had waited with increasing anxiety for the tank commander who eventually found them at 5 am.[28] Orders were not issued until 8.30 and by the time they reached the people most concerned one company commander 'had less than 15 minutes to assemble his men and explain the attack to his officers'. The Ulstermen's first experience of fighting alongside armour went from bad to worse. As a preliminary it was essential for the 15th Royal Irish Rifles to 'roll up' a stretch of the Hindenburg Support line and reach the canal but one of two tanks on which they were relying broke down as soon as it arrived and the other made off in the wrong direction and was never seen or heard of again. This mishap was regarded as 'nothing short of a calamity'[29] and did nothing to encourage troops who had been worked hard before the battle and engaged in strenuous operations since it began. The men who went over the top in November, 1917, were not the same enthusiasts who had marched through bunting-clad streets and cheering crowds to Belfast City Hall in May, 1915. The other battalions involved advanced at zero hour but 'the infantry, owing to the intensity of small arms fire, were unable to keep up with the tanks'.[30]

Eleven Mark IVs 'cruised about fruitlessly all day' inflicting heavy losses but attracting considerable attention from the opposing artillery. The young commanders of 'E' Battalion seemed to find Round Trench irresistible.[31]

'Esme' got there first but was quickly knocked out, her crew taking cover in shell holes. Soon afterwards 'Eclipse II' arrived but every gun was put out of action in a storm of bullets. A corporal repaired the broken hammer of a six-pounder but 'five minutes later a shell passed through the rear end and exploded on the left side, setting the (stowed) camouflage net on fire.' The sole survivor, Private Dove, the driver, stayed by the wreck.

'Explorer' came up about the same time as 'Eclipse II' and found 'perfect targets as the trenches were fully manned . . . I gave orders to my gunners to use grape shot and when we opened up with this the Boche put their hands up.'

A red and yellow flag was hoisted to call up infantry who either did not see or could not understand the signal. The Germans picked up their rifles and the battle recommenced. Soon only one six-pounder and a Lewis gun remained in action. Four of the crew were wounded and the section commander, a captain who had chosen to ride in 'Explorer', was also hit. Having used up all his ammunition, Second-Lieutenant Lenard drove back to replenish.

'I think we must have killed from 300 to 400 Germans.'

Round Trench was still holding out at 3 pm. An irrepressible second-lieutenant called Fairbairn, who had 'travelled right across the strongpoint several times' in 'Eve', drove back to the nearest infantry and brought up a company commander to show him 'what was in front of him'. The passenger decided he did not have enough men and would ask his colonel for more. Fairbairn took him back and returned to 'roll out the wire in the interval', i.e. until the troops arrived. A few minutes later a shell set his tank on fire and he and his crew 'evacuated' to the nearest craters.

At this time the Ulstermen were still battling house by house through Moeuvres. A third battalion was brought in to the fight but the Germans were also receiving reinforcements. The left-hand punch had been blocked.

The 51st Division's attempt to work round the other side of Bourlon Wood had also run into difficulties, though there had been none of the contact problems experienced by the 36th Division. Well before dawn the sunken road that runs for more than two miles between Graincourt and Marcoing was alive with kilted figures. A line of tanks, engines ticking over, noses cocked against the embankment, stood ready to climb out. Early assembly had been necessary to escape the observers on Bourlon Ridge.

At zero hour twelve machines led the 1st/6th Seaforths into the gap between the wood and Fontaine, twelve more headed straight for the village, followed by the 1st/6th Gordons.[32]

The attack began well 'though the divisional practice of keeping the infantry well behind the tank advance was unfortunately again in evidence'.[33]

Also murderously obvious were the machine guns in La Folie wood. Caught in the cross-fire between the wood and Fontaine the Gordons could make no headway; it is doubtful if they could have succeeded had they been within ten yards of a tank. They dug in 500 yards short of Fontaine.[34]

The Mark IVs moved steadily towards the village. There was no drill for street fighting and the experience gained in the previous days had not been disseminated. Later Fuller wrote that it 'never occurred to me that our infantry commanders would thrust tanks into such places'. His surprise is hard to understand as they had been 'thrust' into swamps and pulverized woods at Ypres. The machines were also at a disadvantage in having lost the 'overwhelmingly demoralizing' effect which made them so potent on 20 November.[35]

Crouched in cellars or watching from the upper storeys of houses, the Silesians of the 46th (von Kirchbach) Regiment saw their outpost line overrun in the fields but held their fire; mobile anti-aircraft gunners waited on their lorries. Tank tracks were clattering in the streets before fire was opened at point-blank range. Armour-piercing bullets from attic windows tore through the 8 mm tank roofs and hammered on the thicker sides and sponsons. Melting on impact, hot lead from ordinary rounds spurted through joints in the plates. Tiny flakes of metal few across the fighting compartment, gashing hands and faces. The vulnerable barrels of many Lewis guns, which had replaced the armoured Vickers of earlier models, were riddled. Those still serviceable blazed back and six-pounder shells made matchwood of the furniture barricading the windows.

As soon as the first wave of tanks left the sunken road eleven more drove across the fields from Flesquières to take their place. Followed by infantry reinforcements, six of them headed for Fontaine and three for the edge of Bourlon Wood nearest the village. As they approached heavy shells burst around them and a barrage came down. The supporting Scots scattered in confusion, fired on by machine-guns at the edge of La Folie wood. A section of Mark IVs had been detached to deal with these and two females had entered the trees where they scattered enemy posts but could not silence the Germans holding out in the château. A six-pounder tank, supposed to accompany them, had been knocked out en route, but even if it had arrived its presence would not have been decisive. It might have suppressed the fire from the château windows but it could not chase the enemy from the cellars. Nor could it have overcome the big bunkers in the grounds. These great cubes of concrete were 'blind' – without weapon slits – but the occupants could sit out almost any weight of fire. Short of foot soldiers climbing onto them and dropping bombs down the air vents (and these may have had shutters) or going in by the door, there was little to be done. When the tanks withdrew the Germans re-occupied positions on the fringes of the wood and blazed away. It is unlikely that the crews of the Mark IVs even noticed the double bunker which had been tucked in behind the gothic gatehouse.

Along the northern edge of La Folie was a very deep sunken road in the banks of which the Germans had tunnelled dug-outs.[36] It was an ideal position from which to take the Highlanders in the flank.

Twelve more Mark IVs crawled down the slope from Flesquières to renew the attack. No one could be in any doubt that the Tank Corps meant business, but the Scots were tiring. Fresh troops were called for.

CHAPTER ELEVEN
Ordeal of the HLI

If Major-General Geoffrey Feilding[1] felt uneasy it was understandable. The Guards Division had been moving by tiring marches nearer and nearer the front and he had a growing impression that all was not well. On the 16th, at a secret briefing, he had been told by Sir Julian Byng that his men would not be used in the offensive unless Bourlon Wood was captured on the first day of the attack. If it did fall into British hands the Guards 'would pass through the gap in the enemy's defences and would attack north in the rear of the German front line in conjunction with the 40th Division'.[2]

Bourlon had not fallen but the approach march continued. The leading Guards brigade had reached Doignies that morning in the steps of the 40th which by then was in violent action at Bourlon. At 8.30 Feilding had asked IV Corps, under whose orders he had been placed, if he would be required to relieve any of the divisions in the line but had been told 'most unlikely'.

At midday, however, a signal warned that he might be required to replace the 51st Division that night. The day became one 'full of orders – countermanded orders – new orders – and lack of orders'.[3]

Early in the afternoon the Guards learned they were definitely to carry out the relief and began an exasperating search for the headquarters of the Highland brigades. From the direction of Bourlon came the roar of battle. In the early afternoon the first German counter-attack forced the Welsh brigade from the edge of the wood into the trees. A sergeant crept back from the houses where Symes's detachment was holding out and found a tank to

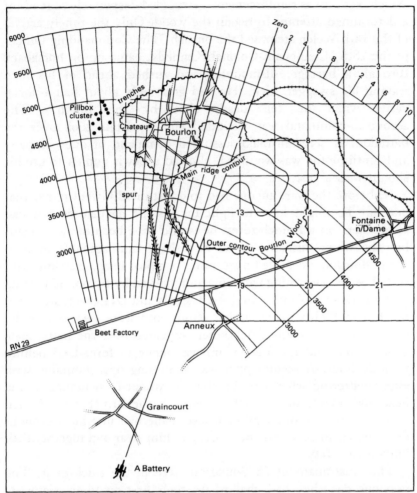

Simplified outline detail of a trench map used by 19-year-old 2nd Lt John Sinnett, FOO (forward observation officer) of 'A' Battery, 181st Brigade, Royal Field Artillery, during the 40th Division's attack on November 23. The battery position is shown S of Graincourt together with distances and degrees of the arc of fire. Young Sinnett who survived the war, reached one of the sunken roads W of Bourlon (which is not certain) on the 23rd. As the 40th Division's artillery remained in action throughout the battle, after the infantry were withdrawn, it may be assumed the map was in constant use. Note example of squares marked in degrees for map references.

cover its withdrawal. Soon all South Wales Borderer officers who had started the attack had been hit and the Fusiliers also suffered many casualties. In mid-afternoon two companies of the 17th Welch, sent up as reinforcements, struggled desperately to fend off a determined attempt to regain the wood. Only the timely arrival of the 18th Welch stemmed the onrush. The Commanding Officer of the 18th, Lieutenant-Colonel Kennedy, came up on horseback through a barrage, dismounted and rushed ahead of his men waving his swagger stick. 'He had gone only about half-a-dozen yards when he fell dead, shot by the Bosch.'⁴ The second-in-command was wounded and a captain took over the battalion. A sergeant-major assumed command of one company and, until he too was wounded, allowed a Lewis gunner to use his shoulder as a rest.

If, before the war, anyone had told a stunted Gwent miner that one day he might have to fight for his life against Pomeranian Grenadiers⁵ in a French forest he would have been declared mad, but the whole scenario would have been unimaginable even in 1914. Bourlon resembled a steaming compost heap, crawling with scaly beetles, swarming with ants and marked by a cloud of darting midges. Drab biplanes – SE5 As, Camels and DH 5s – roared over the hill in flights up to fifteen strong and were swooped on by gaudy Albatros scouts. Richthofen appeared over the battle zone about 1 pm and his first victim was lucky to force-land behind friendly lines. A second pilot was skimming over Fontaine with guns chattering when the Red Baron swooped. Wounded in the head and unable to pull out of his dive, the British flier crashed into the trees. Another pilot, whose plane had just been brought down by an anti-aircraft shell, dragged him clear and together they limped to safety.

The Australians of 68 Squadron were in the thick of it. The previous day they had chalked up their first air-to-air victories. Lieutenant F. G. Huxley, gained height after strafing a column of infantry, found himself 1,000 feet above and behind an Albatros. He dived to within fifty feet, fired thirty rounds and saw it plunge to earth where it lay 'four wings flat on the ground and a tail sticking up into the air'. An hour later a two-seater DKW received 100 rounds from the machine gun of Lieutenant Howard and glided down behind the British lines.

Major-General Hugh Trenchard, the Royal Flying Corps' field commander, visited the squadron on the 22nd and wrote to

Birdwood, commanding the ANZAC Corps, congratulating him on the conduct of the squadron which was 'very much shot about' but, at that time, had suffered only one fatality.

The pilots 'apparently revelled' in flying 'amongst the treetops' strafing 'the Hun' from fifty feet.[6]

Ground attacks by the RFC were appreciated at a much humbler level than that of major-general. Huxley reported on 23 November:

'I saw three tanks in the wood. On the eastern edge I saw two guns which were apparently holding the tanks up. I dropped four bombs on the gun positions one by one, from 100 feet, which silenced them. The three tanks advanced and three others south of the wood also. I saw a stronghold WNW of Fontaine which was holding up infantry. A Camel joined me and we dived several times. I fired 500 rounds and each time I dived the infantry advanced.'

Lieutenant Albert Griggs, an American-born pilot serving with 68 Squadron, had attacked a field gun near Fontaine on the 22nd, dropping a 25lb bomb within a few yards of it before scattering the detachment with his Vickers. On the 23rd he saw British infantry pinned down west of Bourlon and dived repeatedly on a strongpoint, coming as low as fifty feet. The Maxims on the ridge were firing down on him at times and plane and pilot were eventually riddled and crashed.[7]

Another member of 68 Squadron was posted missing and Australians were landing tattered DH 5s at airfields throughout the region all day. Many were beyond repair.

While the scouts clashed above the ridge, the DH 4 and Martynside two-seater squadrons struck at the German rear. Railway stations at Dechy, Douai and Somain were hit by 112 lb bombs which were also dropped at Denain, once battered by Marlborough's cannon balls. Observation planes reported many troop trains which 'left no doubt that the full flow of reinforcements to the Cambrai front was in full tide'.[8]

Yet even on the afternoon of the 23rd Sir Julian Byng was still contemplating a breakthrough. The Cavalry Corps was warned once again that it might be required to sweep north of Bourlon and operate against Cambrai from the west.[9]

Some RFC pilots were more optimistic than others. One was confident he had seen British troops north-east of Bourlon Wood and others on the eastern outskirts of Fontaine, which seemed to have been captured. He had heard a big explosion in the centre of Cambrai above the noise of his aircraft's engine.[10]

'Another terrible day,' recorded Abbé Delval. 'From morning to night shells whistle over our heads, the whining of the English is shrill, the Germans replying to them have a deeper note. The stations are no longer exclusive targets . . . missiles have fallen in the Place au Bois, in the park . . . and quite a few houses have been wrecked.'

The Hospice had been hit and a number of occupants hurt, though most of the sick had been moved to the cellars. Few people dared go out and those who did ran the risk of being stopped by soldiers and asked for their identity cards. Anyone between 17 and 48 was promptly arrested and sent to Germany or Belgium for forced labour.

Archbishop Chollet and the mayor had been released from their precarious prison in the attics of the Hotel de Ville but were still under arrest.

'There has been no gas since yesterday and we have been warned to stock up with water. Nearly everyone is living in their cellar. As for myself, I hardly dare go into the kitchen which has only a zinc roof.'

The Abbé had moved his bed to the ground floor. He reflected that even if the British did take Cambrai the Germans would start shelling it.

'There is still a constant rolling bombardment to the south, south-west and west.'

To develop the situation, the British had to have all of Bourlon ridge and quickly. If Fontaine could be taken and the tanks pressed behind the hill the way might still be open for the cavalry. Mullens was back on the scene with the 1st Division. It had been placed under Harper's orders and its leading brigade stood by at Flesquières all day while the battle raged in Fontaine.

The twelve tanks of the first wave 'went through the village several times'[11] but eleven of them received direct hits. The second wave fared little better. The third wave left the sunken road about 2.30 but by the time they reached Fontaine the light was going. The ruined streets were lit by the flashes of six-pounders and 77mm cannon and a blazing tank. Germans crept forward to throw bundles of grenades under the Mark IVs, blowing off links so tracks snaked into the air and machines slowed to a halt. Figures were seen hanging on the sponson guns to prevent their elevation and traverse. Without infantry support the tanks could only withdraw . . . if they were functioning. Of twenty-three in the second and third waves only eleven came back. The group was estimated to have fired five hundred 6-pounder shells and more than 40,000 rounds of small arms ammunition. An equally liberal expenditure of German ammunition was responsible for the repulse of the Highlanders who were back where they had started from, mostly, and still striving to establish contact with the troops in Bourlon Wood on their left. But could anyone still be alive there?

Once his troops had been driven from the wood, the enemy switched all his artillery onto it. 'Boney' Fuller, who had come up from Tank Corps HQ to watch developments, stood on the Bapaume-Cambrai road mesmerized by 'an incessant tornado'. Millions of sparks arose as a smoke barrage was fired. At Graincourt Brigadier-General John Campbell of the 121st Brigade received word that 'the Yorks and 21st Middlesex are practically obliterated'. There was little he could do to help.

He had sent up the 12th Suffolks in the late afternoon to thicken the line on the left. This meant that both assault brigades had committed their entire strength. The intermingled Welsh battalions held a series of posts on the crest inside the edge of the wood where warrant officers commanded companies, corporals platoons. The firing line was placed under the overall command of Lieutenant-Colonel Benzie, Scottish CO of the South Wales Borderers.[12] Enemy patrols probing the slopes were driven back and the scattered British tried to maintain contact while awaiting the arrival of reinforcements.

The 119th Brigade having sent forward its last remaining reserves, its salvage section and works company, the 120th began to check over its equipment in anticipation. It had started the day near Graincourt where large stocks of captured soda water and rations were distributed. Many soldiers ate a picnic lunch while watching large shells bursting in Bourlon Wood which 'did not look at all pleasant'.[13] Reports of heavy losses filtered back. Two companies of the 14th Argyll and Sutherland Highlanders marched off. Then two companies of the 11th King's Own.

In the evening the 14th Highland Light Infantry were placed under the command of the 121st Brigade and told that they and the Suffolks were to clear Bourlon the next day. A dozen tanks would help and the 36th Division was to resume its attack left of the village. Shortly before 1 am on the 24th the order went out from IV Corps 'for the ground gained to be held at all costs'.[14] The rest of the Argylls were sent forward during the night.

In the early evening it became obvious that the cavalrymen at Flesquières were not going to need their horses. The 9th Brigade trotted to Graincourt, dismounted and formed a battalion 620 strong, the 15th and 19th Hussars and the Bedfordshire Yeomanry each providing a company. Minus spurs, collars turned up against the sleet, the troopers trudged along the roads taken by the 40th Division not 24 hours earlier. With them, picking their way through deepening mud, went pack animals carrying a dozen Vickers guns and ammunition. At Anneux the 15th Hussars went into reserve, sheltering in wrecked houses. Guides led the others across the Bapaume road to relieve the Green Howards. The battalion had gone into action with twenty-five officers and 450 men at 10.30 am. About ten hours later hussars and yeomen began to make cautious contact with the few still dug in near Bourlon village – less than 100 unwounded men. It was midnight before the last Yorkshiremen began stumbling back over the bodies of comrades killed that morning. They found shelter in the trenches around the ruined sugar factory and tried to sleep. Drifting snow piled up against the shadows in the fields.

The flakes were soft and water streamed off the ground-sheets worn by the 1st Guards Brigade advancing to relieve Harper's Highlanders. The staff of the 51st Division said they had received no warning from Corps headquarters so had made none of the usual arrangements. Roads were blocked and the Vickers of one incoming machine-gun company were stranded on the line of march along with the Lewis limbers of the 2nd Grenadiers. The guns of a Scots battalion at Graincourt were borrowed and Vickers already in position were taken over. Between midnight and dawn three Guards battalions were in the line, having marched 15 miles, much of it across unknown country. The snow turned to rain and chalky mud smeared everyone and everything.

Zero hour for the clearance of Bourlon village was fixed for noon but the enemy struck first – at the wood itself. At 8.45 swarms of Germans appeared 'without any particular formation',[15] driving back the British outposts. The line of defenders at the edge of the

116

1. Bourlon Château in the years immediately before the Great War. It became a German headquarters in 1914.

2. Bourlon Château in 1918. It was considered beyond repair and demolished.

3. Comtesse Bernard de Francqueville in 1918. She came to Bourlon as a bride in 1914.

4. Comte Bernard de Francqueville, weari decorations. Twice wounded in the Great W he was arrested as a member of the Resistance the Second World War and died in a conce tration camp in Germany.

M. Vicq. M. Jacquart. M. Trépont, M. Lebas, M. Gosquereile, Cte de Francqueville, Cte de Forceville, M. Gatoire, M. Dessein, préfet du Nord. maire de Roubaix. de St-Quentin. maire de Bourlon. maire de Lavaux. maire de St-André-lès-Lille. ingénieur, à St-Quentin.

DIX OTAGES FRANÇAIS RENDUS PAR L'ALLEMAGNE

5. A newspaper picture of French hostages returning to France in 1916. Comte Roger de Francqueville is seventh from the left.

6. The gatehouse of La Folie wood. The Germans built a pillbox behind it.

7. La Folie Château. Men of the 4th Dragoon Guards raided it on 20 November, 1917. The picture was taken in 1930. The tricyclist is Bernadette de Francqueville (now Comtesse le Bault de la Morinière).

8. This contemporary aerial photograph of Bourlon Wood gives no indication of the rugged contours within.

9. La Ferme de l'Abbaye, home today of Comte Pierre de Francqueville. The entrance to a German pillbox (right) was formerly a weapons aperture commanding the village. Comte Pierre enlarged it to make a door. Legend has it that a German general was captured in it in 1918. The Canadian Grenadier Guards used it as a headquarters that year.

0. La Ferme de l'Abbaye soon after the Great War.

. A German postcard of Bourlon village in the summer of 1918. Note church with spire moved to avoid giving an aiming point to hostile gunners.

12. The outskirts of Bourlon where furious fighting took place.

13. The dry Canal du Nord with damaged machinery. This sector, near Moeuvres, was attacked by the Germans two days after the picture was taken (note the shadow of the photographer in the foreground – he was using a tripod) on 28 November, 1917. In September, 1918, it was stormed by the 52nd Scottish Division.

14. A Mark IV tank moves forward to support the 40th Division's attack on 23 November, 1917 past a field gun (left).

5. German prisoners being marched through Ribécourt on 20 November, 1917.

16. Villagers leaving Noyelles, 22 November, 1917. A fortnight later their homes were again in German hands.

17. Back to the soil in 1919. A peasant works on his land in Bourlon having fenced it off with barbed wire.

9/12/17.

Dear Mr Dame.

I am afraid I have this very sad news to tell you that your son is missing.

I have done everything to find news of him, and what I have got is from Private soldiers whose information is not always very reliable. He was seen wounded during the attack on Nov 27th, but as the Germans are back now on that ground it is impossible to find out further.

I hope very much he has been found by them and is now a prisoner.

He was a splendid officer and we are all very fond of him in the Regiment, so naturally feel very anxious about him.

I feel most deeply for you, as I know how dreadful it is, not to know the truth.

But, I will do all I can to help you and if I hear anything further, I will telegraph to you at once.

If he is a prisoner the Regimental Orderly Room in Buckingham Gate will be the first to be notified from Germany.

Please accept my sincere sympathy. Yours sincerely.

Lt Col Commanding 2nd Bn. N.R. Alexander

18. A poignant letter from Lieutenant-Colonel Harold Alexander to the father of a young Irish Guards officer, John William Malvern Dame, reported missing in action. He was the only son of Mr and Mrs J. M. Dame, had been educated at Downside and was 19 years old. His body was never found.

19. Beaurepaire Château near Montreuil. From 1916 to 1919 this was Haig's personal residence. It was chosen because, according to his requirements, it had central heating and was surrounded by a wall. It has hardly changed since he occupied it. The château is still in the hands of the family from whom it was rented in 1916. The picture was taken in 1986.

20. A monument recalls the death of an American officer who was killed while serving in the Grenadier Guards. Thieves stole the original plaque so Monsieur de Francqueville replaced it. Lieutenant Windeler's body was never found.

21. The Comte de Francqueville knows Bourlon Wood intimately – and each of the surviving oaks which contain shrapnel. He is pointing to a splinter scar. The trees cannot be cut down for timber because they would wreck the saw when processed. Monsieur de Francqueville was wounded during the second World War clearing a wood in the Vosges.

22. Beyond the memorial to the 62nd West Yorkshire Division with its pelican sign, behind the trees, lies a rarely visited cemetery.

23. Graincourt church today. The entrance to the underground workings is on the other side, but air vents can be seen in the gardens opposite.

24. A piece of modern sculpture marks the site of Anneux chapel. The road to the right curves across the exposed plain which the machine guns of both sides swept with deadly results.

25. Officers of 68 (Australian) Squadron RFC, pictured on 7 December, 1917, at the entrance to a hangar. The central figure with cane is the CO, Lieutenant-Colonel W. O. Watt. Immediately behind him is the head of Lieutenant Richard Watson Howard who was a captain with an MC when he died of wounds in March, 1918. The figure hands in pockets on the right is believed to be Lieutenant Harry Taylor, killed in an accident in August the same year. Captain F. G. Huxley, in flying suit had shot down a German plane the day before this picture was taken. The officer propped on a bench beside him is Captain Gordon Campbell Wilson, DCM, MC. (*Australian War Memorial picture*).

trees waited until the enemy was only 150 yards away, then let fly 'with tremendous effect'.[16] The assault collapsed but a heavy and accurate barrage drove the British back some 300 yards to the sunken road in the middle of the wood. When the shelling eased they hastily re-occupied their old positions and the German guns resumed their bombardment. At 11 am another mass attack was caught by the British artillery – but the enemy, regardless of his loss, drove back the right flank.

The Welsh regiments, Argylls, 15th Hussars and machine-gunners, who had come up during the night, were inextricably mixed. At the height of the struggle part of the line gave way. According to the commander of the 119th Brigade: 'A few men with less staying power than the rest lost their heads and some of them their lives as a consequence. They fled from danger only to encompass disaster. A revolver "emptied into the brown" accounted for five; a Lewis gun fired into the panic-stricken mass put many on the grass and in the undergrowth.'[17]

Brigadier-General Frank Crozier was a colourful and controversial figure. While a battalion commander in the Ulster Division, he had insisted on a death sentence being carried out when he might have secured a reprieve. Executions held an unpleasant fascination for him. In West Africa before the war he had ordered a condemned soldier to be shot at close range with a machine gun as he did not trust the marksmanship of his native troops. Give him an order to hold a position at all costs and it would be carried out to the letter. He took the view that 'funk in itself is nothing. When unchained it becomes a military menace, and for that men die at the hands of their comrades'. An officer who made his way back to brigade headquarters with a slight wound was pounced on and 'forced, with others, up the hill, there to die'. Crozier recorded with approval that one of his battalion commanders had shot some men from another brigade in order to restore a dangerous situation.

There were limits to what even Crozier's panache and drive could achieve. During the afternoon the British were forced back to 'a line facing east and in the middle of the wood'.[18] Summoning their remaining strength the defenders under Lieutenant-Colonel Plunkett of the Royal Welsh Fusiliers made a despairing effort which pushed the enemy off most of the high ground and re-established posts along the northern edge of the trees. Pockets of Germans still held out.

The massive German attacks on the wood had unfortunate consequences for the 36th Division. It was to have had the support 'of practically all the IV Corps heavy artillery' but the big guns had to be switched to protect the creaking front of the 40th. Without a heavy preliminary bombardment the Ulstermen did not stand a chance. The commanding officer of the 1st Royal Irish Fusiliers due to lead the attack refused to launch his men on such a forlorn mission and the operation did not take place.[19] This allowed the Germans in Quarry Wood and on the left of Bourlon to enfilade any assault over the spur against the village.

Their artillery was also becoming stronger and, as the 14th HLI left Graincourt where they had been picking up tools and grenades, a gun ranged on them. Its second shell exploded in the midst of a platoon in column of fours and when the smoke dispersed only the subaltern in command and his servant staggered to their feet. The 14th had been raised in September, 1914, not as a Kitchener battalion but as a duplicate of the 4th (Special Reserve) HLI[20] and been a training unit for some months. It shook out into artillery formation and marched on. A party sent ahead to locate the 119th Brigade 'saw nothing of the Welsh regiments except a lot of dead'.[21]

The Corps Commander had second thoughts about an assault on Bourlon village that morning. Zero hour was postponed and after a discussion with Ponsonby at Havrincourt it was decided to call it off until the next day when more tanks would be available. The cancellation order went out at 3 pm, but, 'owing to the wires being cut between the division and the brigades, this message did not arrive and the Brigade Commander . . . rightly decided to carry out the attack.'[22]

At 3.30 a dozen Mark IVs headed for Bourlon Village, followed by the 12th Suffolks on the left with the 14th HLI moving through the edge of the wood on the right. The 121st Brigade operation order laid down 100 to 200 yards as the distance to be kept between tanks and infantry and once again the gap proved too wide. The tanks drove into the village but withdrew as they could see no signs of any support and, in any case, eight had been put out of action from one cause or another.[23]

The Suffolks came under machine-gun fire at an early stage but as far as the HLI were concerned the omens were at first good. The Scots pushed through the trees and streets and reached the railway cutting and trenches north of the village with only thirty-five casualties. The Suffolks, however, found it almost impossible to clear the enemy from the cellars and houses and eventually fell back to an old trench running along the south-west edge of the village.

The news that three companies of the HLI had reached the railway had unexpected repercussions – it rekindled hopes of cavalry action. The railway passed through a cutting; the cutting could shelter horsemen; it could be the route to the open country beyond. Haig had been talking of mounted action when he visited Byng that morning; Third Army headquarters informed IV Corps that if a way could be found the Cavalry Corps commander would use all five of his divisions to exploit the situation. Infantry formations would be placed under his command. Greenly's division was ordered to Flesquières to be ready to advance as soon as Bourlon was firmly in British hands. Haig's hopes were expressed in a Special Order of the Day which began:

'The capture of the important Bourlon position yesterday crowns a most successful operation and opens the way to a further exploitation of the advantages already gained.'[24]

Yesterday? If anything, the situation on the 24th was worse than on the 23rd.

News from Bourlon arrived only slowly at British headquarters, runners being picked off by snipers in the trees. If a message did reach the underground complex at Graincourt the telephone links to the rear were likely to be cut by shell fire. At Havrincourt Ponsonby had only a sketchy idea of the true situation. About 9 pm he was under the impression that Bourlon village had been captured. Only gradually did it emerge that the three companies of the HLI were cut off and prisoners were warning of counter-attacks being prepared for the morrow. On the right the position was precarious, in some eyes 'critical'.[25] A gap existed between the Welsh brigade in Bourlon Wood and the Guards Division before Fontaine.

Ponsonby had gone into action with twelve strong infantry battalions. On the night of the 24th his reserves were down to the 13th East Surreys, the remaining companies of the 11th King's Own having been sent to the 119th Brigade.

Extra men had to be found. On a blustery night two more battalions of troopers made their way from Havrincourt towards the wood. The last of the 1st Cavalry Division had been dismounted. The new arrivals were to back up the next attempt to clear the village. Ponsonby was also sent the 2nd Scots Guards and as its leading troops entered the wood the German machine-gunners, 'who were exceedingly well posted on the high ground,'[26] sent harassing bursts through the dripping undergrowth. Patrols suffered heavily. Quite a number of Guardsmen would never have Haig's Order of the Day read out to them.

Could any improvement in the situation reasonably be expected? From previous experience of trench warfare there was little reason to believe that once a promising attack bogged down success could be achieved by sheer obstinacy. General Fayolle, when required against his better judgment to press an offensive in 1916, had written: 'The third days of battles are never worth anything.'[27] The 40th Division was entering its third day of action.

The 13th East Surreys waited in captured German trenches less than a mile from Graincourt while their commanding officer was receiving his orders under the church. He was to mop up Bourlon and reinforce the HLI holding out on the railway. A dozen tanks were expected to support the operation. Lieutenant-Colonel Herbert Warden, then 40,[28] promptly set out into the darkness to find out what he could, having sent word for his troops to report at Anneux Chapel at 3.30 am. The information he gleaned was not encouraging. The HLI were thought to have been wiped out. No one knew of any friendly troops near Bourlon village. It was the Germans themselves who convinced Warden that at least some survivors were holding on. They started to bombard part of the wood as if to prevent reinforcements reaching the last known positions of the HLI. Anneux being another likely target, he hurried back to divert the battalion and, in a sunken road just south of Anneux, called his officers together. Warden, an Edinburgh lawyer, had thought over this brief carefully and decided to attack with three companies. Each was given a specific sector of Bourlon village to mop up. A platoon from each was to go through it in darkness to reach the HLI. The fourth company he held in reserve.

Tanks expected at 6 am had not arrived by zero hour but Warden gave the order to advance. Within a matter of minutes he had located Lieutenant-Colonel Battye, the tough regular CO of the HLI, in a house on the southern edge of the village. While they were talking heavy fire was opened on the building by Germans still in the wood and the Surrey reserve company had to deal with them. Explosions, shouts and long bursts of fire could be heard in Bourlon itself. One of the mopping-up companies was driven out but rallied at the edge of the wood. Soon after 7 am, in the half-light, Battye left the house to check a Lewis-gun position. He was hit in the chest by a machine-gun bullet, staggered back and died before Warden's eyes. The lawyer, who had founded a patriotic body called the Edinburgh Military Training Association in 1914, assumed command of both battalions. He was posting riflemen at loopholes driven through the walls of the house when a runner arrived with an order for the HLI to capture the stretch of railway north of Bourlon 'in order to allow the cavalry to get forward today'.[29]

It was timed 5.20 am, addressed to Battye, and came via Brigade headquarters from 40th Divisional HQ. Even as Warden read this fanciful message tiles were hurtling from the roof, bullets were flying in all directions and the HLI and East Surreys around the house and in the wood were digging and firing for dear life.

Oh, for the sanity of the law courts; oh, for news of the 119th Brigade. Patrols sent to explore the wood on Warden's right found only scattered groups of Germans. Remnants of the Welsh and the units sent to their aid had attacked early that morning in support of the Scots Guards intending to eliminate the bellicose machine-gunners of the night. Some high ground was regained but Warden's position was still in advance of the British line. Not until early afternoon was contact established.

Further attempts by the Scots Guards to advance made little headway. Tanks were needed. General Ponsonby had asked for a dozen to support Warden's attack and thought they were being made available, but on the 24th the Third Army had ordered all machines into reserve for a refit.[30] This message seems to have been overlooked at IV Corps HQ, perhaps failing to register with a worn-out staff captain, or mislaid by a weary clerk. The Chief Staff Officer, De Pree, wrote later: 'It was hoped to mop up the village with the help of twelve tanks but these tanks were not forthcoming.'

About mid-morning German observers directed salvoes on detachments moving at wide intervals up the Graincourt–Bourlon road. The bursts were creeping nearer when hail squalls obscured these inviting targets.[31] The 4th Grenadiers, on their way to support the Scots Guards, were duly grateful for their good fortune. Some hours later many men on the same melancholy road considered their luck was right out.

CHAPTER TWELVE
Toll for the Brave

As his Yorkshiremen marched back to rest billets on the morning of the 23rd General Braithwaite heard one call out: 'This wipes out Bullecourt, sir.'[1] The troops seemed to have regarded the bloody repulse south of Arras as a personal reflection on their courage. An advance of more than four miles in 24 hours had shown their true capabilities.

What the troops said when the news arrived late on the night of the 24th that the 62nd Division was to replace the 40th in Bourlon the next day is not recorded. Would they be carrying out a normal relief? Was the battle dying down? Or did they wonder: 'Why us? Again!'

If there were grumblers, if some hearts sank, Braithwaite was confident that his men would 'go in' again. Yet in a war in which 'attrition' was a recognized policy – Haig's published despatches on the Somme, 1916, are actually entitled *The Wearing Out Battle* – prospects for a foot soldier were bleak. Except to themselves there was nothing special about the 62nd Division. It had been raised (without a number) from units intended to supply drafts for the West Riding Territorial Division (which fought in France as the 49th) and saddled with the official description of 'second line', though eventually this tag became meaningless.

What its originals had in common was their background – they came from a Yorkshire that was the heart of the Roaring North, with thriving factories, rich broad acres and a population proud of their county to the point of obsession.

York, Leeds and Bradford filled the ranks of the 185th Brigade's

West Yorks battalions, men coming from the big banks and merchant houses as well as the weaving, spinning and engineering plants.

The 186th Brigade (all battalions of the Dukes) absorbed volunteers from the woollen, cotton and worsted mills around Halifax and Huddersfield, from the Colne Valley and from Skipton.

The heavy industrial districts, which included Wakefield, Dewsbury and Battley, Doncaster, Sheffield and Rotherham, provided the troops for the KOYLI and York and Lancs battalions of the 187th Brigade.

On the whole they were sturdy, steady men, most of whom had been raised in the Sunday School tradition and were not given to bad language. They were proud of their accent, their home towns and had a blind faith in their county's cricketers. They didn't really want to be anywhere else than Yorkshire but on 24 November quite a lot of them must have realized that their chances of seeing home again were slim. Every distant thump emphasized the fact.

In Cambrai the echoes of battle had been heightened by explosions in the town itself, some driving Abbé Delval to his cellar. He tried to venture out to say Mass but the Germans were stopping all movement. A distressed refugee priest sought shelter with him. While he was attending a funeral a shell had penetrated the ground floor of his lodgings, burst in his study and blown out the house front. A maid had been deluged in plaster but escaped unhurt.

Delval learned that St Géry church had been badly damaged and nine Germans killed in the Rue des Anglaises. He recorded a macabre affair:

'M. Mussault died on Thursday and the body was on its death bed; a shell burst in the room, demolishing everything, and the corpse, thrown into the air, was buried under a mass of débris from which a single hand emerged.'

Throughout the day the Germans continued to search Cambrai for men of working age and threatened the city with a heavy fine if they were not produced.

'The situation is far from pleasant.'

The 25th was a Sunday. By noon the Yorkshire battalions were filing past Graincourt church where there would be no service that

day. In the West Riding they could be sure the chapels were full –
the ministers reading out the names of the men killed a few days
earlier. There would be prayers, too, for those who were still alive
and they were going to need them. As the troops came into view
German guns opened fire.

That night not a great many of the 40th Division were left to be
relieved. Of the Welsh Brigade a handful of armed scarecrows
remained – the 12th South Wales Borderers alone had lost
twenty-two officers and 388 men killed, wounded or missing.[2]
What had happened to the HLI was anyone's guess. Only tenuous
contact had been maintained with Warden and the East Surreys.

As the newcomers gleaned what they could from sketchy
reports, enemy shells scoured the area. Forty men of the 2nd/4th
Dukes were hit while waiting to take over a quarry from the 4th
Grenadiers who insisted they were not to be relieved (they were
later relocated in support of their own division).

The 2nd/7th Dukes replaced the Scots Guards opposite the
highest point on the ridge – which was in no-man's-land. Battalion
headquarters moved into the Chalet where the night passed to the
sound of 'sniping and desultory machine-gun fire with intermittent
shell fire which at times became almost intense'.[3]

Monday dawned bright and with a nip in the air. Quite early,
staff cars began to line up near a hut in the grounds of Havrincourt
château where a signboard bearing a pelican proclaimed the
headquarters of the 62nd Division. The commander of IV Corps
was about to hold a conference there.

If only they hadn't rung the bells different decisions might have
been taken, but the whole country had heard them – bells which
had welcomed Henry V after Agincourt, bells which had pealed
for the defeat of the Armada, bells which had swung, rung and
chimed for Waterloo and the Relief of Mafeking had said it all
again in Grandsire Triples and Bob Doubles.

It was not the first time bells had been rung during the war.
Under Regulation 12d of the Defence of the Realm Act permission
to ring church bells had to be obtained from the 'Competent
Military Authorities', but by 1917 normal activity was generally
allowed during daylight. In October a campaign by ringers to be
allowed to exercise their ancient skills after dark had met with little
success.[4]

'It just happens that the present is an unfortunate time for applications of this nature,' wrote the editor of *The Ringing World* on 26 October. The 'unwelcome attentions of enemy aircraft on moonlight nights' was so persistent that the authorities were 'bound to decline anything that might possibly be a guide to hostile machines.'

The bands of ringers felt thwarted. After a 'great triumph in Flanders' there had been newspaper inquiries as to why the bells had not rung and it was felt that there was a marked desire on the part of the public to hear them on such occasions. It was suggested that 'ringers should be ready to do their part, as they have done through the great wars of the past, to signalize the successes of the troops'.

After the opening of the Cambrai offensive the pent-up frustrations were released and *The Ringing World* reported:

'Last week, with the great smashing blow at the enemy which reconquered about 40 square miles of territory, and brought in nearly ten thousand prisoners and a hundred guns, came the opportunity, and the newspapers calling loudly for the bells. Needless to say the ringers were not behindhand in doing their part and it is gratifying to find that St Paul's Cathedral gave the lead. The ringing there was done at the request of the authorities, while the Bishop of London himself issued an appeal for the bells generally in his diocese to be rung.'

Southwark Cathedral had been first, ringing on Thursday the 22nd.

On Friday, as the 40th Division was attacking, it was the turn of other churches in the metropolis. A huge crowd gathered round the west front of St Paul's where 'emotions were stirred as this grand peal crashed out the strains of victory. When the bells stopped the crowd sang the National Anthem and then the ringing started again, and there were scenes of real rejoicing'.

The Londoners in the 20th and 21st Middlesex would have been startled to learn their bloody reception at Bourlon had earned such recognition.

A ripple effect developed. Peterborough Cathedral's bells 'which had long been silent' rang out, as eventually did those in Bristol, in churches throughout Surrey, Sussex and Kent and many other parts of the country. On the day of the Havrincourt conference bells echoed across the great Wiltshire plain where the New Armies had trained, the churches responding to a special call by the Bishop of Salisbury. The joyous clamour proclaimed that after a year of prodigious slaughter for small gains a sensational advance had been made at little cost (so long as your own kith and kin did not figure in the casualty lists). It is not the nature of iron clappers to be subtle; ringers tolled with a will, spreading news which had already gone far and wide. As early as 22 November General Fayolle had confided to his *cahiers*:

'This morning we learned that the English have had a great success with tanks at Cambrai. At last there was surprise. This could have important consequences.'

The President of France sent congratulations to George V and the King despatched a personal message to Byng. Eton wired its congratulations in Latin. The Lord Mayor of London sent a telegram on behalf of the City.[5] They were not to know that the Germans were hanging on to the outskirts of Bourlon Wood and still occupied the village. All Britain was heartened by the tone of Sir Douglas Haig's Order of the Day of the 24th. Apart from announcing the 'capture of the important Bourlon position', it also gave the impression that the fighting had been rounded off:

'In the operations of the Third Army during the past four days the troops engaged were called on to advance under conditions different to anything ever attempted before. The manner in which they adapted themselves to the new conditions was in all respects admirable, and the results already gained by their efforts are of far-reaching importance.'

More adaptation was going to be required if the facts were to fit the glowing picture painted by the high command. The man to be least envied was the commander of IV Corps who, from the beginning, had favoured a limited operation. Whatever credit was due to him for the success of his troops on 20 November, General Woollcombe had fallen from favour. Privately Haig was unhappy at the way things were working out and even suggested to Byng that he should take over personal control.[6]

An almost hysterical spasm must have afflicted the normally phlegmatic Scot. As commander of the Third Army Byng was responsible for co-ordinating the operations of six corps (seven if the Cavalry is included) and had a duty to concern himself with the broader perspective. Moreover, there was nothing in his record to show that he could produce magic solutions to knotty problems. His known metier was meticulous preparation. As a corps commander his operations after the capture of Vimy had been uninspired. There was no reason to believe that he would do any better than Woollcombe who had been praised the previous autumn when, under his command, the 11th Division captured the notorious Wunderwerk bastion on the Somme.[7]

Poor Woollcombe, if anything he was suffering from a surfeit of high-priced help in November, 1917. Everyone had a finger in the pie. Haig might descend at any time from his special operations centre at Bavincourt (only 12 miles from Albert). Byng had an advanced HQ at Bapaume just three miles from Woollcombe at Villers au Flos. The whole Cambrai salient was overrun with main and battle HQs for divisions attacking Bourlon and Fontaine. On top of that were the HQs for the divisions of III Corps, now on the defensive. They did little to improve the British grip on the battle.

From experience Haig should have known better than anyone when an offensive was moribund and his effort to give the operation the kiss of life hints at desperation. Though urging Byng to take personal charge, Sir Douglas himself had inevitably become the battle controller the moment he departed from his original plan to call a halt within two days if there was no breakthrough. The decision to go on meant defining different objectives, devising a new policy. Only he, not Byng, could do that. But Haig had no contingency plans, merely hopes. Not renowned as an original thinker, he saw the completion of the capture of Bourlon as the only way ahead. On the Somme, at Arras and at Ypres he had given orders to at least two army commanders who had in turn directed several corps commanders. At Cambrai the Field-Marshal reached a point at which he was concentrating his efforts on the operations of a single corps. Everyone in the chain of command was breathing down everyone else's neck but Sir Douglas's breath was hottest of all.

The Havrincourt conference stemmed from a visit made by the Chief Staff Officer of IV Corps to the Guards commander the previous afternoon. When De Pree announced that the Division was to take part in another attack on Fontaine while the 62nd tackled Bourlon, Major-General Feilding objected strongly. Ten days earlier he had been told by Byng that the Guards would not be committed to an assault unless Bourlon Wood was captured on the first day of the attack. Further, that in the event of failure 'there was no intention of continuing the operation and that the plan was to withdraw to a line through Flesquières'.[8]

Feilding could see no grounds for optimism. His division, reputedly the best-trained and led in the BEF, could not work

128

miracles. Six weeks earlier it had left Ypres, the infantry alone having suffered 2,264 casualties.

Feilding's view that his troops would not have a fair chance of success could not be lightly dismissed. He had commanded a battalion during the Retreat from Mons, been wounded at Ypres in 1914, and fought in almost every major battle since then. When, as a brigade commander, he was given a dubious task at Loos, he personally reconnoitred the enemy position and pronounced it 'too strong for the operation to be successful'.[9] The Corps Commander had cancelled a certain bloodbath. Being wise in the ways of the Army, Feilding arrived at Havrincourt armed with a written appreciation of the situation. At 9.30 am, when the conference began — Braithwaite was the other divisional commander present — Feilding outlined his objections.

Briefly 'the Guards were holding a long line . . . If the attack were to take place they would be called upon to advance across a stretch of country in full view of the enemy's gunners . . . to capture an undemolished village which would be stoutly defended.'

To stand any chance Fontaine would have to be subjected to a crushing bombardment by heavy artillery.

Feilding pointed out that, as his men would be 'attacking from a salient into a salient', the further they went the more they would be exposed to shellfire from three sides. If it had been impossible to capture the Bourlon position at the beginning of the offensive when the enemy was disorganized and had lost much of his artillery, why should it be any easier now he had recovered? German batteries across the canal from Noyelles and at Rumilly could fire on the backs of the attackers. If these positions (opposite III Corps) were not included in the operation it would be better to abandon isolated efforts to carry Bourlon and retire to the Flesquières Ridge.

Whatever Woollcombe may have thought of Feilding's suggestion, there was no decision he could make. That was up to the Army Commander who, it was revealed, was going to join them. While the meeting waited, Feilding tried to discuss other aspects of the proposed attack but gave up in disgust when he discovered that the Corps Commander 'was unprovided with any plan, or artillery programme, or objectives, or divisional boundaries'.[10] At 11 am all present pushed back their chairs and stood up respectfully as Sir Julian Byng entered.

Quickly it became clear that talk of withdrawal was going to receive short shrift and this became a certainty when amid a further scraping and shuffling – it was a small hut[11] – the Commander-in-Chief arrived.

Sir Douglas Haig declared that, as he did not have sufficient troops, there would be no extension of offensive operations, but the attack proposed for the next day would probably enable the main objective to be secured 'to capture and hold the best line for the winter'.

Sir Douglas then mounted his horse and rode off to study the prospect from Flesquières ridge.

In view of Haig's statement about a lack of reserves, no strategic reason remained which required the capture of Bourlon. No one had suggested what would be done with the position if it did fall completely into British hands. But could a withdrawal be contemplated? If only they hadn't rung the bells. Byng decided. The attack would go ahead.

The meeting rose as he left and, snatching caps and sticks, the divisional staffs hurried off. Zero hour was once again 6.20 am. Feilding's brigadiers, waiting at his headquarters, learned this when he arrived early in the afternoon. Twelve tanks were to join the attack which was to be made by the 2nd Brigade. Three battalions were to advance in line abreast with their left flank well inside Bourlon Wood and Fontaine as the main objective. The 1st Scots Guards were to cover the exposed right flank.

The COs concerned did not learn of their mission until 4 pm and the company commanders only at midnight by which time it was snowing steadily. The 2nd Brigade was moving up for a normal relief and 'no one engaged had ever seen the ground'.[12] About 1 am half-frozen, mud-covered Irish Guardsmen were stumbling across the Bapaume–Cambrai road through a blizzard thickened by shell fire which claimed forty of them.

The 62nd Division had more experience of the area but much had to be done after the conference – 'little daylight was left to make final preparations; the scheme therefore had to be explained verbally by staff officers'.[13]

Late in the evening a grimy individual found the headquarters of the West Yorkshire brigade and revealed the whereabouts of Colonel Warden. He had spent the 25th fortifying his headquarters, linking it with his companies in the wood behind and looking in vain for Suffolk and Middlesex remnants on his left.

The arrival of two mortars increased his fire-power and finally provoked the enemy to bring up a minenwerfer to reply. Fortunately by that time the light had gone.

News of the approach of the 62nd Division had been followed by a message stating that 'the relief was not to begin until some tanks should arrive, and pushing through Bourlon relieve the three companies on the railway line.'[14] By that time all hope for the HLI had gone, but Warden had no option but to remain where he was in a badly-lit building crammed with wounded men. The advanced dressing station was three miles away at Graincourt and the handful of regimental bearers were exhausted. The arrival of fresh stretcher parties brought much-needed relief.

It was impossible to bury the many dead and they were 'got out of the way',[15] but a grave was dug for Lieutenant-Colonel Battye in the garden of the house and a cross improvised. The living settled down at their loopholes and listened for the promised tanks. Any attempt at movement in Bourlon brought bursts of fire, every road being covered.

At daylight on the 26th there was still no sign of Mark IVs and about the time the Generals were gathering at Havrincourt Lieutenant-Colonel Warden sent back a request for orders. All the exits of his strongpoint were under small-arms fire and it was 'being gradually demolished' by the minenwerfer.

After dark Warden's men withdrew in small parties to join the East Surreys still in the wood. They learned they were on the line selected for the British barrage due to precede the attack the next morning and were pulled back still further.

Ignorance of British positions in and around Bourlon had prevented the heavy artillery firing on the village on the 26th, a lack of 'preparation' that made the role of the tanks all the more important. Twenty Marks IVs lined up on the Bapaume–Cambrai road and at 2 am guides appeared to lead them to their 'jumping-off' places. Crawling behind a pinpoint of light through the middle of a wood lashed by gale-force winds, some did not get into position until an hour before zero.

There was no rest for anyone. West of Bourlon the 36th Division's infantry were staggering into a horizontal blizzard after handing over to the 2nd Division. They found every shelter, dug-out and hut in their 'billeting' area crammed with support and service troops and many of them 'spent what was left of the night in the open, in the snow'.[16] Towards morning the snow gave way to rain.

CHAPTER THIRTEEN
Greenhouse in a Hailstorm

In the grey dawn of 27 November 'F' Battalion, the Tank Corps, attacked with unbridled fury through a German counter-barrage, the Mark IVs heading straight for the various entrances to the village.[1] Scores of machine-guns roared a greeting. Fighting Mac slowed to a stop, guns silent and fragments flying from the hull. The hatches remained shut. Falcon jerked clumsily round a wounded khaki figure and stuck in the marshy verges of the village pond. Flirt, close behind, took emergency avoiding action, stripped the teeth from its abused secondary gears and also came to a standstill. Figures darted about the stranded monsters unshackling towing wires for use by Firespite creeping cautiously to the rescue over the treacherous ground.

Feu d'Artifice backed away from a virulent machine-gun nest with flames licking round the exhaust. Three wounded had been removed when thick black smoke gushed from every aperture. The rest of the crew made a hurried exit.

Fervent and the unnamed FS 2 (promoted from supply duties) rumbled belligerently into the chaos, followed by a handful of crouching infantry. Flaming Fire and Frivolous chased scores of Germans up a sunken road.

The commander of a Mark IV watched another back out of a garden with German soldiers on top of it. One was hanging on to the barrel of a six-pounder, while another pumped pistol bullets into the silencer. These men were hosed off by Lewis fire. A field gun firing from a garden hit the unditching beam of the reversing tank, which replied with two six-pounder shells. They missed the

ATTACK OF 2ND GUARDS BRIGADE ON FONTAINE NOTRE DAME 27 NOVEMBER 1917

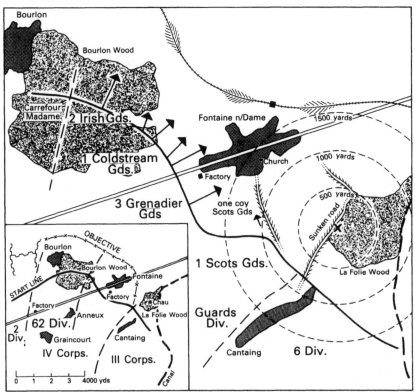

Sketch map showing the effect of machine guns in the sunken road skirting La Folie Wood. The German 1908 Maxim was sighted up to 2,190 yards. The slopes falling gently towards Fontaine which the Grenadiers had to cross were within easy range of even a single gun at 'X'. The enemy had many guns there and fired into the backs of the Scots Guards pushing up another sunken road running N and S. Enfilade fire also plagued the 62nd Division's western flank.

gun but exploded its ammunition store in a cottage behind it. The front of the building blew out. Machine guns rasped unchecked.

The previous day, untroubled by artillery, the enemy had dug pits and improvised barricades. Having intercepted a wireless message confirming the arrival at the front of the Guards Division, an attack was expected and soon after 6 am likely assembly places were heavily shelled. Half an hour later the British laid a smoke screen in front of Moeuvres, heavy howitzers pounded Quarry Wood and the advance began behind a rolling barrage of shrapnel and HE.

York and Lancasters and KOYLIs of the 187th Brigade had to clear Bourlon village while Bradford's Dukes pushed through the fringe of the wood, maintaining contact with the Guards. Companies of the West Yorkshires followed in support. By 8 am fighting was going on in the streets of Bourlon and the railway had been reached, though the only signs of the HLI were corpses. On the right the Guards reported themselves on their objectives everywhere, including Fontaine station. Why, then, did the British find themselves back almost on their start-lines at dusk? The plain truth would appear to be that the attack was doomed from the beginning by inadequate preparation.

The experience of the 2nd/5th West Yorks provides an example. The battalion did not reach its allotted position until 10 pm the previous night, too late to carry out a reconnaissance of any value. The troops waited on the southern edge of the wood, aware that they were to support an assault timed for 6.20 am, though 'nothing was known of the position of the first line' and 'no instructions' were received. The Adjutant searched vainly for brigade headquarters but could only make contact with a Guards battalion which was unable to enlighten him.[2]

The first firm news of the battle reached the battalion only after the attack had been in progress 'about an hour'. Forebodings were confirmed soon afterwards when a subaltern of the 2nd/5th York and Lancasters reported that he was the sole surviving officer of his battalion's attacking force and had withdrawn the remnant of the men to 'the ridge just south of Bourlon village'. Brigade HQ had ordered that the high ground be held 'at all costs'.

To ensure this the 2nd/8th West Yorks moved hurriedly from the beet factory and took shelter in a sunken road while the commanding officer, Lieutenant-Colonel A. H. James, conferred with the COs of 2nd/5th West Yorks and 2nd/5th KOYLI.

'I was informed . . . that the attack on the village had failed and that the position was critical.'[3]

Advancing to see for himself, Colonel James found 'the trench which runs on the top of the crest on the 100-metre contour . . . full of men of the 2nd/5th KOYLI. There was no question of reinforcing them as the trench was crammed.'

The other COs expected a counter-attack but, 'looking down the slope into the village, I could see no sign of the enemy massing'.

Colonel James deployed his companies in depth and watched them dig in with 'light' casualties.

An opportunity missed – or a massacre averted? No one will ever know, though there was plenty of evidence elsewhere that the enemy was thick on the ground and full of fight, as the 2nd Irish Guards found to their cost.

The Battalion had come up during the night over unknown country. They were 'given a compass bearing and despatched at dawn into a dense wood on a front of 700 yards, to reach an objective 1,000 yards ahead'.[4]

Struggling uphill through the undergrowth, slithering and slipping on the waterlogged ground, the 'Micks' reached their goal but were heavily shelled and raked by German machine guns still operating from high ground within the wood. The companies lost touch with battalion headquarters where at one time Lieutenant-Colonel Harold Alexander feared a total disaster had befallen them.[5]

The 3rd Grenadiers ran the gauntlet of the machine guns in La Folie wood, which had survived a feeble bombardment, and fought their way into Fontaine where they made contact with the Coldstream. They, too, were badly mauled by fire from enemy strongpoints and one company lost all but one of its officers in a bitter fight for a chalk pit where 'in addition to killing forty of the enemy with the bayonet' 200 prisoners were taken.[6]

Though the tanks were 'late in crossing the line . . . some of them caught up the infantry during the advance' and, shaken by the overall ferocity of the assault, some of the German garrison of Fontaine withdrew. Just as many, however, remained in cellars and in the crypt of the church. A handful fired persistently from two derelict tanks. When the 4th Grenadiers and the 1st Scots Guards tried to relieve the pressure the enemy counter-attacked. Twice they were repulsed but a third attempt, from La Folie, succeeded in reaching Fontaine where concealed Germans emerged to resume the battle.[7] At this point all three Guards battalions were in danger of encirclement. The Coldstream and Grenadiers withdrew, so reduced that many of their prisoners escaped for lack of men to escort them. By around 1 pm they were back where they had started; the survivors of the Irish Guards made a precarious escape through the woods somewhat later, moving whenever the enemy shellfire was heavy enough to drown the noise of their retreat. By early afternoon one officer and seventy-nine men had returned.

The tanks also limped back from Fontaine, one commander reporting that, when he left, Germans were swarming all over his machine 'trying to fire through the loopholes'.[8] One Mark IV remained – Fray Bentos – smouldering after being hit by a shell.

The ordeal in Bourlon village was even worse. Some enemy machine-gun rounds were said 'to have gone through brick walls as if they were paper'[9] and a tank officer described his experience as 'like being in a greenhouse in a hailstorm'.[10] Unable to close up to the Mark IVs in such an inferno, the infantry were out of the village by 9.30. Bradford's men, having forced their way through the wood with difficulty, held some outlying houses until 4.30 when shelling and counter-attacks drove them back into the trees.

The fighting in the village and the wood was reported as being 'of so confused a nature and the opposition so severe that it is difficult to follow what happened'.[11]

The 62nd Division, for all its efforts, could record only a slight advance, the casualties suffered in those few hours – 1,648 officers and men – being almost the same as the total for the period November 20–22. The Guards' losses amounted to thirty-eight officers and 1,043 other tanks. Of these 490 were reported missing, many being killed or disabled in the final German counter-attack. Among the Grenadiers was a young officer called Windler whose parents lived in the United States. He was shot by a tree-top sniper.

Feilding's forecast had been fulfilled almost to the letter. There had been no time to carry out proper reconnaissance – even aerial photographs were not available and the artillery preparation was insufficient. It was 'highly questionable whether a local attack, arranged in such a haphazard and casual manner, against a position of such strength as Bourlon Ridge could have been successful, even if it had been possible to utilize twice the number of men available.'[12]

Unknown to the Third Army staff, the enemy had been

preparing to counter-attack the same day and had strong forces on the spot.

Despite this unforeseen opposition, the greater part of the wood remained in British hands, though its capture was never fully completed. At that period of the war, unless conventional trenches were dug and wired, any front line remained fluid.

After the repulse of the attack on the 27th a large-scale wiring operation was planned. Captured enemy supplies accumulated for work on the Hindenburg Line rear area had already been used, so 56 lb coils had to be brought up, slung on poles between two men. While reconnoitring the route for the carrying parties, three sapper officers were ambushed in the wood by a dozen Germans. One of them was hit immediately but two crawled back by a roundabout route through the undergrowth only to be spotted again. A shot through the neck killed Major Frederick Johnson who had won the Victoria Cross two years earlier in Flanders.[13] His body was brought back that night to the hunting lodge as the sappers moved up to erect substantial entanglements.

Having cracked the whip for a week and enjoyed deafening applause, the lion-tamer then turned his back on the lion. Though still considering the position very favourable,[14] Haig conceded that his reserves did not allow him to continue battering away at the enemy line. The curtain could be rung down. Byng ordered Woollcombe to do everything to defend the Bourlon position 'the retention of which is very important'.[15]

Two more divisions were to replace the 62nd and Guards but the Third Army instructions stated that 'the relief of these troops should not, however, be unduly hurried as other fresh troops cannot be made available for some days and our resources must be economized'.[16] Even when they were relieved, the 62nd and Guards were to be kept behind Bourlon and organized for immediate counter-attacks.

All tanks were to be withdrawn. Though some dismounted battalions remained temporarily under IV Corps, arrangements had already been made for the cavalry to go into winter quarters.

The withdrawal of the French from Péronne had been put in hand on the 25th and the 1st Brigade, Royal Flying Corps, which had reinforced the equivalent Third Army formation, was released to return to its bases in the north the following day. On the 27th the specialist 9th Wing which had been bombing selected targets went back to its normal duties covering the whole front. That day reconnaissance flights reported heavy train movement converging on Cambrai from Lille, Douai and Denain.[17]

On the evening of the 28th, as the 62nd Division was handing over to the newly-arrived 47th, the unmistakable dull belching of gas shells was recognized amid a severe HE bombardment. A stretcher-bearer belonging to one of the dismounted battalions holding the line feverishly helped his charges don their respirators and then scrambled along a line of posts giving the alarm. He was killed by a shell fragment while tending a wounded man. Private George Clare, of the 5th Lancers, became the only man to be awarded the VC for bravery at Bourlon Wood in November, 1917.[18] Though others were gained in the vicinity there were none for the warriors who fought their way into the village.

The weather had improved, winds died down and temperature risen, ideal conditions for delivering a gas bombardment. General von Moser had received 16,000 chemical shells and proceeded to use them.[19] They were of the 'non-persistent' variety, the effect dispersing after two, three or four hours, but, by keeping up a steady fire, enemy gunners created a dangerous haze which hung about the undergrowth. Phosgene fumes sank into the shell-holes and sunken roads. Ypres veterans may have wondered at the absence of mustard gas which, because of its persistent nature, was dangerous for days. Yellow Cross[20] could have made the wood uninhabitable. Were the Germans short of it? Or did they think it would get in their way if they attacked? The latter was the more likely explanation.

The 47th Division found elements of seven battalions in the wood and a total of forty-seven Vickers guns. Its commander, Major-General Sir George Gorringe,[21] decided to thin out the troops on the ground.

The relief of the Guards Division took longer than the 62nd because the incoming troops had to travel farther, but by the evening of the 29th all of its brigades were in billets, the 3rd in the ruins of Trescault which had been just behind the British front line on 20 November.

A glance at the situation map showed that a great change had taken place in ten days. A slightly curved ten-mile stretch of line had been pushed forward so that it ran nearly 18 miles from a point near Louverval, in the north, towards Cambrai before bending back to Bantouzelle on the St Quentin Canal.

Elements of three corps were actually in the salient. Forming the left hinge where it had been employed since the beginning was:

The 56th (1st London) Division.

This Territorial formation had been in France since early in 1915. It had been given a sacrificial mission at Gommecourt on the first day of the Somme in 1916, been involved at Arras and lost more than 2,000 officers and men at Ypres in August, 1917.

From 20 November the division had been fighting under IV Corps in the Tadpole Copse sector of the Hindenburg line on the left of the 36th Division. By the 29th it was under the command of VI Corps. On its right was:

The 2nd Division.

This was an original component of the 1914 BEF and had seen three years of gruelling service, being reconstituted several times. Half of its battalions had been exchanged for New Army units. It had been engaged on the Scarpe in April but missed Ypres. After relieving the 36th Division, it became involved in sharp clashes west of Bourlon. It was deployed to cover the hotly-disputed valley running from the Crucifix down to the Bapaume–Cambrai road. On its right, responsible for Bourlon, was:

The 47th (2nd London) Division.

Six months after reaching France in 1915 it played a notable part at Loos, went through a severe trial on the Somme and was employed in the Messines Ridge battle in June. Alongside it at Fontaine was:

The 59th (2nd North Midland) Division.

This was another Territorial formation, a late arrival in France, though it had taken part in the Ypres operations where it suffered losses of more than 3,000 in September in the Polygon Wood sector. The divisional boundary was also the boundary with III Corps and it had as its immediate neighbour:

The 6th Division.

Hurriedly created from regular battalions in 1914, it arrived in

France in time for the Aisne battles and had seen arduous service, the Somme included. It had been spared the worst of the 1917 battles and had been fresh on 20 November. A third of its units were New Army service battalions. It held Cantaing and Noyelles next to another nominally regular formation:

The 29th Division.
Serving at Gallipoli before coming to France for the Somme battle, the 29th had been in action in the later Arras battles and suffered 4,000 casualties at Ypres. At Cambrai its units included the 1st Royal Guernsey Light Infantry, the 1st Royal Newfoundland Regiment and two Kitchener battalions. The 29th held the bridgehead at Marcoing–Masnières. On its right rear was:

The 20th (Light) Division.
Formed of Kitchener battalions, mainly of rifle regiments, it had been in France since the summer of 1915 and lost heavily on the Somme. At Ypres, in the appalling conditions of mid-August, it suffered 3,204 casualties, followed by another 1,400 in September. Alongside it was the much-tried East Anglian formation:

The 12th (Eastern) Division.
Its Kitchener volunteers had been in most big battles except Ypres, 1917, and when it moved to the Cambrai sector that autumn had recorded a total of 31,079 casualties since reaching France in summer 1915. Its nearest neighbour (under VII Corps) was:

The 55th (1st West Lancashire) Division.
The Territorials had fought on the Somme in 1916 and lost nearly 6,000 men at Ypres in August and September 1917. Next to it, on the right wing of the whole British line and also under VII Corps and in contact with the French, was:

The 24th Division.
This was one of the two New Army formations thrown in recklessly on the second day of Loos. Since then it had seen much fighting, been involved at Messines and lost 2,200 men in the opening stages of Third Ypres.

The recital of losses indicates the problem facing divisions trying to assimilate replacements while carrying out operational duties. To add to their problems they had to cope with a pernicious drain on manpower for posts behind the lines. In autumn, 1917, a battalion with a 'paper strength' of 600 was found to have only 107 available for trench duty. True it had a strong headquarters and a large number of effectives in the transport lines, but there were also men attached to the divisional headquarters as clerks, draughtsmen, orderlies, signallers and a cook; five were on traffic control, some working with a tunnelling company.

'There were clerks to town majors, camp wardens, guardians of coal, straw and ration dumps, cooks and servants at the Rest Camp.'

There were also about twenty sick not evacuated, men absent on leave and twenty on courses at various schools![22]

This state of affairs may not have applied everywhere but it is symptomatic of the debilitating effects of static warfare on fighting units.

'Static' was theoretically the condition to which the divisions of III Corps had been reduced when Haig 'shut down' the battle on its front. In the bridgehead east of the canal regular shelling did not prevent 5,000 yards of trench being dug and wired; the 29th's divisional canteen opened just behind the lines and 'life began to settle down to much the usual trench existence. Rations and parcels arrived regularly. There was even a light railhead in Marcoing'.

Infantry and engineers laboured on billets for a reserve brigade at Gouzeaucourt, five miles behind the bridgehead. To the man at the front it seemed that 'those in authority expected the Germans to acquiesce in the general situation' and that 'the weak southern flank of the salient could be put into a state of defence at leisure'.[23]

CHAPTER FOURTEEN

Twenty-Two Ravine

The Adjutant of the 7th Royal Sussex was enjoying bacon and eggs in a dug-out in the support line when the thunder of a distant bombardment disturbed him. Climbing the steps, he joined the Regimental Sergeant-Major on the parapet. Through the grey of the morning they could see crowds of British troops coming away from the front line where it ran in front of the village of Gonnelieu on a ridge overlooking the St Quentin Canal. It was the first time the Adjutant had seen 'a rearward movement on so large a scale', and he 'quickly finished breakfast.'[1] It was just after 7 am on 30 November.

Soon afterwards, Major-General Beauvoir de Lisle[2] was smoking his pipe as an orderly cleared the table when a shell exploded in the quarry where the 29th Division had its headquarters. More followed and someone called out that the artillery brigadier had been hit in the knee. Hundreds of men were reported to be trailing across the chalk downs 'not unlike Epsom on a race day' and when bullets began to crack overhead General and Staff decided to run the gauntlet of a barrage to reach Gouzeaucourt about three-quarters of a mile away. The wounded brigadier was left in the care of an orderly.

Officers, servants and cyclists took their chance among the shell-bursts while a captain and three troopers of the Northumberland Yeomanry, attached to a headquarters as despatch riders, galloped off and were killed charging the enemy.[3]

'In addition to the barrage, there was a machine gun sweeping

GERMAN COUNTER-ATTACK NOVEMBER 30 1917

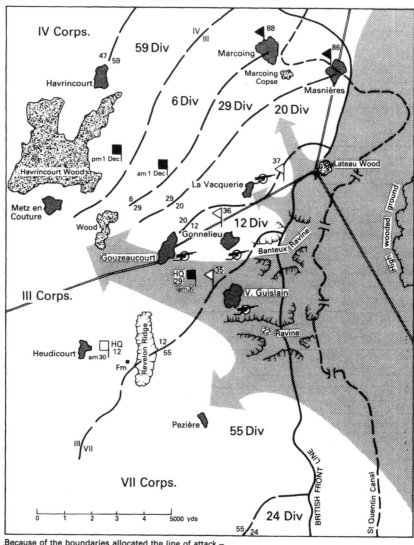

Because of the boundaries allocated the line of attack —
objective Metz en Couture — threatened the rear of five divisions

Formation boundaries
III Corps heavy artillery locations
Examples of divisional HQ moves (29 Div)   29 Div's bdes
Examples of distance between HQ Div (12 Div) and bdes

the road. . . . Worst of all, three low-flying aeroplanes fired on all who stopped for breath in shell-holes.'[4]

The mess waiter was among the casualties.

The Australians of 68 Squadron had just eaten when the alarm sounded and two flights took off to intercept the enemy. Near ground level they could see little, but soon met opposition as they climbed into banks of fog and smoke. One pilot sent a two-seater Aviatik diving into the ground, its observer slumped over his machine gun. Another plane, 'resembling an Albatros but with a clipped tail', was also destroyed. Two Australians crashed after being hit but escaped from their wrecks unhurt. On a later sortie the pilot who shot down the Aviatik saw a crowd of Germans round its remains and dropped a 25 lb bomb on them.[5] When gaps could be found in the mist there was no shortage of targets.

The Germans appear to have had their first thoughts of a counter-offensive on 23 November when reinforcements began to accumulate. Units were concentrated under a headquarters at Busigny about 20 miles south of Cambrai and another at Caudry mid-way between Cambrai and Le Cateau. These became the Caudry and Busigny 'Groups'.

On the 25th the Staff of Second Army issued preliminary instructions and two days later von der Marwitz conferred with Crown Prince Rupprecht and General Ludendorff at his headquarters at Le Cateau. Their plan was simple – a blow at the base on each side of the salient. The main effort was to be made on the southern sector of the battlefield in the direction Banteux–Gouzeaucourt 'while a subsidiary attack was to be made west of Bourlon in a direction due south'.[6] The bombardment was to be intense but brief, the attack timetable staggered along the front and aircraft used on a scale not seen previously.

The Banteux–Gouzeaucourt thrust was delivered towards Metz-en-Couture (south of Havrincourt Wood), situated on the only good road to the Bourlon position. By about 9 am on 30 November the Germans were only three miles from Metz and the Third Army was facing disaster.

Bantouzelle, found deserted on 20 November, had been used as an assembly point for enemy troops. The bridges had remained intact and, despite costly attempts, the 12th Division had been unable to secure Pelican Trench which overlooked the crossing. From Banteux-Bantouzelle the Germans had access to a Y-shaped valley, variously called Twenty-Two or Banteux Ravine, which drained two small streams into the canal. This feature figured prominently on British maps as, contrary to staff teaching, it lay at the junction of III and VII Corps and of the 12th and 55th Divisions.

On the 12th's side of Twenty-Two, Gonnelieu topped one spur; on the 55th's side Villers Guislain topped another. Not quite two miles further south, another ravine complex stretched into the British positions like a bird's claw, its branches dubbed Pigeon, Targelle and Quail by some sporting staff officer. The defence of such important ground put an added strain on the 55th Division. Because of the fighting on its left, it had been required to hold six miles of trench, though it could muster only two reasonably-strong brigades (the 165th and 166th). The third (the 164th) had not been brought up to strength after its losses at 'the Knoll' on the 20th. At this time the 12th and 20th Divisions were both holding three-mile sectors – the nearer to Bourlon the shorter the front.

In the early hours of the 30th the Germans emerged from cellars and dug-outs in Bantouzelle and other villages, crossed the canal undetected and formed up at the entrance to the ravines (there was another on the 55th Division front accessible at Honnecourt within the enemy lines).

When the barrage opened the gullies filled with gas, forcing the defenders to wear respirators. Heavy mortars demolished the strongpoints. In a short sharp fight the 1st/5th South Lancashires and two platoons of the 1st/5th King's Own were overrun. Taking advantage of the mist and smoke, the Germans pushed up the southern arm of Twenty-Two Ravine to enter Villers Guislain and take the 1st/5th Loyals in the rear. They used the other branch of the 'Y' to reach Gonnelieu. Roads from both villages led to Gouzeaucourt.

Alerted by SOS signals before dawn, the gunners of the 270th Siege Battery at Vaucelette Farm, about a mile and a half from Villers Guislain, fired their 6-inch howitzers at 'excellent targets'. When the German masses were only 200 yards away they made off with their sights and instruments. Enemy aircraft drove them from a trench when they tried to make a stand and finally they dug in alongside some infantry.[7]

Only 400 yards from Gonnelieu the 377th Battery, Royal Field Artillery,[8] had been firing on its SOS lines since 7 am. About 8 o'clock a patrol reported that the Germans were heading for

Gonnelieu, having taken Villers Guislain. Two guns were immediately dragged out of their pits so they could be swung in any direction.

Soon afterwards a major dashed up, announced that his 6-inch howitzer battery had been captured and pointed to grey-clad figures swinging two guns in a highly undesirable direction. Six shells from one of the 18-pounders put an end to this menace but by that time the other was engaging riflemen at 800 yards. Bullets cracked off its shield. A liaison subaltern brought news that he had been using his revolver and hand grenades to defend a battalion headquarters and 'on the information received from him the fire of the Section was shortened considerably'.[9]

With the two guns still in their emplacements firing on SOS lines at distant targets, the others dealt with the immediate menace.

'Time after time the enemy's infantry attempted to advance, but the stopping power of the 18-pounder, firing over open sights with Fuze 1, proved itself too much for them and they fell back . . . with heavy casualties.'[10]

When machine-gun bullets damaged the recoil glides of one of the exposed guns a third was pulled out of its pit and by 11.30 the range was down to 150 yards. Three detachments withdrew after disabling their weapons, leaving the fourth to cover their retirement. Three men were captured, one of whom escaped later. Thanks to this stand some 300 British wounded got away but the Germans were after a tremendous prize – eighteen howitzers were located in and around Gouzeaucourt, four 6-inch, eight 8-inch, four 9.2-inch and two 12-inch. There was also a supply train in the sidings. General de Lisle tried to organize a stand when he got there but the Germans were close behind. The quartermasters of the 18th Brigade of the 6th Division had already moved their transport details to a covering position behind the village alongside a company of pioneers (11th DLI) and a Royal Engineer field company. A detachment of the 11th US Engineer (Railway) Regiment, which had been working north of Gouzeaucourt, joined in. They had only their shovels to begin with, 'but by the end of the day every survivor was armed with a Mauser rifle and bayonet'.[11] Some Americans were captured but a few escaped later.

On the right of Gouzeaucourt the defence was maintained by Brigadier-General Berkeley Vincent who had been driven from his

HQ near Villers Guislain about 7.30 am, having lost all touch with his battalions. Two clerks had been killed by an enemy grenade while burning papers in the headquarters dug-out.[12] Vincent, an Irishman who had begun his career in the Royal Artillery and later transferred to the Inniskilling Dragoons,[13] established thirty men about 200 yards from his old command post. Ground-attack planes quickly reduced the party to four.

Collecting other stragglers as he went, Vincent reached Gauche Wood south of Gouzeaucourt, but was shelled out of it. He lined up about 100 men along the railway line further west and fired on advancing Germans until cartridges ran out. The little band trailed up another ridge and helped themselves at an ammunition dump in a farm. This time they stayed put. Revelon ridge became a rallying point. Pioneers, hussars, corps cyclists, the band of the Royal Dragoons, anyone capable of using a rifle was put into the firing line. Field gunners continued to use their 18-pounders at point blank range.

The mixture of troops at Gouzeaucourt – 12th, 20th and 29th Divisions – is revealing. Within ninety minutes of the enemy assault divisional generals were rendered powerless and brigadiers reduced to the level of platoon commanders. In some sectors links between higher and lower echelons were severed almost at once.

'The congestion of the various divisions in the salient formed by the success of the 20th (November) had made the allocation of Divisional Headquarters difficult and in the case of the 12th the lines of communication ran parallel to the front line.' The capture of Villers Guislain and Gouzeaucourt 'destroyed all the cables to Brigade Headquarters'.[14]

The 29th's headquarters was five miles from its bridgehead at Masnières, but only two and a half miles from the German posts outside Banteux. De Lisle's phone lines were broken immediately by the enemy barrage. Orders filtering through from above were often contradictory or quickly countermanded because of changing circumstances. No sooner did news arrive of serious developments on Byng's southern front than large bodies of troops were observed massing against the north-western flank of the bulge.

'A whole division was reported as moving into Moeuvres, while battalions and regiments were moving in waves across the open slopes between Moeuvres and Bourlon'.[15]

General von Moser had six divisions under command, plus 508 guns, a ration strength of 130,000 which he later pointed out was equal to the Crown Prince of Prussia's force at Worth during the Franco-Prussian War.

Three assault divisions assembled under a ragged smoke screen, intending to thrust down the western flank of Bourlon and swarm over the ridge past the Crucifix to the sugar factory on the Bapaume–Cambrai road. Once there, the British field batteries massed around Graincourt would be in jeopardy. Bourlon Wood itself could be cut off. Unhappily for the German troops, their leaders had learned little from the experiences of their opponents attacking in the opposite direction. They too were ordered into a horse-shoe re-entrant ringed by the Vickers guns of three divisions – the 47th in the wood, the 2nd along the pavé and around the factory, and the 56th in the trenches before Moeuvres and along the Canal du Nord.

Whatever criticism may have been directed at Woollcombe, there can be no doubt that the decision of IV Corps not to risk the heavy artillery beyond the canal after the original attack was crucial. Every German attempt to advance was enfiladed from their right by big guns. The 18-pounder brigades met them head on.

Moser's troops had no ravines in which to gather and their tactics would not have come amiss at the battle of Worth itself.

'Great attacks were delivered at 9.20 am, 11.25 am, and again at 2.30 pm.' All were repulsed with heavy loss. One group of eight Vickers guns fired 70,000 rounds 'at close quarters' during the day.[16]

'Their front ranks were shot to pieces . . . But as one wave was swept away another took its place; in one part of the line no less than eleven waves . . . followed one after the other . . . all were bloodily repulsed.'[17]

Gunners reported that they could 'fire into the brown, it was not necessary to select targets, the enemy formations being so dense; it was in fact like the early days of the war when they attacked arm-in-arm'.[18]

From time to time reports reached IV Corps HQ that the enemy had reached the RN 29 but all were false; 'he never really dented our line and took only a few advanced posts, and forced our line back some two or three hundred yards on the crest near the wood in the afternoon'.[19]

Those 'few advanced posts' saw ferocious fighting. One of them, a sap-head off a trench known as the Rat's Tail, was occupied by a company of the 17th Royal Fusiliers under orders to withdraw to a less exposed position. Captain Walter Napoleon Stone sent back three platoons and held off the enemy with the fourth until the others were in position. Field telephone in hand, he stood on the parapet sending back information until the last minute and was shot in the head as he and his men tried to fight their way back.[20]

A party of the 10th DCLI, staggering up to the main line with boxes of bombs and cartridges, observed a company cook of the Fusiliers 'standing on the parapet of a trench, amidst a hail of bullets, hurling bandoliers of fresh ammunition to the men around him'.[21]

On the banks of the Canal du Nord, just outside Moeuvres, a serious situation arose when the enemy overran a company of the 1st King's and cut off one of the 13th Essex in a trench at Lock 5. They were eventually held.

Phosgene shells continued to flood the centre of Bourlon Wood, reducing the 1st/19th London[22], in support on the lower slopes, to only seventy effectives and putting an entire machine-gun company out of action. The enemy drove the 1st/6th and 1st/15th London Regiments[23] (who lost 600 men between them) into the trees on the western edge, but there they stayed. Try as they may, the Germans could no more capture Bourlon Wood than the British could take the village. It was a similar story opposite Fontaine from which the enemy emerged but was driven back by the 59th Division with heavy loss. Cantaing went up in flames during the fighting.

Despite these important defensive successes, it looked at noon as though they might merely add to the scale of impending disaster. The staggered timing of enemy assaults 'wrong-footed' the British commanders. The first, by the Busigny Group on Byng's right, mainly affected VII Corps and the 55th Division; an hour later the Caudry Group swarmed over the front of III Corps, advancing in thick mist against the pronounced salient held by the 20th Division where the canal bent sharply round to the British bridgehead at Les Rues Vertes-Masnières.

The 20th's outposts were out of sight of the crossings and its main defence zone was incomplete, with little wire and no communication trenches.

Earlier, when the storm broke at Banteux Ravine, the commander of the 20th generously sent his reserve brigade to help his neighbour. Within an hour he was trying to recall it. The enemy had appeared out of the mist in his own sector, entered Lateau Wood from the rear and cut off three battalions – the 10th and 11th King's Royal Rifle Corps and the 10th Rifle Brigade. All were overrun and the men killed or captured.[24] A strongpoint at Rue des Vignes cemetery, on which much energy had been spent, also fell. This virtually took the 59th Brigade out of the 20th's order of battle and its survivors rallied on the neighbouring 61st.

As the line cracked on the left it became desperately urgent to protect the flank of the 29th Division exposed in the Masnières bridgehead. The garrison had been alerted during the night by unusual movement and noises behind enemy lines but they were not expecting Germans to attack their rear. Once again the divisional boundaries had been badly drawn so that responsibility for Les Rues Vertes, the twin village to Masnières, was divided between the 20th and the 29th. Germans appeared at 'LRV' before 9 am, capturing a field company of sappers asleep in cellars under the old brewery.

The troops in Masnières on the other side of the canal would have been cut off had it not been for Captain Robert Gee, 22 years in the ranks of the Royal Fusiliers before being commissioned. Gee was a man of great stamina, one of only two members of his 169-strong company who paraded fit to fight after the killer blizzard at Gallipoli in November, 1915. At Cambrai he was on the brigade staff and when the Germans entered Les Rues Vertes he and half-a-dozen signallers threw a barricade of furniture across the street just short of a house used as an ammunition dump. Knocking a hole through an adjoining wall he emerged in a bomb store where two Germans tried to capture him. One he killed with an iron-shod stick, the other with his revolver.

The grenades provided welcome reserves for two companies of the Royal Guernsey Light Infantry which came panting up. From the roof of the local château Gee next spotted an enemy machine gun about 100 yards away and crept up on it with an orderly. Revolver in hand, he waited for a British mortar to distract the detachment, then rushed over and shot them. The orderly fell, one of four killed or wounded alongside Gee that day. Gee himself was wounded while organizing the destruction of another machine gun and went reluctantly back to the dressing station.[25]

While the battle of 'LRV' was being fought, the 2nd Royal Fusiliers, 1st Lancashire Fusiliers and 16th Middlesex beat off all attacks on the bridgehead. At one time the Germans actually reached Marcoing Copse, well behind the British canal line. About 10 am the master cook of the 2nd South Wales Borderers appeared at battalion headquarters to report the enemy approaching fast. He was being rebuked for spreading rumours when bullets ended all doubts.[26] A counter-attack was hastily organized and, while the Welshmen gave covering fire, elements of the 1st King's Own Scottish Borderers, 2nd Hampshires, 4th Worcesters, 1st Essex and the Royal Newfoundland Regiment drove the enemy back.

By 11 am the 29th Division's forward units were again in touch across the canal at Masnières, thanks to the spontaneous action of the troops on the spot. General de Lisle regarded their achievement as all the more remarkable because 'the attack on the 30th came as a complete surprise'[27] and the men were very tired, having had no rest since the night of 17/18 November when they entrained for the area. One incident in particular seized his imagination – a solitary private in the KOSB was discovered firing one gun of a deserted 18-pounder battery laid to cover Masnières.

Such simple and inspired solutions to the problem whether to fight or run were not available to the staff of Third Army headquarters who had great difficulty in deciding where to direct their scanty reserves as conflicting reports came in.

The Guards Division began the day under IV Corps, was placed under VII Corps about 8.30, expecting to move south, but at 11 o'clock found itself under III Corps and ordered to march on Gouzeaucourt, the fate of which was then unknown. It was quickly revealed to Brigadier-General Champion de Crespigny, who rode on ahead of his men. Troops from every arm were streaming across the fields saying the Germans were already in the village looting the supply train. Without waiting to arrange artillery or tank support, the 2nd and 3rd Coldstream Guards were deployed to attack from the south while the 2nd Irish Guards approached from the north.

The Guardsmen concentrated in low ground near Gouzeaucourt Wood and moved over the ridge in artillery formation (dispersed to avoid casualties). As they went downhill the pioneers and other details who were still holding out went forward with them. The 20th Hussars, who had come up mounted but sent back their horses, advanced on their right. Gouzeaucourt was cleared in quick time and 100 prisoners captured, but a further advance was prevented by the enemy 'making effective use of some captured British guns and firing at very short range'.[28] British artillerymen who followed up the attack recovered four abandoned 6-inch howitzers and re-opened fire.[29]

In mid-afternoon tanks appeared. Four were knocked out, the crews removing their Lewis guns and joining the Guards. Elements of the 5th Cavalry Division also arrived but a mounted attack on Gauche Wood miscarried when squadrons of the 8th Hussars and 12th Lancers collided. Despite this incident, Gouzeaucourt had been saved (the Guards finding the looted supply train a convenient source of rations) and the thrust on Metz-en-Couture halted. To the south the line began to stabilize along the position taken up by Brigadier-General Vincent. To the north the front was patched up to link with the 29th Division at Masnières. In IV Corps sector little ground had been ceded. Troops from other Armies began to move to Byng's aid and the withdrawal of the French cavalry from Péronne was stopped. Pétain ordered up two infantry divisions in lorries, though they would take a day and a half to reach the scene. In the meantime, the 186th Brigade of the 62nd Division, which had spent only one night in rest billets after being relieved, began a six-mile march to a position near Graincourt behind the 2nd Division. Brigadier-General Bradford set up headquarters in a dug-out but was caught in a sudden burst of shelling as he went forward to reconnoitre. He died immediately – only twenty days after he had taken over his command.

Even more remote from the battle area than the 62nd, the horse transport of the 36th Division, en route to a rest area, was halted by cyclists and ordered to retrace its steps. Officers who had gone ahead to organize billets near Arras were sent hurrying back to their units which had already begun the long return march, there being 'no time to provide trains upon the congested railways'. The road took them once again across the barren expanse devastated by the enemy in the spring of 1917. Not surprisingly the Ulstermen appeared 'very fatigued'.[30]

The move of the tired troops was part of Byng's response to advice given him by the Commander-in-Chief to use his reserves 'energetically'.[31] There was nothing else available.

Haig had arrived at Albert shortly before midday after hearing of the enemy's success against VII Corps. He outlined the steps already taken by GHQ to transfer divisions from other parts of the front but he faced the same problems that Ludendorff had encountered on the 20th when he succinctly observed that 'the order to entrain (a division) is by no means the same thing as its arrival'.

Until new formations appeared, Byng had to do the best he could with what he already had. The Cavalry Corps and such tanks as could be put into running order were moved up during the day and the staff spent a sleepless night making counter-attack arrangements.

Information was now accumulating from survivors drifting back under cover of darkness, among them the garrison of Limerick Post, a strongpoint which had been attacked from Pigeon Ravine. A mixed collection of the Liverpool Scottish, 1st/5th King's Own and 1st/5th Loyals had held out throughout the day, rejecting all attempts to 'induce us to surrender'.[32] Severe hand-to-hand fighting occurred when the enemy tried to storm the sandbagged redoubt but he was driven off. At dusk, after the Germans had brought up a minenwerfer, the Lancashiremen crept away.

The weather had turned warmer and was dry for once. North of Gouzeaucourt and around Gonnelieu a flurry of flares and the noise of prolonged machine-gun fire erupted as units of the 6th and 20th Divisions tried to surprise the enemy. The Germans were on the alert and, when the excitement died down, activity on the southern part of the front was mainly confined to outbreaks of artillery fire. Only at Bourlon did the shell-storm continue unabated. When it ceased about 4 am the medical officers of the 2nd/6th South and 2nd/6th North Staffordshires had to solve the problem of evacuating 680 gas casualties from the wood. Under the existing instructions suspected phosgene victims had to exert themselves as little as possible.

CHAPTER FIFTEEN
'Draw swords . . . gallop'

The Germans worked through the night of the 30th to consolidate captured trenches – new fire steps had to be built as the existing ones faced the wrong way. For entanglements they relied on those originally intended to protect the British support line. Carrying parties humped ammunition up the ravines to Gauche Wood and to Gonnelieu and Villers Guislain. On the saddle of the ridge that linked the villages, a sugar factory was turned into a strongpoint. Opposite, across a valley, columns of horsemen were assembling around the straggling linked villages of Peizière-Epéhy. The low conversation of the riders was in Pushtu, Hindi and Urdu as well as English. Most of the regiments in the 4th and 5th Cavalry Divisions belonged to the Indian Army – relics of the old Iron Rations of 1915 to be used only in an emergency. Their objectives were the ravines and the high ground outside Villers Guislain. Tanks were to lead the way.

The 1st Guards Brigade lining up to assault Gauche Wood heard that they too were to have tank support and cavalry on their right but a number of machines had not arrived at zero hour and there was no sign of the horsemen. It was a situation that occurred time and again during the Cambrai operation. With the light improving to the benefit of the enemy infantry, commanders had to decide whether to wait for support or to go ahead without it.

The Guards attacked with such help as had arrived. Four tanks proved invaluable to the 3rd Coldstream assaulting trenches on the open slopes north of the wood, but the 2nd Grenadiers had none. They overcame the problem by covering the 1,000 yards to the trees in one mad scramble rather than in the manner prescribed by regulations.[1] The Germans shot high and, before they could recover, the guardsmen were upon them and the wood changed hands. Some Mark IVs made a timely arrival and, though the machines were quickly knocked out or broke down, the crews removed their Lewis guns and formed a flank guard until the cavalry arrived.

The 3rd Guards Brigade also attacked Gonnelieu on time – 6.20 am – but only one of nine promised tanks was present. It enabled the Welsh Guards to seize the high ground to the south-west but the 4th Grenadiers had no such assistance as they left the cover of the railway line and advanced up a bare slope towards the village. Not a shell was seen to burst on the enemy position.

The fighting for Gonnelieu was confused and costly. One platoon was annihilated by machine guns in the first few minutes. Another reached the cemetery and took a heavy toll of the enemy; then its Lewis gun jammed, there was a furious mêlée among the tombstones, and only a subaltern and a sergeant made their way back. A company commander controlled a withdrawal from the village, helping back several wounded and walking up and down giving orders within 50 yards of the enemy. Finally he led a handful of men in a counter-attack and was killed.[2]

After two and a half hours Viscount Gort, commanding the Grenadiers, decided that there were too many machine guns in Gonnelieu for it to be taken without a bombardment or tanks. Some survivors of the 20th Division's abortive night attack had been discovered in a trench west of the village and the Grenadiers joined them. Gort was inspecting the position when he was severely wounded. It was later learned the enemy had been gathering in Gonnelieu to renew their attack when the British struck.

While the Guards had been heavily engaged, Jacob's Horse of the Lucknow Brigade made a dismounted attack along the road to the sugar factory. By that time the light had improved and the enemy could see the Indians clearly. Little progress was made. German artillery began to range on the regiments 'drawn up in mass' around Peizière-Epéhy.[3]

Major-General Kennedy could see little point in sending further regiments of his 4th Division against an unshaken enemy, even though tanks were expected. 'Corps', however, would consider no arguments and in a heated telephone conversation Lieutenant-General Kavanagh 'insisted' on mounted action. The

156

Commander of the Mhow Brigade thought as little of his men's prospects as Kennedy, but had to comply. He assumed the situation must be 'a desperate one'.[4]

Squadrons of turbaned horsemen filed down Catelet Valley and reined left to prepare for the charge. Lances for Gardner's Horse had to be brought up in waggons as they had been left behind that morning. Soon after 9.30 the Germans occupying the old British second line covering Targelle Ravine and its offshoots saw lines of horsemen galloping up the slopes towards them, pennants fluttering. They watched the Indians leap trenches, burst through some thin wire and run down fugitives. The same onlookers kept their fingers on the firing mechanism of their machine guns and made the dust and soil fly. Riderless mounts galloped away and dying animals writhed, kicking and neighing. After a frenzied stabbing and hacking at a handful of Germans, Gardner's Horse pulled their mounts into cover and occupied Kildare Post. A lance dafadar made three daring rides to report that his comrades were engaging the enemy with rifles and Hotchkiss guns.[5] Targelle and Pigeon Ravine remained in German hands.

'Draw swords . . . form line . . . gallop!'

The Inniskilling Dragoons attacked straight up the road towards the sugar factory soon after the Lancers charged. The lead squadron was riddled by cross fire and a machine-gun section which accompanied it lost its entire strength, fifty-five men and eighty-four horses, plus all four weapons. Those 'Skins' who reached the factory were captured. Seeing the futility of the action the other squadrons wheeled round and trotted back.

Dismounted cavalry attacks were made throughout the day but the Jodhpur Lancers, Central India Horse and Lord Strathcona's Horse (of the Canadian Brigade) only added to the casualty list. It was believed at the time that their efforts had barred the enemy's way; it was not known until later that he 'intended no fresh advance in this part of the field'.[6]

The troops in the canal bridgehead were in much graver peril; the 86th Brigade was still threatened with encirclement. From early morning Les Rues Vertes and Masnières were heavily shelled but another sugar factory became a stumbling block, this time for the Germans. East of the canal they were mown down by Vickers of the brigade machine-gun company in and around the building.

'Possibly 500 fell and the German Red Cross were kept busy for the rest of the day.'[7]

In the afternoon, as if stung by this loss, the enemy unleashed a stupendous bombardment on 'LRV' and Masnières. To Brigadier-General Ronald Cheape,[8] who had been on active service since 1914, it was 'like nothing I have ever seen'. Houses collapsed, splintered timber caught fire; for an hour and a half all was enveloped in smoke and dust. Then Germans began working their way forward through the débris. For a moment panic threatened to stampede raw British reinforcements[9] brought up the previous day and thrown into action without joining their own units. They were rallied by all available officers and, helped by a handful of Guernseys, pushed the enemy back.

The 29th Division now stuck out like a sore thumb with Les Rues Verte and Masnières forming a broken nail. The position was two miles long, less than a mile across but its perimeter stretched for nearly six. Down the centre ran the waterway. To attempt to hold the villages meant more casualties and the division had by then lost half of its strength. Major-General de Lisle raised the question of withdrawal but Byng was still 'most anxious not to give up ground'.[10] As no reinforcements were available, de Lisle left it to his brigadiers to decide – and they organized a retirement that night. All moveable wounded were evacuated and the smouldering rubble abandoned. 'The thumb' below the joint remained in British hands.

By contrast to the flame and fury elsewhere, Bourlon Wood was comparatively quiet, though west of it the Germans began pushing down the Hindenburg Line in much the same way as the 56th and 36th Divisions had been trying to bomb their way up it ever since 20 November.

The state of relative calm enabled Byng to carry out a change of management in the Bourlon–Fontaine sector. Woollcombe and his staff were to have been relieved the previous day but their replacement in the middle of the great German attack was impractical. It was not until 6 pm on 1 December that they handed over to Lieutenant-General Sir Edward Fanshawe and the staff of V Corps.[11]

The next day the Commander-in-Chief began discussions at GHQ on the possible withdrawal from the most exposed parts of the Cambrai salient. Prince Rupprecht and von der Marwitz were also in consultation. The British counter-attacks had taken a heavy toll and some German divisions were very tired. Artillery ammunition was insufficient and communications bad.

Surprise was a card that both sides had played. Before it could be tried again there would have to be a period of static warfare. Only sporadic fighting occurred on 2 December. In Cambrai the civilian population began to circulate again. Abbé Delval wrote:

'What grief and disillusion for us. The Allies were at our gates and we were awaiting our deliverance – more than that, we were counting on it! Now truth has given the lie to our hopes. Are we to have more disappointments? Having done little to help them, the German yoke is going to be more painful and intolerable than before.'

While the Germans concentrated on securing the ground before attempting anything more, the British were reorganizing and waiting for reserves. Byng was still thinking of hanging on to what remained of his gains. Retire? He made no suggestion 'that such a course was necessary or even advisable'.[12] When Haig visited him on 3 December the Third Army Commander said he would need two extra divisions to retain the Marcoing–Bourlon salient permanently. It was wishful thinking. That morning the Germans laid a tremendous barrage on the stump of the Les Rues Vertes–Masnières position. Half of it was occupied by the 2nd South Wales Borderers and the Royal Newfoundland Regiment of the 29th Division and half by the 14th DLI and 1st KSLI of the 6th Division, units which had been in the original advance on 20 November. All manned hastily-dug trenches in which 'the shells threw up such clouds of dust that the rifles positively jammed with it'.[13]

Twice the Durhams were driven from their positions and twice, led by a company commander, they retook them. In a third attack he was captured but escaped.[14] The CO of the Durhams was 27-year-old Lieutenant-Colonel John Rosher, a solicitor in civilian life. He pressed every spare man into the defence of the bridges over the canal and the two light infantry battalions fell back to Marcoing. Informed opinion in the 29th Division was that Rosher's action had prevented 'a complete catastrophe'. As it was, the units in the bridgehead lost heavily. The South Wales Borderers held their ground but were taken in enfilade and reduced to the CO, Adjutant, one officer and seventy-three men, plus the medical officer. An entire company of Newfoundlanders was wiped out. The Durhams and KSLI eventually recrossed the canal and took up a position covering Marcoing but there was little to gain from hanging on. While this fighting was taking place Haig was instructing Byng to withdraw.

It had been a trying day for Sir Julian. He told the Commander-in-Chief that he was not particularly worried about holding La Vacquerie, the fortified hamlet a mile north of Gonnelieu on 'Welsh Ridge' but a brigade of the 61st (2nd South Midland) Division was driven out that morning. The 61st had relieved the 20th and 12th Divisions under difficult conditions, no one being sure where the front lay. The 2nd/4th and 2nd/6th Gloucestershires clung to a strongpoint called the Corner Work and prevented a further enemy advance. Hundreds of grenades flew as the 2nd/7th Warwickshires disputed Ostrich Avenue, part of the old Hindenburg System.

After their morning conversation Haig's instructions to Byng were explicit: 'The Third Army front will be withdrawn with the least possible delay from the Bourlon Hill–Marcoing salient to a more retired and shorter line of defence to be selected by you.'

The second paragraph of the three-paragraph GHQ Order issued on 3 December and signed by Kiggell hints at some reluctance by the Army Commander to comply:

'The line chosen should be the best available with a view to obtaining security of ground combined with economy of troops. The abandonment of ground recently won is quite secondary to these considerations.'[15]

The final paragraph drew 'particular attention' to the importance of Byng's right flank 'about la Vacquerie, Welsh Spur [Ridge] and to the south of those places'.

The evacuation of Bourlon Wood and the Marcoing position took place on the night of 4 December under appreciable moonlight. As at Suvla, which Byng had left with more enthusiasm in December, 1915, the British kept up the pretence of normal conditions. The 23rd London Regiment, in trenches on the immediate left of the wood, heard of the retirement 'accidentally', no message having reached it, but in general all went according to plan. Burdened with surplus ammunition and bombs, the infantry of the 47th Division withdrew through the gas-drenched undergrowth and slithered down the slopes stormed eleven days earlier by the 40th. Sections stumbled down the sunken road which marked the limit of the first attack of the 62nd. 'In it there sprawled large numbers of German dead. No one knew the occasion of their death but it was probably the attack of 30 November.' The previous night officers who had been occupying this open grave for two days were startled to hear a low groan. A badly wounded German had regained consciousness.[16]

German shelling of the rear areas during darkness helped to blanket noise of movement, and the gunners of the 270th Siege Battery chose this, of all nights, to indulge in a piece of private enterprise. Borrowing four eight-horse teams from another unit and fitting rubber tyres to their limbers, they prepared to recover their abandoned 6-inch howitzers from the edge of the German positions. Enemy troops were using the pits as outposts. Helped by a small detachment of the 10th KOYLI, the raiders carried out a pincer movement to persuade the opposition to withdraw. They discovered preparations had already been made to destroy the guns. Sandbags, charges and detonators were removed from the barrels, the howitzers pulled from their emplacements, signals made to the rear. Two teams galloped up and made off with their rightful possessions. The enemy began raking the area with heavy shells and machine guns and, as the next teams arrived, a driver was hit and the plunging horses became unmanageable. Once they were quietened the guns were hooked on and were careering over the ground when the lead detachment came to grief in a shell crater. Four horses of the second team were hitched to the first. All twelve took fright, but bolted in the right direction. The last gun, with only four horses attached, was recovered with the aid of every man of the infantry covering party heaving on drag ropes.[17]

As the moon rose, about 11 o'clock, all appeared as usual on the Cambrai front. By 4.30 am only skeleton forces remained at Bourlon 'moving from point to point, to fire rifles and Verey lights, just as if the normal garrison had been there'.[18] Wreckers moved into the dug-outs under Graincourt church to ensure that the Germans could not quickly make use of them again.

The following day troops watched the enemy bombard and attack deserted positions. They 'came over in waves and, on finding the trenches empty, halted irresolutely. After a little while they settled down.'[19] Two miles away the British remained hidden and silent. For once the PBI on both sides were happy.

Near La Vacquerie bombers again clashed in Ostrich Avenue and the 9th Inniskillings went to the aid of the 2nd/7th Warwickshires. They reported the old Hindenburg Support Line 'a filthy place. Corpses were touching, laid along the fire step, all men of the 61st Division'.

The next day a young lieutenant of the Inniskillings inspired the recapture of 400 yards of trench before being killed.[20] Along with the 36th, another familiar numeral reappeared on situation maps – the 51st Division moved up to the Moeuvres front. The last Guards units pulled out on the night of the 5th, the 1st Irish having lost an officer and thirty-five men in a sharp farewell fight near Gonnelieu.

'The Commander-in-Chief has announced this afternoon in his official communiqué the news of our withdrawal from part of the ground captured in our advance on 20 November, in order to avoid holding the sharp salient made by Bourlon Wood and our line running down east and west of it.'

Philip Gibbs in his despatch dated 6 December added that the enemy bombardment of empty trenches had seemed 'a huge joke to our men, whose sense of humour was sharpened by their sense of safety'.[21]

On the 7th he declared that to the troops the withdrawal from Bourlon was a 'relief from a place of horror . . . the big black belt of trees on the ridge above Graincourt and Anneux' had seemed different from all other woods.

'It was such a forest where, in old days lonely knights would have crossed themselves as they went through, the rider expecting to meet witch-women and evil creatures.'

These demons he likened to the gas shells poisoning 'all its glades'. Once troops left the place the spell was broken.

'They pulled off their masks these white-faced weary fellows of ours – and breathed freely again.'

The grim scene made its impact on both sides. Abbé Delval wrote on 7 December:

'An officer [German] reported in the house where he is billeted that there had been a bitter battle in Bourlon Wood where both sides had suffered very heavy losses; the wood is full of pieces of bodies and the trees are ripped to pieces. The English have been pushed back as far as Havrincourt.'

The 'English' had certainly pulled back. According to one calculation: 'Out of sixty square miles and fourteen villages (captured) the British retained but sixteen and three respectively, while the Germans had secured seven square miles and two villages held by us before the battle.'[22]

The line finally selected by Byng partly followed that suggested by

Feilding at the Havrincourt conference on 27 November. However, by the time it was occupied the villages of Villers Guislain, Gonnelieu, La Vacquerie and the ravine complex had fallen into enemy hands. The Flesquières position formed, if not as pronounced a salient as before, still a vulnerable one. For this doubtful gain 46,600 men had been expended, of whom slightly more than 5,000 were known to have been killed, though there were more dead among the 10,000 officially listed as missing. Bourlon's bramble thickets hid many a tragic secret.

The enemy claimed to have taken 6,000 prisoners on 30 November and put his own total loss of killed, wounded and missing (presumably including those captured) at 41,000. Disputes over the means of reckoning German losses have never been satisfactorily resolved (lightly wounded were said not to be counted), but a reasonable British calculation based on enemy regimental histories after the war put the figure at 45,000. Another total estimate by the British Official Historian is 53,000. The Germans stated that 14,000 of their casualties were suffered on or after 30 November. To sum up, it is likely that in a period of two weeks the blood of more than 90,000 soldiers of the British and German empires was spilt on the approaches to Cambrai, the greater part in and around Bourlon.

Both sides had lost many guns – the British admitted to 158, the Germans to 145. Morally the gain lay with the enemy. For more than two years his troops had stoically borne hammer blows in the West but on 30 November they had shown they too could execute a major offensive.

Ludendorff: 'We had won a complete victory over a considerable part of the British Army. It was a good ending to the extremely heavy fighting of 1917. Our action had given us valuable hints for an offensive battle in the West if we wished to undertake one in 1918.'[23]

The British infantry, sorely tried throughout the year, began to react to their long ordeal. A 24-hour delay in relieving the 1st Welsh Guards and 4th Grenadiers, holding the front after their attack at Gonnelieu, put 'a severe strain upon troops who had been through such severe fighting and suffered such heavy losses'.[24]

The 36th Division was reduced to its lowest physical condition since it landed in France – the men 'became indescribably dirty; lungs, throats and hearts were affected. High as were the battle casualties, the sick wastage was higher.'

It became doubtful if the Ulstermen could withstand a full-dress assault on Welsh Ridge.

'Morally the infantry had survived far better than the authority which left them in the line had any right to expect. The men kept surprisingly good hearts. Walking round these much harassed outposts one was still greeted with a grin when one inquired how many "pine apples" had come over in the last twenty-four hours from the German blocks a little further down the trenches. But physically they were wrecks. They were living on their nerves.'[25]

The staff of the 63rd Division noticed on arriving in the Third Army area 'an atmosphere of disquietude bordering on alarm, which was new in their experience, and which reflected the gravity of the disaster by which the fighting troops had been so nearly overwhelmed.'[26]

Rumours spread. Major-General 'Billy' Heneker, commanding the 8th Division at Ypres (where he had just lost 600 men in an operation he had strongly opposed), wrote in his Field Service notebook on 4 December:

'The Bosche offensive and fighting west of Cambrai has developed into a big thing and various divisions are going south from here to take part. Here the Bosche broke our line south of the Cambrai salient and captured a lot of ground. 12th and 55th Divisions bolted. Cavalry were late in first push and Kavanagh, Cav Corps Commdr has been sent home – also Dick Mullens 1st Cav Div.[27] Putty's seat is slippery as his was the Corps concerned.'

Suddenly a lot of seats seemed to be 'slippery', not only General Pulteney's.

CHAPTER SIXTEEN

Questions in the House

Lloyd George was on the warpath;[1] that was how Sir William Robertson put it. The Prime Minister could not understand why GHQ was taking so long to supply the War Cabinet with details of the 30 November débâcle. Days after the defeat Lord Derby, War Secretary, had said lamely that Haig himself was 'probably . . . ignorant of the causes of this reverse'.[2]

By contrast a disquieting picture was building up in the press. In his despatch dated 1 December Philip Gibbs had already given what proved to be a highly accurate report. It stated that the enemy had intended to 'pierce southwards to the Cambrai road, past the west side of Bourlon Wood, while what was possibly a heavier attack was delivered suddenly on our eastern or right flank in the direction of Gonnelieu and Villers Guislain.'

The northern attack had failed but the other 'had a success' which put 'a most severe strain on our generalship' and allowed the enemy to capture some guns.

By chance Gibbs had been on his way to Gouzeaucourt on the morning of the 30th and had turned back after meeting retiring troops. According to him, 'it was there that the surprise was greatest that Friday morning.' An officer serving in a field ambulance had fled from his bath clad in only a towel. Even when Gibbs was driving to the rear troops, unaware of the situation, were still cooking breakfast and some were playing football.[3]

The Cabinet read between the lines and at a stormy meeting on 5 December nothing Robertson said – 'and I said a good deal' –

GAINS AND LOSSES NOVEMBER - DECEMBER 1917

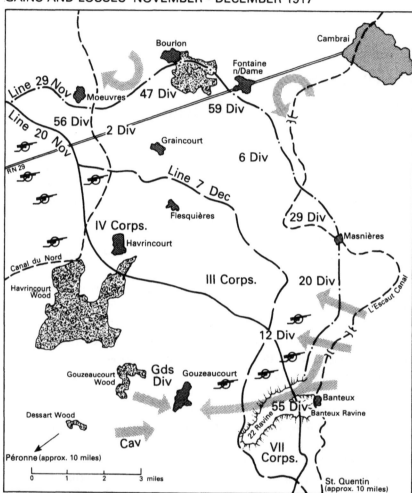

The numerals indicate the positions of the Third Army formations at the limit of the British success.
Arrows show the direction of the enemy thrusts on November 30.
The line shown as being occupied on December 7 produced the salient to which Byng clung too long on
March 21, 1918.

Indicates the position of the heavy artillery on November 30th.

could convince the Prime Minister that difficult conditions at the front were hindering the collection of information. Lloyd George pointed out that if a similar blow had been dealt to the enemy, London would have been informed in a matter of hours. In any case, how could such a surprise have been brought off when, according to GHQ, German morale and strength were in decline after their battering at Ypres? Was the Commander-in-Chief trying to play down the extent of the reverse? Derby and Robertson indignantly repudiated the suggestion.

After the meeting Sir William sent off an official telegram to Haig asking for the Field-Marshal's opinion on the events of 30 November and followed it up with a personal letter, on 6 December, hoping that the telegram 'did not seem to be asking too much'.[4]

The CIGS considered the Cabinet were making a fuss to cover up the fact that they had neglected to supply enough men for the Army. Two days later he wrote again to Haig expressing disgust because Lloyd George and 'his creatures' had been re-examining the weekly summaries provided by the War Office and 'had marked a curious collection of statements showing that I had underestimated the enemy's power'.

Haig replied that if Lloyd George wasn't happy with his conduct of operations he ought to replace him. Otherwise he should stop complaining and back him up.

At the same time Sir Douglas took a less cavalier view of the criticism of Charteris's work as the BEF's Director of Military Intelligence, and he refused to consider inefficiency as grounds for replacing him. Haig thought no one could do the work better[5] but he instructed Kiggell, still Chief of the General Staff at GHQ, to interview Charteris, said to be disliked by subordinate headquarters.

Whatever his faults, Charteris had correctly calculated that everything would depend on the first 48 hours at Cambrai and that by the third day enemy reinforcements would bring parity in numbers. He managed to put this across to Haig but his ability to communicate with his master seems to have failed him some days later. Though by the 27th Charteris believed the Germans were receiving 'large reinforcements', Haig was under the impression that the enemy was 'thin on the ground everywhere except Bourlon'. The shortcomings of the GHQ intelligence branch were not, however, Lloyd George's main concern. As time passed he became certain the War Cabinet was being 'kept in the dark' and that after the victory bells the Staff were ashamed to admit the huge loss in men and guns.[6]

The Commons was uneasy. Mr John Dillon, the Member for East Mayo and leader of the Irish Nationalist Party,[7] complained on 12 December that the Prime Minister was failing to tell the House 'the condition of the war'. MPs were disturbed by rumours about Cambrai. Speaking in the debate on the Vote of Credit (for financing the war) he quoted at length from a hostile article in *The Times*, generally friendly to the General Staff and party to 'inside knowledge which . . . is denied to Members of this House'. That criticism should come from such a usually sympathetic source was convincing evidence that 'there were blunders'.

Mr Dillon said: 'The official communiqués were more than usually laconic. The correspondents have so far been limited almost entirely to details of amazing individual gallantry.' *The Times* article had declared that its readers could 'no longer be satisfied with the fatuous estimates e.g. of German losses in men and morale which have inspired too many of the published messages from France'.

The official version of the battle was being amplified every day by 'innumerable and most disquieting accounts' from officers and men who took part in the actual fighting'. *The Times* had even demanded that the blunderers be removed.

Labour's Mr Jimmy Thomas, the railwaymen's leader, representing Derby, showed something of the broad-minded patriotism which Haig had discerned during his visit to GHQ. If firm, his tone was reasonable. He asked the government to make a statement, 'to allay the very strong feeling existing in the country today'. It was common property that 'as a result of the last offensive very many lives were lost and heavy casualties inflicted upon us'. The army of the day was 'comprised of the great mass of the civilian population'. There was a feeling growing up among soldiers and working men that 'so far as the blunders of the people at the top are concerned they are not dealt with in the same way as the bottom'.

Just as Mr Thomas wanted a fair deal for the private 'so equally there must be a fair deal and trial for the general, whoever he may be'. No position 'social or otherwise' should prevent the Government dealing with people guilty 'at the top'.

Mr Bonar Law, Leader of the House (and Chancellor), replied cautiously. In his view much of the discontent voiced was 'due to the entirely exaggerated hopes with which the initial success at Cambrai was received in this country'.

An Irish voice: 'Who was responsible for that?'

Mr Bonar Law really did not know. He confessed that when Members had burst into spontaneous cheering at the first announcement of the successful attack on the 20th he had been tempted to get up from the Front Bench and say:

'This was nothing like a breakthrough, that it was not intended to be a breakthrough and that it was simply an operation which stood more or less by itself.'[8]

As far as the 30th was concerned the Germans had made three different attacks,[9] the smallest, as regards to the numbers engaged, being at the point where 'owing to surprise' they broke through. The other two attacks had been repelled 'with great loss on the part of the enemy', Mr Bonar Law said. He assured the House that 'a full official inquiry would be made' and, rambling on, declared, 'Accidents of this kind are inevitable in war, even surprises. A misty morning might happen for which blame cannot be attached to anyone.'

Bonar Law's public performance projected a complacency on the part of the Cabinet which was completely belied behind the scenes. Sir William Robertson was being pressed for more and more information. On 15 December he visited Montreuil with Major-General Robert Hutchison, Director of Organization at the War Office. The CIGS said that the Cabinet had every confidence in Haig but there was a lot of loose talk about the 'mishap' at Cambrai and the sooner he sent in his official report the sooner the gossips could be silenced.[10]

The delay in producing it was attributed to the great blizzard sweeping Northern Europe; despatch riders could not negotiate the roads between front and GHQ. (There was a deal of truth in this – the horse transport of the 36th Division, which had at last been relieved, reported that some of the country tracks off the Doullens–Arras road 'simply could not be found'. Double teams were being used to haul wagons from deep drifts.)[11]

As the required reports were not to hand Sir William proceeded with another task – persuading Haig to replace his Quartermaster General, Sir Ronald Maxwell. Within a week of his 65th birthday he was considered too old to do the travelling his job entailed even when there were no snow drifts. Haig had no wish to lose him but yielded in the end.

Robertson dined with Sir Douglas on the 16th and the following day left for London. While he was en route an MP asked in the Commons on whose authority orders were given that joy bells should be rung and flags displayed to celebrate the victory of Cambrai; whether this was done on the authority of the War Cabinet.

Mr Bonar Law replied cryptically that the answer was 'in the negative'.[12] In the meantime, the object of these ephemeral plaudits, Sir Julian Byng, was writing his own account of the events of the 30th. The first paragraph has often been quoted:

> 'I attribute the reason for the local success on the part of the enemy to one cause and one alone, namely – lack of training on the part of junior officers and NCOs and men.'

This needs to be read in the context of the whole passage, sub-titled 'Reasons', which continues:

> 'As stated above [i.e. in the body of the report], I estimate that the number of prisoners captured by the enemy in the area of their success amounted to about six or seven thousand, of whom some five hundred or more were non-combatants (road makers, railwaymen etc). This number of fighting men alone should have been sufficient to have at least delayed any thrust on the part of the enemy sufficiently to allow the reserves of infantry and cavalry to be brought up to the vital spot.
>
> 'Individual acts of gallantry and resource were plentiful and the old divisions of the Expeditionary Force stood the test as well as heretofore – but that fact remains that some divisions were over-run and that their powers of defence were not fully realized. In this respect the action of the machine-gunners is conspicuous. Villers Guislain and Gonnelieu had been turned into strong defended localities with machine guns sweeping all approaches but in the critical moment these machine-gunners were carried away by the retirement of the infantry from the front trenches.
>
> 'With very few exceptions the artillery remained fighting to the last but the machine-gunner did not appear to have the same confidence in his weapon. The cause is not far to seek. The German machine-gunners are the pick of the infantry and therefore a *Corps d'Élite*. Our machine-gunners, on the other hand, are enlisted as such and are not brought up with the same *esprit de corps* that is found in a regiment.

'The gallantry of the young soldiers was conspicuous on 20 November when all was going well with them, but the amount of discipline they had imbibed could not stand the ordeal of the heavy massed attacks of the enemy in superior numbers on the 30 November.

'The remedy seems to be a longer period of training and in this connection it is to be noted that in the Guards, where the course is longer, there is no likelihood of any lack of staunch behaviour.'[13]

If Sir Julian genuinely believed badly-trained troops were at the root of the matter he was obliged to say so, but his conclusions contained serious implications. Training was the Army's own responsibility. Critics were entitled to ask what had gone wrong and at what level. His citing of the higher reliability of the 'old divisions of the Expeditionary Force' also raised questions as to the extent of his knowledge of them. None of the so-called Regular divisions of 1917 remotely resembled those which had gone to France in 1914 or early 1915. All but a handful of 'Old Contemptibles' had become casualties. Ranks had been replenished time and again; formations had changed. Of the battalions of the 2nd Division which had repulsed the enemy west of Bourlon, a third were from the New Army.

The 'Regular' 29th Division numbered the volunteer Royal Guernsey Light Infantry, the Royal Newfoundland Regiment and the 16th Middlesex (New Army) among its twelve battalions.

Comparisons having been made, they required analysis. Were the London Territorial units of the 47th Division, praised for the defence of Bourlon Wood, really superior to the West Lancashiremen who had lost Gonnelieu? If so, why?

And did Sir Julian actually mean it when he attributed the 'local success' of the enemy to 'one cause alone'? Had the higher echelons of command made not a single error? Even a small one? Had the Staff of the Third Army reached such a state of perfection?

Byng's report was signed on the 18th and a summary of it arrived at the War Office that day in a Special Operations Priority Message to Sir William Robertson. The contents had been telephoned from snow-bound Third Army HQ at Albert to GHQ. A moderating influence can be detected in the version prepared for transmission. Signed by Lieutenant-Colonel John Dill,[14] of Haig's Staff, O.A.D. 731/1 was from 'Chief France' to 'Chief London' and began by stating that the inquiry into events on 30 November was

171

still incomplete. The attack from the north of Masnières to and including Honnecourt had been made by five German divisions on the 29th, 20th and 12th Divisions and the left brigade of the 55th. It went on:

'Attack was not a surprise. Intelligence reports for two previous days had indicated abnormal railway movement. Considerable movement of troops had been observed for days previously on Seventh Corps front. Reinforcements in Moeuvres sector and increase of artillery had been noticed also increase in enemy's wireless activity the last being chiefly on front Masnières-Quéant.

'Enemy's low-flying aircraft had also been very active on Seventh Corps front, commanders concerned had realized probability of attack. Troops had been specially warned, extra machine-gun defence had been established in villages of Villers Guislain and Gonnelieu and other precautions had been taken.

'The Army Commander [says] that anticipating some such attack as occurred he had disposed his reserves where he considered they would best be situated to assist whatever portion of the salient might most require reinforcement after the enemy's attack had developed.

'In his dispositions he gave full consideration to possibility of attack on Gouzeaucourt-Epéhy front. Troops on Bourlon front where previous fighting had been severe and where main hostile attack was expected and delivered were relieved by three fresh divisions which had been brought up to reinforce the Army. Details of fight are not yet clear, and the following outline is given subject to any correction found necessary on completion of enquiry.'

According to prisoners, their first objective had been shelled severely for between 30 and 50 minutes before their guns lifted onto villages behind the British front and they advanced in 'deep masses'. The attack on the front of the 29th Division had been contained.

'To the south of that resistance appears to have been effective at some points where the enemy's attack was held up until defenders were compromised and overcome through troops on their flanks giving way. Our wire did not delay the enemy. This must be ascribed to hostile bombardment and conditions of continuous fighting.'

The summary went on to describe the enemy's rapid progress

up Twenty-Two and Banteux ravines where 'any resistance offered was quickly broken'.

After referring to the counter-attacks the message stated that guns and troops behind the front were taken unawares and did not appear to have received warning from troops in front 'on whose resistance in case of attack they were relying'. Had the warning been received it was probable that the British artillery would have broken up the attack. Guns deliberately placed well forward to protect the front and 'to reach enemy's artillery' had been overrun before the danger was realized. As for the infantry:

'Many of the troops fought well and there were many individual cases of heroism but others seem to have given way quickly, probably overborne by weight of numbers, this enabled the enemy to surround those resisting.

'With few exceptions also resistance of machine-gunners on front which broke appears to have been ineffective. This in some cases at least was probably due to their fire being masked by our own men falling back on them in front of the enemy.

'The divisions concerned including the 29th had been engaged since the 20th and were fatigued. On the other hand the rapidity with which resistance was organized by troops in the rear and the enemy's advance brought to a standstill was creditable. Revised calculations indicate that total prisoners taken from us on 30th do not exceed from 6 to 7 thousand. Enemy's published figures evidently include prisoners taken in previous fighting at Bourlon, Fontaine and elsewhere.'

Having digested 'OAD 731/1',[15] the War Cabinet wanted to know more and the next day, through the CIGS, compiled a list of specific questions to be put to Byng – in particular 'whether any commanders, and if so which, were to blame for the loss of the front system of defences on the right flank'.

Even as the Government sought more information, MPs were increasing their attacks on the military leadership in France. Lieutenant-Commander Josiah Wedgwood (representing Newcastle under Lyme), who had served at Gallipoli and in France, been wounded and won the DSO, was scathing: 'If there is going to be an inquiry into Cambrai it is ten times more reasonable to have an inquiry into Passchendaele'.

He accused Haig of 'super-optimism', which, he said, 'must make him value rather the carrying-out of his promise to statesmen at home than his responsibility to his own troops in the field.'

Haig had 'believed persistently' that it was possible to use cavalry to break through.

'Look how the Cavalry have been used at Cambrai . . . What on earth can any reasonable person who has seen fighting imagine that cavalry can do in modern warfare?'

Wedgwood had personally used machine guns against German cavalry and they had made a 'beautiful' target. However, thanks to the 'trade unionism' of the generals the cavalry had been preserved and brought forward into situations 'where their use is obviously absurd'.[16]

Though Wedgwood could be ignored, the Cabinet could not. Byng found himself obliged to expand on his views, which seemed to be changing. He informed GHQ on 22 December that: 'The 12th, 20th and 29th Divisions had all taken part in a very successful attack (on the 20th) and were correspondingly elated, although undoubtedly weary, were in good heart and full of fight. 55th Division had been holding a quiet part of the line. I regarded it as a good division and in a very fair fighting condition.'[17]

Except for a 'minor operation against The Knoll' the 55th had not been actively engaged since it came out of the line in Flanders. He was satisfied that the frontages held by the divisions attacked on the 30th were 'not more than they could justifiably be expected to hold, at any rate sufficiently to delay the enemy until the reserve divisions could come into action'.

In the absence of Pulteney and De Lisle (both on leave) he was unable 'to explain General De Lisle's statement that the attack came as a complete surprise'.[18]

Haig adopted many of Byng's deductions when he replied to the Cabinet in a classified document which went off on Christmas Eve and referred blandly to 'the mishap of November 30'.[19] (If the loss of more than 100 guns and thousands of prisoners was simply a 'mishap' well might Lloyd George wonder what would constitute a defeat!)

In preparing his report Sir Douglas said he had considered whether it had been reasonable to expect the divisions to hold the lengths of front assigned to them, bearing in mind their strength and the condition of the troops. He had also sought to establish whether 'adequate protective measures' had been taken (German prisoners had commented on the lack of barbed wire) and if reserves had been disposed correctly. His conclusion:

'After consideration of all the factors, I find no reason to criticize adversely the dispositions made, which in my opinion were

174

adequate to meet an attack of the strength anticipated and actually experienced.

'I further consider that if there were miscalculation it was not of such a nature to reflect adversely on the competence of the commanders concerned.

'As a matter of fact, no specific request for more troops to meet the expected attacks was made either by the Army or the Army Corps, Divisions and Brigades concerned.

'Whether the break on our front was due to the fighting value of the troops at that point being below average or to the task assigned to them being greater than they could reasonably be expected to carry out, are matters which, in the nature of things, it is impossible to determine. Risks have to be taken at reducing force at some points in order to be stronger at others.'

All superior commanders had to take these risks on a close calculation of the probable action of the enemy. On 20 November the British had succeeded in concentrating 'a superiority of 9 to 5 Infantry Divisions . . . without counting our 5 Cavalry Divisions and the tanks'.

On the 30th the enemy had brought up thirteen divisions (eight in line and five in reserve) against ten British (eight in line and two in reserve) exclusive of tanks.

Haig considered that the risk was 'legitimate' and 'that with this margin of superiority the enemy should not have succeeded in penetrating any part of our defences'.

He concluded: 'Whatever view may be held on the foregoing, I feel, after careful consideration that all the blame for the mishap of November 30 must rest on my shoulders. It was I who decided on the 22nd that the Bourlon position should be attacked and occupied, in the belief that the enemy's forces in the defensive sector lying to the North-West as far as the Sensée River would find their communications cut and so be forced to withdraw.'

This had expanded the front and thrown extra work on the troops, many of whom were very tired by the 30th and unable to resist 'as I believe they would have done had they been fresher'.

The frank acceptance of all blame may be read as a generous act[20] or a statement of the obvious. As Commander-in-Chief no one else could be ultimately responsible. Furthermore, by the time Haig prepared the report he knew there was no risk to his personal position. He had been assured by Sir William Robertson that there was no question of the War Cabinet replacing him.

With the explanation of the 'mishap' Haig sent a separate report summarizing the result of the Cambrai operation between 20 November and 7 December when it was deemed to have ended. It was a document reflecting complacency, even self-satisfaction.[21] He considered that: 'We have demonstrated that the strongest possible defences made by the Germans may be completely pierced in a single day, given careful and secret preparation.'

Even after the Third Army's withdrawal, 12,000 yards of the Hindenburg system remained in British hands and the enemy would 'be compelled to dig winter positions in haste on very disadvantageous ground, particularly as regards communications and artillery positions'.

Another paragraph stated:

'The general effect of the above must be to engender a feeling of insecurity in the enemy's Higher Command regarding sectors of his front which he has hitherto regarded as secure. He cannot in future thin out the infantry and artillery on any front, however quiet, without a risk he had never contemplated before November 20.'

The Cambrai battle had made large inroads into German reserves, possibly diverting 'at least one division' from transfer to Italy.

The 'moral effect of the success at Cambrai upon all the Allied armies, in Italy and elsewhere, was also without doubt considerable.'

Against such gains had to be set a loss of some 3,000 yards of British line, about 6,000 prisoners and 166 guns.

Ludendorff could have reported the events of 30 November to Hindenburg and the Kaiser using almost the same phrases. He would also have been able to add a pungent postscript.

On 29 December, as Haig arrived in England on leave almost a year to the day since his promotion to field-marshal, German stormtroops in white smocks led an attack north of La Vacquerie. They used flame throwers in the struggle for Ostrich Lane and the remains of the Corner Work. The enemy actually set foot on the sensitive crest of Welsh Ridge before being repulsed. A small salient, Eagle Trench, remained in their hands. The price paid for 'the defence of a very indefensible position'[22] was high – the 63rd Division lost sixty-two officers and 1,355 men killed, wounded and missing.

Before news of this further reverse reached London, the Cabinet had asked its military advisers to examine the despatches, appendices and maps which had thus far arrived. On New Year's Day, 1918, they were studied at the War Office by Robertson, as CIGS, Major-General Frederick Maurice, Director of Military Operations, and Major-General Sir Charles Callwell, his predecessor, an intelligence expert.[23]

They expressed unanimous approval of Haig's operations during the offensive period of the battle and accepted his conclusions and reasons for the break in the front on the 30th. Any weaknesses in the 55th Division's defences were put down to units being under strength and having taken over a sector devastated in the German retirement to the Hindenburg Line. Many of the troops were in need of training. Otherwise there was hardly a word of criticism from the trio.

It was not good enough for the Cabinet which was particularly concerned about Haig's statement that 'As a matter of fact' no request for reserves had been made by any commander down to brigade level. Three further questions were posed:

(a) Had the generals commanding the 12th and 55th Divisions asked prior to 30 November for reinforcements of men, guns or both?

(b) If so were the requests verbal or written?

(c) If they were refused – by whom?

There was a final paragraph:

'Following also required. Names of Commander of the right Infantry Brigade of the 12th Division and left Infantry Brigade of the 55th Division and of the 8 Battalion Commanders in these two Brigades. Were any of these officers killed, wounded or missing in the fighting of November 30–December 1? It had been suggested that although requests for reinforcements may not have reached the Army Commander they may have been made to his subordinates and it is desired to clear this matter up definitely once and for all.'[24]

The message was forwarded from Montreuil to the Third Army by Lieutenant-Colonel Dill on 4 January. That afternoon Sir Douglas Haig took his family to see 'Aladdin' at Drury Lane but he had much on his mind. He had learned of moves, temporarily frustrated, to remove Robertson; that the Cabinet thought Kiggell a sick man who must be replaced. Lord Derby had turned down Haig's suggestion that Major-General Richard Butler,[25] the

Deputy Chief at GHQ, should take over. On the other hand Sir Douglas had been warmly received by the King at Buckingham Palace and been handed the field-marshal's baton which had been made for him. After asking about 'the Cambrai mishap' – mishap was proving a most useful term – the Monarch had agreed the country must be prepared for more hard times.

By the time the Cabinet's supplementary questions about requests for reinforcements reached France the staffs of both VII and III Corps had been withdrawn into reserve. Lieutenant-General Snow had gone back to Britain on sick leave but from Pulteney came a short response:

'I have no recollection of any demand from the 12th (Division) for either men or guns: there is no official demand in our records, on the contrary the 12th had troops in reserve at Heudecourt.'

Major-General Jeudwine's reply on behalf of the 55th Division was longer.[26] He quickly disposed of any doubts about the tenacity of the men who had been on the spot. In the 166th Brigade, which bore the brunt of the action, the commander and three COs had been wounded (one falling into enemy hands as he tried to fight his way back) and a fourth lieutenant-colonel had been killed at the head of a battalion sent up in support; no lack of staunchness there.

As far as asking for more men was concerned Jeudwine stated that as early as 21 November, General Snow had called at his headquarters and 'discussed the probability of attack about Villers Guislain and the troops available for defence and informed me he had no reinforcements to give me'.

It was agreed to locate a battalion at Vaucelette Farm (from which the 1st/4th Loyals made a costly but effective counter-attack on the 30th) but in view of what had been said Jeudwine saw no point in pressing the Corps Commander for what did not exist. He did point out his weakness in artillery and the following night was given a battery which Snow had borrowed from the 24th Division (on the 55th's right) with the prophetic words that its rightful owner might not see it again.

By the 28th, after observing the enemy from the British front line, Jeudwine was convinced an attack was imminent and reported this to VII Corps HQ. He was told that 'it had been arranged with III Corps that I should have a call on a brigade of the 12th Division on my left . . . about Heudicourt'.

On the 29th, however, he was told by Major-General Arthur Scott, commanding the 12th,[27] that he had no orders from his own Corps on the subject, that he had not a Brigade available, and that what troops he had he required for himself'.

All Jeudwine could do was to report back to VII Corps. During the day he arranged for five batteries of heavy artillery which had been placed at the disposal of the 12th Division to 'bring annihilating fire at dawn' on likely German assembly places and bridges over the canal. This was agreed between the artillery brigadiers of the two formations. Late the same evening, while, unknown to the British, the enemy assault troops were gathering, he had been told that III Corps, which controlled the guns in question, would not allow them to be used.

The controversy about the heavy batteries (9.2-inch, 8-inch and 60-pounders) was recalled and drawn to the attention of Third Army HQ on 20 December. Jeudwine mentioned it when replying to inquiries from Byng's Chief Staff Officer and felt so unhappy about the reaction that he promptly picked up pen and paper:

'Dear Vaughan, As telephone conversations are often unsatisfactory, and as ours ten minutes ago was carried on under some difficulty, I think I had better put my answer in writing.'[28]

An impression of uneasy relationships between the various senior staffs begins to emerge. From Jeudwine's account of his meeting with Scott, the two men may not have been on the best of terms, though they must have known each other for years. Both were professional gunners of similar age – 56 – though Scott was a few months older and had gone to Woolwich a year earlier.

Perhaps the most remarkable thing to emerge from Jeudwine, whose words have a ring of solid truth about them, is the revelation of General Snow's Cassandra-like utterance of 21 November.

Snow was a tried and tested soldier who had spent his regimental career in the infantry. He had commanded the 4th Division at Le Cateau and during the battle of the Marne until injured in an accident. He returned to France at the head of the 27th Division with which he went through the Second Battle of Ypres. He had taken over VII Corps in 1915 and later been employed in the Somme and Arras battles. At Cambrai during the week preceding the attack of the 30th he made daily visits to observation posts along his extended front and was in no doubt that a heavy blow was about to fall. In as much as Haig's official report said that the Third Army was not 'surprised' by the enemy it was literally true. Snow had been sounding warnings for nine days. On the evening of 28 November, his Chief Staff Officer, Brigadier-General 'Jock' Burnett-Stuart[29] had passed on a warning emanating from the 55th Division, but Third Army headquarters[30] seemed to think it enough that VII Corps and III Corps were in touch and 'on the alert'.

Snow must have been baffled at the indifference shown, most of all by his fellow old Etonians Sir Julian Byng and Sir William Pulteney.

In the circumstances it was hardly surprising that rumours persisted in London. On 15 January, a few days after Sir Douglas Haig returned to France, an MP asked for information about the result of the 'Inquiry into the incident at Cambrai'.

Mr Bonar Law said all the relevant documents had been seen by 'a committee of the Imperial General Staff presided over by Sir William Robertson,' plus a committee of the War Cabinet and War Cabinet itself.

'As a result . . . the War Cabinet are of the opinion that the Higher Command was not surprised by the attack of 30th November, and that all proper and adequate dispositions had been made to meet it.

'They consider it highly detrimental to the public interest to have a public discussion of the breakdown which undoubtedly occurred, and are satisfied that all proper measures have been taken to deal with similar situations in future.'

A Member asked: 'Has anyone been sent home over this incident?'

Bonar Law avoided giving a direct answer, merely saying the Higher Command was not to blame.

Mr Noel Pemberton Billing, the irreverent Member for East Herts: 'Will the Right Hon. Gentleman take this opportunity of dispelling the rumour that Sir Douglas Haig is being relieved of his command in France?'

Bonar Law: 'That is quite unnecessary.'[31]

Sir Douglas, in fact, had already initiated a further inquiry about which the House knew nothing.

CHAPTER SEVENTEEN

A Shell Hole in Glass Street

Boots like mirrors, buttons gleaming, puttees immaculate, 3445 Gunner Petty, W. F., must have wondered what he was doing facing a panel of British Brass Hats in a French town hall. He could not know that the Adjutant-General himself, Lieutenant-General Sir George Fowke, had been against a Court of Enquiry, arguing that 'the necessary information could be obtained without such a formal procedure'.[1]

The existing chain of command had been used to acquire the details on which Haig based his report to the War Office in December. Why then did the Commander-in-Chief insist on a further enquiry? Had the political criticism stung him? Was it a subtle attempt to anticipate allegations of a cover-up? Or was he genuinely puzzled by what had occurred? Haig had implicit faith in the British soldier, perhaps too much on occasions, and it is not unreasonable to believe that he wanted to get to the bottom of the Third Army report.

The enquiry was to be held into 'The Action fought South of Cambrai on November 30th', at first sight a natural label though, in effect, it narrowed the field. It was as if Board of Trade inspectors investigating a shipwreck were told to concern themselves with the behaviour of the crew after the vessel had struck the rocks and not how the ship got there in the first place.

The convening order was issued on 17 January.[2] Lieutenant-General Alexander Hamilton Gordon, of IX Corps, was appointed President of the Court and sat with Lieutenant-General Sir Ivor Maxse, XVIII Corps, and Major-General

Reginald Pinney, of the 33rd Division. Their terms of reference were to report their opinion on

    (a) the sequence of events, and

    (b) the causes of the German success.

At 59 Hamilton Gordon was the 'decent old buffer' type of senior officer.[3] A grandson of the 4th Earl of Aberdeen, he had joined the Royal Artillery in 1880, seen active service in Afghanistan and South Africa and been to Staff College. Reluctantly taking over Aldershot Command at the beginning of the war, he had been delighted to obtain an appointment in France in 1916. His Corps had been engaged mainly in Flanders. The General was not specially noted for his intellectual qualities and a young divisional commander who 'tried to get some sense out of him' during the planning stages of Third Ypres confided to his diary that he was 'useless'.[4]

Maxse, aged 56, was one of the few commanders to score a success with combined infantry-tank operations at Ypres and had a reputation as a training expert. He had joined the Royal Fusiliers in 1882 and switched to the Coldstream Guards about ten years later. A veteran of the retreat from Mons, he had been present at almost every major engagement.[5]

Maxse's father had been an admiral; Pinney, the other member of the Court, was a parson's son.[6] He had spent his regimental service with the Royal Fusiliers and commanded a brigade in 1915. The 33rd Division had a good reputation (though its soldiers complained that their commander had substituted coffee and tea for the rum ration). He was a year younger than Maxse.

The Court was held in the Hotel de Ville at Hesdin, about 15 miles from Montreuil. For more than two days the trio studied documents, then, after lunch on 23 January, started to examine witnesses. They began with a gunner officer whose battery commander (on leave) had made a statement that on 30 November he had seen 'between 1,000 and 2,000 British troops falling back in disorder down the slopes of Villers Guislain and that they were 'in the artillery'. The witness himself put the figure at about 700.[7]

Gunner Petty was then called.

'Are you Major Johnson's servant?'

'Yes, sir.'

'Were you with him on the 30th?'

'Yes, sir.'

'I want you to tell me what you know took place, and what you think Major Johnson does not know, about meeting some infantry falling back.'

Undismayed by the legal jargon, Gunner Petty was brief.

'On the morning of the 30th I got up as usual about 6.30 am and went to prepare breakfast. The mess from the battery would be about 100 yards, and, on arriving there shelling started with 4.2s.'

Petty had taken cover in a dug-out and then 'heard fellows saying the infantry was coming back on the road'. Going out he saw batches of British troops making their way down the slopes near Villers Guislain cemetery. Someone said the Germans were less than 500 yards away and 'the major gave orders for the battery to fall back'.

Petty: 'On the way . . . I came across some infantry near Epéhy going away from there and asked them what had happened, and they said the Germans had broken through and they were not strong enough to hold them. I asked them what division they belonged to and they replied "12th Division" and said they [had been] in the advance [of the 20th November].'

Officer: 'Can you tell me what regiment they belonged to? Did they say they were Devons?'

'No they said they were 12th Division. I thought I saw some Devon badges.'[8]

He had not seen anyone from his own division, the 55th.

'Did you see anyone running away?'

'Yes, I saw gunners running in every direction.'

'Were they heavy or field artillerymen?'

'They were heavy artillery,' replied Petty, who perhaps out of fairness felt it necessary to add: 'When I was running away I saw Germans in the cemetery.'

Unsensational in its content, Petty's words must have been encouraging to Major-General Jeudwine whose Lancashire Territorials[9] had looked like being saddled with the blame for the collapse. In an earlier report he had stated that on the 30th, between 7.45 am and 7.55 am, 'a great number – estimated between 1,000 and 2,000 – of disorganized British troops were seen falling back from the direction of Gonnelieu down the slopes of the cemetery north-west of Villers Guislain.'

Realizing that this was being misinterpreted he felt it necessary to send a message to Third Army HQ on 3 January asking that it be made clear that 'None of these troops belonged to the 55th Division; they came in from the rear of the Division on the left of the 55th'.[10]

Gunner Petty's evidence supported that claim.

In all twenty-five witnesses were listed, Petty being the lowest rank. Also called were a corporal, nine junior officers, three majors, three lieutenant-colonels, five brigadier-generals and three major-generals (Scott of the 12th, Douglas Smith of the 20th and Jeudwine).

Where it was considered appropriate they were reminded that under Rule of Procedure 124 f of the 1914 *Manual of Military Law*:

'Whenever any inquiry affects the character or military reputation of any officer or soldier, full opportunity must be afforded . . . of being present throughout the inquiry.'

Individuals had the right to make additional statements and, if they felt their character or military reputation was being impugned, to cross-examine witnesses. The citing of this rule indicated the serious nature of the investigation but opened the way for representatives of the Machine Gun Corps to defend themselves.

A Scots lieutenant[11] attached to the 61st Machine Gun Company (20th Division), having listened to an extract read from the third Army report:

'I do not agree that the machine-gunners of my company did not have confidence in their weapon. I have gathered from infantry who came back that the machine-gunners fought to the end with their revolvers after their guns had been put out of action.'

He had been in charge of an anti-aircraft battery on the 30th but had dismounted his high-angle Vickers to engage the German infantry. Only one officer of the whole company had returned from the forward positions unwounded and most of the men were casualties.

The Machine Gun Officer [primarily an adviser] of the 12th Division[12] explained that the three brigades each deployed a company according to their own defence requirements. A fourth company was given tasks by the divisional commander. Four guns had been placed in reserve at Villers Guislain ready to be moved forward in the event of a major attack. On the morning of the 30th the bombardment was first taken to be 'ordinary routine shelling' and by the time the reserve guns were deployed they could not reach their assigned action stations. They fought instead from

184

positions just outside the village until, outflanked, they fell back. In the Machine Gun Officer's opinion: 'Villers Guislain was not a defensive position.'

He added: 'I totally disagree with the opinions expressed. All the officers and men to my knowledge behaved with the greatest gallantry and did not retire until completely isolated.'

A lieutenant in the 35th Machine Gun Company[13] told the Court he had kept four guns in action from a support position until forced to cease fire to let them cool down. He had served for two years with the company (and won the MC) and was 'absolutely satisfied with the way the men fought on November 30th'.

Undeniably the evidence of officers as to the behaviour of overwhelmed forward detachments was opinion and hearsay rather than fact – the witnesses had been in reserve or support positions. No such criticism could be made of Corporal Goacher of the 196th M.G. Company.

'On the evening of the 29th I was put into position . . . near Glass Street, just north of Villers Guislain, in a shell hole . . .

'About 6 am on the 30th we were "standing to". The bombardment began about that time and soon after a brown-bodied aeroplane flew over me and shot at the detachment. There were about 20 other aeroplanes doing the same. When the aeroplane fire ceased, I looked to my front and saw . . . troops about 800 or 900 yards away coming towards me. At first I thought they were our boys because some of them wore our steel helmets . . .

'When . . . about 400 yards distance from me, I saw they were not our infantry. I fired about seven or eight belts[14] of ammunition into them and killed about 200. They then divided . . . and some got into the low ground on my left, and came round into Glass Street and outflanked me. I continued to fire until they were close to me and then blew up the gun and retired.'

Other witnesses might have testified to the efficiency of British machine-gunners. Prisoners taken from a battalion of the 6th German Reserve Infantry Regiment estimated they had lost half their number by 11 am on the 30th. The 109th Infantry Regiment also found itself opposed by stubborn machine guns as it approached the second line and was held up there until it outflanked them.[15] It was a pity the prisoners' stories and Corporal Goacher's evidence could not have been made available to a distinguished body meeting in London that evening.

By coincidence the adjournment debate in the Commons on 23

January was on the Cambrai affair. The record shows that by the beginning of 1918 MPs were not the gullible lobby fodder they are sometimes held to be.

The Cabinet was in a curious position. Lloyd George, Haig and Robertson had endured an uncomfortable relationship for some months and the November fiasco had fuelled the atmosphere of suspicion, distrust and even contempt which existed.

However, having decided to change the supporting cast instead of the principal role at GHQ, the Prime Minister was obliged to tread warily.

The attack on the Higher Command that evening was led by Major David Davies (Liberal, Montgomeryshire), a philanthropic landowner with warlike tendencies.[16] He had seen service in France with the 14th Royal Welsh Fusiliers before becoming, in 1916, Parliamentary Private Secretary to Mr Lloyd George. Having held the post during 1917 the 'Honourable and Gallant Member' could be expected to know a thing or two.

'The Leader of the House promised us an inquiry into the whole of the circumstances surrounding this operation. Then we were told that an inquiry had been instituted by the Commander-in-Chief in France on his own account and that afterwards the documents were placed before the Chief of the General Staff and communicated to the War Cabinet through General Smuts, who is usually turned on to do these unpleasant tasks.'

Using an argument which is familiar today,[17] Major Davies declared: 'Here is a case in which a general whose conduct was coming under review institutes an inquiry on his own account. Therefore the element of impartiality, at any rate, would appear to be lacking.'

The Major had obviously researched the subject. He had heard that 'repeated warnings' were disregarded by the Higher Command; that 'no proper arrangements were made' and that the French who had reserves at hand were not called on to help.

The House's attention was drawn to a previous statement by the Government that 'no superior officer had been retired as a result of these operations'. Yet according to *The Times* a process of change was going on in the Higher Command which had nothing to do with the Cambrai 'set-back' but would have been justified 'if that had never occurred'.

He continued: 'The question arises why, if these causes were operating some time ago, these officers were still in command when the Cambrai operations took place?'

No specific mention was made of Kiggell, Maxwell or Charteris, but Major Davies referred to a newspaper article which, having 'eulogised' the Commander-in-Chief, introduced an important point. Haig's position depended in large measure on his choice of subordinates but 'his weakness, if it be weakness, is a devotion to those who have served him longest, perhaps too long, without any rest'.

In Davies's opinion, no more damaging statement could be made about a Commander-in-Chief – that he was incapable of appointing suitable officers to his Staff. He was shocked to think that changes being made at GHQ might be 'due to newspaper pressure . . . by the powerful Press which exists in this country.'

Major Davies sat down after asking the Government to supply the House with 'a little more information' and to take the Commons 'more fully into its confidence' at a time when they were calling on the country to supply more men for the Army.

These were shrewd thrusts and after the rapier came the cutlass. Mr King, another Member,[18] declared that Haig 'told us that during the 1917 campaign he would break through the Germans at many points, that the campaign of 1917 would be decisive, and that he would pursue the policy of striking against the German army until they were utterly broken.'

When, in breach of regulations, Sir Douglas had made these statements, in an interview with newspapermen, Mr King 'felt hopeless about him'.

As for the ringing of the bells to celebrate a victory which turned out to be a disaster 'what confidence can we have left in General Haig?' Describing him as a boaster who did not make good his boasts, King called on the Cabinet 'to get a new Commander-in-Chief'.

His words stirred into action Mr Kennedy Jones (the Member for Hornsey). He called on the War Cabinet to declare before the House that, after taking into account the 1916 and 1917 campaigns, they were satisfied that the current General Staff and Commander-in-Chief were 'the best possible men'.

He claimed that most people knew that after the Somme campaign in 1916, there was 'the gravest dissatisfaction' with Haig. When the Coalition Government came to power at the beginning of 1917 'they had it in contemplation to dispense with the

Commander-in-Chief'. Only fear of great newspaper opposition had prevented them. [Kennedy Jones was co-founder of the *Daily Mail*.][19] He went on that it was common knowledge that Sir Douglas had said that 'if he were left alone, that if he received so many men, and if he was permitted to pursue the campaign he had devised, he could guarantee certain results by October, 1917'.

Echoes of after-dinner conversations in distant châteaux could be heard faintly in the chamber.

'He told that to nearly every person who went to France to see him.'

It was left to Mr Ian Macpherson, Under-Secretary of State for War, to reply.[20] A Scottish lawyer who sat for Ross and Cromarty, Mr Macpherson is a shadowy figure in the annals of the Great War but he was obliged to play an important part at the time. Lord Derby, the Minister, was conveniently situated in 'another place'. The Upper Chamber has its uses.

Macpherson represented a lower strata of government, but was a member of the Army Council and hit back: 'Nothing could be more cruel than . . . an attack . . . upon probably one of the most distinguished generals at the present time in the world when he has no opportunity of defending himself.'

Major Davies (in an implied reference to the censor's powers): 'May I ask the Government why they allowed the attack in the Press against the Commander-in-Chief during the last two or three weeks while we are to keep silence?'

It was a fast ball which Mr Macpherson fumbled until another Member came to the rescue by interjecting: 'Has the Government ever contemplated dismissing Haig?'

Happily the Under-Secretary could speak only for the Army Council which had never lost confidence in the Commander-in-Chief. As for the Cambrai incident: 'It is true that the joy bells were rung, and I am not sorry, in many ways, that they were.'

He sympathized with 'those people who unfortunately might be wrong in the last analysis', but had been right to show their feelings of thankfulness at the time.

Major Davies: 'May I ask whether they were invited to do so by the War Office?'

Avoiding a direct answer Mr Macpherson released a verbal flood touching on other matters. As his Right Honourable Friend, the Chancellor of the Exchequer had said, 'The last part of the action at Cambrai was not so successful'. Mr Macpherson knew, however, with accuracy 'that our General Staff did know on the 28th November that such an attack was coming on November 30th'.

As for Haig's own inquiry, the papers had been studied in London and the War Cabinet had concluded that, 'though an unfortunate breakdown did take place, it was through no fault of the General Staff'.

The Under Secretary's stance exasperated Members. Was no blame to be attached to the Higher Command?

Mr Macpherson gushed on. The House would realize that if at any given moment there was a break in the line it might not necessarily be due to the fact that the Higher Command have made a mistake. He did not know why it was that the House 'the moment a breakdown takes place ascribes it to the Higher Command. There never was a greater mistake'.

Mr Kennedy Jones: 'Can you ascribe it to anyone?'

Macpherson: 'I am not going to ascribe it to anyone.'

Kennedy Jones: 'To the soldiers?'

Macpherson: 'There never was a more gallant lot in the world than our soldiers, but I can only say that I for one, with the information I have got, will never ascribe that breakdown to the Higher Command. I can say no more.'

He did say some more, however, and, when asked despairingly if *anyone* was to blame in *any* quarter, replied:

'It is impossible to say in dealing with two or three Divisions who was responsible.' Reserves? They had been 'ready behind the lines in perfect disposition'. He could only say . . . he had endeavoured to suggest . . . he made so bold . . . but Mr Macpherson revealed nothing.

Mr William Pringle, another Scottish lawyer (MP for North Lanarkshire) reverted to the point that no member of the War Cabinet was present in the House though up to that time there had been only a single statement on the Cambrai incident. He had just got round to the business of the bells when Parliamentary procedure silenced him.

'It being one hour after the conclusion of Government business,' Mr Deputy Speaker adjourned the House.

There had been no mention of the Court of the Three Generals.

CHAPTER EIGHTEEN
Grumbling Appendix

Brevity dramatized evidence heard at Hesdin between 23 and 28 January.

Examiner: 'Can you tell us how many survivors of the South Lancashire Regiment there were?'

Witness: 'Yes, sir. Four, two of whom (signallers) were not in the trenches. Of the two in the trenches one, Private John French, a Lewis gunner, was on the right of the battalion. I know this man and think he is half-witted; the other man, a sergeant . . . was in a strongpoint which connected up with the 12th Division and can only say he came back with the 12th Division.'

'We want some light thrown on the South Lancs.'

'I can say nothing further.'

'They disappeared altogether?'

'Absolutely disappeared altogether.'[1]

(The 1st/5th South Lancashires, 500 strong, had been holding trenches across Banteux Ravine. After the war it was learned that they fought until their ammunition ran out.)

The Signals Officer[2] of the 1st/5th Loyal North Lancashire Regiment said only one man returned from the right front company, two or three from the left. Reinforcements had been sent up via 'Silk' and 'Rag' trenches.

'My impression is that support company put up a good fight there.'

What about two reserve platoons which moved into Silk Trench?

'I don't know what happened to them.'

190

Of the 500-strong battalion, only three officers and fifty-four men had survived the action.

In answer to a question he said that as far as he knew there had been no opportunity for musketry practice since the end of September.

A Royal Horse Artillery major had seen some 500 troops, mainly infantry, retreating through his battery position in La Vacquerie valley: 'About half had thrown away their rifles'. He added: 'These troops were broken and they had a bad effect on our gunners . . . but we steadied them.' His guns had been in action until the enemy were only 200 yards away.

Brigadier-General Vincent described how his Staff carried out an emergency plan when the Germans drew near. 'Captain Sievers of the 9th Essex Regiment led the servant and runner squad up the road to the cemetery but he and several of his men were at once killed.'

Such statements painted a graphic picture but did not answer the basic question – what had gone wrong. It was left to Jeudwine to straighten out one or two crucial matters. When the Third Army Commander's report was read to him – 'Villers Guislain and Gonnelieu had been turned into strongly defended localities' – he declared:

'This statement is evidently based on a misapprehension, as this was not the case . . . From November 27 onwards I had been trying to place a battalion, if possible, in Villers Guislain, but had not been able to quarter even a company there.'

He also refuted General Pulteney's claim that 'the attack on the south was at once successful'. (Pulteney commanded III Corps in the north.)

Jeudwine: 'I submit that no troops of the VIIth Corps or of my Division retired south at all. The troops on [i.e. holding] the left of my division did not retire.'

Any assumption that Jeudwine would accept lightly the mantle of scapegoat was mistaken. He did not hesitate to criticize the boundaries allotted by the Staff at Albert who had adopted a very cavalier attitude to the Hesdin inquiry.

Byng had decided that two lieutenant-colonels from his HQ would constitute adequate representation.[3] One of them found it very difficult to explain away this matter of the boundaries.

Byng's Royal Flying Corps branch also showed reluctance to help the court. On 28 January a message was telephoned to Albert:

'The Court wishes to know what aeroplane reconnaissance was ordered and carried out on the front of VII and III Corps on the morning of 30 November, 1917.

'The 3rd Brigade RFC is required to send an officer to Hesdin with this information as soon as possible.

'The Court is sitting and will continue to sit until this information is forthcoming . . .

'General Hamilton Gordon invites the officer to dine with him at Hesdin this evening.'[4]

Brigadier-General J. F. A. Higgins[5] duly gave evidence the next day from which it emerged that a ground mist had handicapped observation of the two aeroplanes sent up at 7 am. On the front of VII Corps only two gun flashes were reported between 7 and 8 am when 'a great bombardment' extended from Vendhuile northwards.

With regard to complaints about the numbers of enemy low-flying planes, 'it has been constantly represented to the infantry throughout 1917 that the only protection . . . is from the ground.'

The Court wasted no time in preparing its written findings[6]. As far as the 'sequence of events' was concerned, it concluded that the troops in the front line of the 20th Division in the north were overwhelmed by 8 am. So were those in the northern position of the 12th Division 'though the southern portion of that Division fought well for some hours'.

In several places, while front-line units were holding their own, non-combatant troops had retired in crowds, giving the impression of a general panic. They had been influenced by the sight of a large number of casualties coming back – 'walking wounded' hit during the bombardment and by ground attack planes.[7]

The Court set out the causes of the German success. Outpost lines had been surprised and warnings 'from above' had gone unheeded. On the days previous to the assault the probability of an attack was noted by the Higher Commanders and communicated to the troops, 'but these warnings did not produce the desired vigilance for they were undoubtedly surprised . . . Perhaps the frequency of such warnings in general also detracted from their value on this particular date.'

To cover its 11,000 yard front the 55th Division had only 44 guns.

'It should, however, be stated that reasons have been given by the representative staff officer of Third Army (one of the two lieutenant-colonels) to justify the belief that a German attack was more likely to take place on the Bourlon front than in that of the 55th Division.'

The defence scheme had been 'hampered' by boundary lines which did not run at right-angles, 'not even for the 2,000 yards which might have been estimated as the forward zone'.

Subordinate and lower commanders had lacked training and an understanding of the 'method of defence in depth' and this indicated 'a want of supervision on the part of higher commanders'.

In addition 'troops detailed for counter-attack were in many cases exhausted by earlier fighting. They were necessarily employed as working parties and were therefore not in an efficient condition to fulfil the role assigned to them.'

After signing the report General Maxse felt the need to add to it. In an appendix[8] he expressed astonishment that two months after the events of 30 November, general officers 'were still thirsting for information about what had occurred within a mile or two of the sphere of their own activities'.

The lower ranks appeared to be completely 'at the mercy of quartermasters' rumours of the most astounding description', brought up to the trenches with the rations.

It was not to be wondered that the public in Britain were misinformed 'not merely by newspapers and members of parliament' but also through the medium of 400,000 officers and men who had been back and forth on leave during the two months in question.

Indignantly Maxse declared: 'The most prolific propagators of baseless stories are the wounded. Moreover, they get home before the [official] telegrams and rapidly spread the foolish notion that if they had been in charge of the conduct of operations, things would have been very different.'

He suggested that short 'semi-official' communiqués should be issued by senior local commanders as soon as possible after a major battle. GHQ should appoint a soldier to help newspaper correspondents to understand the messages which came in.

It had been wrong for them to have given details of the tank tactics at Cambrai.

Disgusted because 'the battle of Cambrai has now come to be

regarded as a German success instead of a British victory', he could not help thinking that 'we soldiers, with our extreme reticence and horror of all publicity, may be somewhat to blame for this result'.

Maxse was not content with one grumbling appendix (which showed that he was unaware that GHQ already appointed officers to advise correspondents); he produced another, a mini-report of his own.[9] He repeated that the German attack was not a surprise to the Higher Command since 'warnings were sent to the troops betimes'.

In his view the causes of the 'local success' of the enemy were:

(i) lack of battle training in the infantry;
(ii) lack of battle training and discipline in the Machine Gun Corps.

A study of the timetable of the enemy's progress showed that the 20th and 55th Divisions did not put up 'a sufficient resistance'.

There were several indications that the enemy 'walked into two British divisions and proceeded through them without being held up by defended localities', though there had been no evidence of panic among the fighting troops.

The root cause of the problem was ignorance of the rudiments of successful defence and inexperience in handling sections, platoons and machine guns in the field.

'The ignorance arises from the fact that our officers are not taught elementary tactics and that those whose business it should be to instruct them are sometimes themselves uninstructed.'

Only a handful of generals trained their divisions to fight battles.

'The writer of this note is acquainted with one corps which during the past twelve months happened to have thirty divisions in it [i.e. under command at different times]. Of these, two were splendidly trained, a dozen were trying to train and the remainder had little if any system of training at all.

'Moreover, at the present time it would be difficult to discover any particular Corps Commander who could fairly be held responsible for the defective training of any particular division except in the case of the Canadian and Australian Corps which are composed of permanent divisions.' (In other words the Dominion formations remained constant within these corps.)

Maxse's paper raised serious questions. If the Corps Commanders were not to blame, then the fault must lie with the Army Commanders and the policy laid down by the Commander-in-Chief with the approval of the War Office.

194

The report of the Enquiry went to the Adjutant-General who added his own slightly cynical comments[10] before passing it on to GHQ: 'I doubt whether it will be possible to take any steps to allocate blame . . . owing to the nature of the causes to which the Court attribute the German success.'

There had been no evidence 'that lack of vigilance was general thoughout the divisions involved'.

He did not know how far the Third Army explanation for laying down the controversial boundaries 'should be accepted' . . . 'the idea was that VII Corps defensive front should face East and III Corps South-East and that naturally gave Banteux Ravine as the boundary'.

The Adjutant-General did not miss the fact that the Third Army Staff had 'modified' their report dated 18 December, 'and now agrees that the two villages of Villers Guislain and Gonnelieu should not have been described as "strong defensive localities with machine guns sweeping all approaches".'

Two months after the event the truth was beginning to emerge, though it was carefully withheld from the House of Commons.

'The answer is in the negative,' said Mr Bonar Law when asked to hold a Secret Sitting.

Member:[11] 'Will the Right Honourable Gentleman give an assurance that at least the Western Front will be defended as stubbornly as the reputation of those unsuccessful generals?'

Hansard records no reply.

Byng and Pulteney and their Chief Staff Officers would certainly have had difficulty in justifying the artillery dispositions of III Corps as outlined in a contemporary report by the Corps. The field batteries, it conceded, were 'uncomfortably close to the enemy's artillery area in the South-East and most of them were liable to be enfiladed or taken in reverse at easy range.

'These positions, however, were the only places available . . . the whole country to the north of them was in full view from the high ground near Rumilly . . .

'The Heavy Artillery in Villers Guislain and about Gonnelieu and La Vacquerie were equally unfortunately situated but it was imperatively necessary to keep them in those places' (to engage new hostile batteries).

Small wonder Gunner Petty had seen artillerymen running all over the place when shells crashed down on them from every side.

Though the Commons had been assured the Brass Hats were

blameless, the main actors in the tragedy of 30 November soon left the Western Front. Snow, who had foreseen the danger, became GOC-in-C Western Command; Pulteney, who had not, took over XXI Corps in the United Kingdom 'composed almost entirely of youths under nineteen years of age'.[12] Woollcombe, oldest British corps commander, in France, lasted a little longer before being sent to report on affairs in Salonika. The lieutenant-governorship of Guernsey went to Kiggell – attempts failed to get him the better-paid Jersey appointment. At the War Office Sir William Robertson eventually resolved his differences with his civil masters by resigning in a row over the role of the Allied Military Council at Versailles. He went to Eastern Command.[13] None of the divisional generals involved in the 'mishap' was held responsible.

On the eve of the publication of the official Despatch on the battle of Cambrai, Mr Billing, himself a war veteran,[14] asked the Under-Secretary of State for War if what was to be published was the original report from the Commander-in-Chief and whether omission from or addition to its original form had been made.

Mr Macpherson gave him short shrift: 'Yes and No'. This was a bold statement. The Despatch, published on 4 March, was hardly likely to be a replica of Haig's secret New Year's Eve report to the War Cabinet and Macpherson might have said honestly that it contained as much as was consistent with security and intelligence requirements. A blank 'No' was tantamount to a lie.

It was at best a plausible document and, having been produced for public consumption, had understandably to take a confident tone. There were many tributes to the fighting troops, the words 'gallant' and 'gallantry' appearing fourteen times.

It stated that under the original plan the capture of Cambrai was to be subsidiary to the capture of Bourlon and a thrust to the north-west – 'our advance towards the town being primarily to cover our flank and puzzle the enemy regarding our intentions'.

The emphasis on puzzling was something new. The first paragraph of the Third Army plan for Operation GY, dated 13 November, 1917, stated:

'The object of the operation is to break the enemy's defensive system by a *coup de main*; with the assistance of tanks to pass the Cavalry through the break thus made; to seize Cambrai, Bourlon Wood and the passages over the river.'

In paragraph 4 the second stage was to include the advance of the Cavalry to isolate Cambrai while IV Corps captured Bourlon Wood. The third was to include the 'clearing of Cambrai'.

There was no mention of 'puzzling' in the report sent to the War Office by Haig on 23 December. Afterthought and hindsight blurred even the permissible facts.

The Despatch states that on 24 November 'our infantry again attacked Bourlon village and captured the whole of it'. This must have been news to survivors of the Suffolks, East Surreys and HLI. The 40th Division had corrected a mistaken claim to that effect as early as the evening of 24 November. The Germans knew better than anyone that the village had never been in British hands. Why claim that it had? Did someone feel it was still necessary to justify the hasty Order of the Day? And those bells?

As far as the events of the 30th went, 'the signs of a German offensive all pointed to the principal attack being delivered in the Bourlon sector'. On the right flank the reserves immediately available (the Guards and the 2nd Cavalry Division) were located behind the La Vacquerie-Villers Guislain front, in other words behind the point at which the enemy actually broke in.

Two more cavalry divisions were 'within two or three hours march of the battle area' with a third 'but a little farther distant'. These hints at shrewd anticipation were misleading. The Guards were indeed well placed – but whereas all three brigades could intervene quickly on the Bourlon front, only two of them could respond immediately to a thrust in the south. The 2nd Cavalry Division was at Fins because it was reorganizing its dismounted troopers. The 4th and 5th were about seventeen miles from Gonnelieu and brigades were in some cases exercising their horses when the German blow fell. The 1st Cavalry Division was 25 miles from the scene of action.

The sub-title 'Early Warnings' which appears in the section of the Despatch headed 'German Attack' calls for close inspection of the text.

'In view of the symptoms of activity . . . special precautions were taken by local commanders, especially from Villers Guislain to the south. Troops were warned to expect attack, additional machine guns were placed to secure supporting points, and divisional reserves were closed up. Special patrols were also sent out to watch for signs of any hostile advance.'

In a tortuous passage the Commander-in-Chief tries to explain the break-in on Byng's southern flank.

'In short, there is little doubt that, although an attack was expected generally, yet in these areas of the battle at the moment of delivery the assault affected a local surprise.'

The question arises: how 'local' is 'local'?

Once again, one must assume that the Despatch was written to deprive the enemy of any satisfaction and to give the nation only the palatable facts.

Special patrols? We now know that when Haig saw Pulteney at III Corps headquarters on 4 December, the first time they had actually met since the attack, he was told that British patrols had gone out 'as usual' on the morning of the 30th, discovered nothing out of the ordinary and 'all then proceeded to breakfast'.[15]

Early warnings? 'There seems to have been no warning of the attack,' Sir Douglas wrote the same day.

Divisional reserves closed up? 'Luckily' the Guards were near Gouzeaucourt, is what he says in his diary.

That the Guards were present by chance rather than design suggests again that Byng and Vaughan, at Third Army HQ, chose to disregard any considerations which distracted them from Bourlon. General Snow had reported his observations but: 'The intelligence summaries issued by the Army and GHQ, however, gave no support to these suspicions.'[16]

A 'special state of readiness' had been ordered in VII Corps on the 28th and the Narrative of Operations of the 164th Brigade says reserve battalions were at 30 minutes notice to move from 5 am on 29 November. Perhaps these were the units Sir Douglas meant when he said troops were warned, but it was a state of alert that did not apply generally in III Corps, though Scott of the 12th Division declared emphatically in his report: 'I do not consider that the troops in the front system were in any way surprised.'

In the *History of the 12th Division* of which, with the Reverend P. Middleton-Brumwell, he is co-author, Scott says that after his meeting with Jeudwine on the 29th reserve machine guns were placed to cover Villers Guislain. The COs of the 6th Queens and 11th Middlesex were 'informed of the probabilities of an attack and ordered to reconnoitre the ground from Vaucelette Farm to Gonnelieu . . .

'Warning orders were issued by the Division . . . All were therefore on the alert when the German counter-attack commenced.'

If that was the case something must have gone seriously wrong with the divisional communications system. Major H. S. Bowlby, who joined the 7th Royal Sussex in 1914 and served with them until demobilized in 1919, was Adjutant at the time of the attack. In the unit history[17] published in 1934 he states: 'I can vouch for the fact that no warning of a counter-attack ever reached the battalion' (which was part of the 12th Division throughout the war).

Even normal speculation and latrine rumours seem to have been discounted before the 30th as the same battalion history reveals: 'Any fears which we might have had were allayed when details for training when in Brigade Support were given to us. Rifle exercises and platoon drill were included in the curriculum.'

And further and more seriously: 'It is a remarkable fact that no form of defence scheme was ever issued to us and that the duties of the battalion in the event of an attack were entirely unexplained. The lack of any information is fully confirmed by the war diaries of the 36th and 37th brigades.'

Pencilled in an educated hand in the margin of one copy of the battalion history[18] are the words 'And 35 Bde'. In the margin on the opposite page the same hand has written: 'I personally warned the Div Comdr, A. B. Scott. He pooh-poohed the idea of an enemy counter-attack.'

The first hint of trouble to reach the transport officer of the 36th Brigade came from a Machine Gun Corps lieutenant who returned from delivering rations in the early hours of the 30th and spoke of various 'trench rumours' of enemy concentrations and possible attacks. No one paid much attention. The divisional baths had been allotted to the transport that day and, as the order had not been cancelled, half the men were soaped and lathered when a Veterinary Corps officer 'galloped into camp with the news that the enemy had broken through'. The bathers dressed smartly.

Years of trench war had made old soldiers sensitive to atmosphere on particular fronts but at Cambrai novel conditions applied: 'Even the most wary found it difficult to believe that the Germans, after two and a half years on the defensive, were going to launch a really dangerous attack without giving clearer warning.'[19]

Besides, all eyes were on Bourlon. There, says Haig in his Despatch, from Tadpole Copse to Fontaine Notre Dame 'the enemy's main attack' was carried out 'with large forces and great resolution'. Ludendorff states in his memoirs that the bigger blow was made in the southern sector. The preparations in the north had been blatant in order to draw Byng's attention – they were in any case difficult to conceal – and in this they succeeded. British opinion has clung stubbornly to the legend of the main attack being at Bourlon and even the meticulous Guards historian states: 'The weight of troops employed in the northern attack would appear to prove that the enemy meant this to be his principal effort, but General Ludendorff asserts that this was only a subsidiary attack,' and he comments: 'The General's assertion may have been influenced by the failure of the northern attack and the success south of it.'

The facts, according to the British Official History[20], were: Three assault divisions attacked through two holding the line west of Bourlon; one division attacked south of Fontaine. South from Masnières the Germans used 'rather more than six divisions, with three more in support or reserve'.[21]

No matter how many divisions were deployed by the Germans in France in 1917, the growing concentration of enemy formations was what worried Haig in the spring of 1918. Important though Despatches may be, Sir Douglas must have been glad to put his signature to the final account of the Cambrai operations. He needed every minute to prepare for the next round in France.

Among those he could rely on to help in his hour of need was Uncle Harper, whose obstinacy over tanks tactics had been overlooked or forgiven. Knighted and promoted, he commanded Woollcombe's old corps, the IVth, on the sensitive flank of the Flesquières salient.

CHAPTER NINETEEN
Flesquières Again

Now came the trial of strength. For weeks troop trains had rolled across Poland and Germany to feed the Western Front with divisions freed by the collapse of Russia. After a spell on the training grounds, where the unfit and unsuitable were weeded out, units set out for their concentration areas. Reports of the successful November counter-offensive added to German confidence. The Allies could only wait. In the ruins of Flesquières it was the turn of British sentries to stare at the mysterious countryside opposite.

The salient to which the British had withdrawn in December thrust pugnaciously towards Cambrai as if Byng was sticking out his chin and saying, 'You haven't seen the last of us.' Perhaps he saw it as the jumping-off base for another assault – though the bulge invited trouble. Furthermore it stood at the junction of two of Haig's four armies.[1]

In January the British had agreed to French requests to extend their front south and redeployed Gough's Fifth on the right of the Third Army. From Gouzeaucourt to Barisis on the edge of the St Gobain forest the newcomers were responsible for 42 miles of defences. Even allowing that about a quarter of the front was protected by the Oise and its marshy tributaries, the troops were thinly spread. An average divisional sector covered 3.8 miles compared with 2.6 in the Third Army area which ran 27 miles northward from Flesquières. Not only had Byng more men but help was readily to hand. Gough's scanty reserves were perilously far behind the line and included the Cavalry Corps which had been reduced from five to three divisions, the Indian regiments having been transferred to the Middle East.

Believing the enemy's main objective to be the destruction of the British Army, Haig gave priority to the protection of his base area in the Pas de Calais and the Channel ports. His plans were 'so designed that he might be ready to meet a great attack in Flanders at short notice, being prepared at the same time to deal with an attack against the Fifth and Third Armies between the Oise and the Scarpe until reinforcements could reach them.'[2] He put his weight on his left but made arrangements to withdraw from the nose of the Ypres Salient if need be to make three more divisions available for service elsewhere. The Commander-in-Chief also gave instructions, repeated as late as 10 March, that the Flesquières salient should be held only to the extent that German raiders could be repelled; it was to be regarded as a false front. In the event of a serious attack the garrison was to fall back to a position across the base of the bulge.

It was intended to fight the battle in a deep zone in which counter-attack positions had been allocated and masses of wire laid down. Such was the theory, though the further south they ran the sketchier defences became.

Byng either misunderstood, ignored or misinterpreted GHQ's instructions as to the Flesquières salient. The best part of three divisions of Fanshawe's V Corps were committed to its defence. At the beginning of the second week of March they detected practice barrages.

A deliberate bombardment began on the 10th, rose to a crescendo on the 12th when more than 200,000 shells, mainly Yellow Cross, were estimated to have been fired.[3] Mustard liquid, which could remain dangerous for days, stained battery positions, tainted trenches, dug-outs and sunken roads. Even the rays of the morning sun could conjure up corrosive fumes 'and no amount of gas discipline could prevent a growing casualty list among troops bound to remain in the infected area and to carry out their ordinary and laborious duties'.[4]

The 63rd Division having lost 2,580 men and the 2nd even more, it was time to reduce the garrison to a skeleton force. Byng sanctioned the withdrawal of the 2nd Division but replaced it by the 47th. The 63rd stayed put, despite its weakened condition, bolstered by the 17th, which had escaped comparatively lightly. A court was convened to inquire into the reason for so many gas casualties.[5] An expert was on his way to open it on 21 March when the great German offensive began.

A crushing weight of shells fell on the front of the Third and Fifth Armies but no direct assault was made on Flesquières. The Germans, not wishing to suffer from the lingering effect of their own mustard gas, were content to put fierce pressure on both sides of the base of the salient. Immediately to the north, IV Corps was driven back into its battle zone and in the Fifth Army VII Corps was hammered back around Gouzeaucourt. Flesquières faced isolation.

On the morning of the 22nd Byng was still holding the salient, sole remaining trophy of the November fighting, and 'in the hope that after all it might not be necessary, the GOC Third Army did not give any order with regard to retirement until the afternoon'.[6] Shades of the Masnières struggle at the beginning of December. Byng's reluctance to withdraw V Corps increased the danger on its flanks. By the end of the day IV Corps had been driven out of its battle zone.

The Fifth Army south of Flesquières also yielded important ground after bitter fighting. Had the withdrawal been carried out earlier, commanders in the salient might have had room for manoeuvre. As it was, they had to concentrate on escaping from a trap. The troops who had held their ground, unaware that the enemy was deliberately avoiding head-on encounters, were baffled 'as to why and wherefore we had retired'.[7] Ribécourt, Trescault and Havrincourt Wood were evacuated and supply dumps set ablaze to deny them to the enemy. 'Many battalions in these days had the same feeling of complete isolation, as though no one was fighting or prepared to fight but themselves.'[8]

Units of the 2nd Division, back in action despite their weakened state, found the retirement of the 63rd Division 'inexplicable'. The 63rd were astonished to find the 47th had withdrawn.[9] 'The central control of operations appeared to have given way.'[10]

It was as if a tug of war team had suddenly let go the rope and retained its balance while its opponents reeled back. 'The note of these days is not the breakdown of the infantry resistance but of the elaborate organization behind the lines, for which the fighting strength of the front line troops had been ruthlessly sacrificed and on which the infantry had been taught to rely.'[11]

Byng had lost his grip and was unable to aid his weaker neighbour. As Gough saw it on the 23rd, 'Before nightfall the V

Corps was driven out of its positions and forced to retire in a north-westerly direction, thus increasing the gap until by dawn on Sunday, the 24th, 1½ miles of country lay open to an enterprising enemy, in spite of the fact that Congreve (GOC VII Corps) had stretched his line until it was covering three miles of ground which lay in the Third Army's boundary.'[12]

Bapaume fell on the 24th and Third Army HQ had to evacuate Albert which the Germans reached on the 26th. There the attacking armies halted, their lines of communication too long to maintain impetus. They had lost direction. On the Allied side the command structure was reorganized. Gough, whose army had been consumed by the intensity of the fighting, was relieved of his post within a matter of days – an action now generally recognized as unjust.

Many years later Lloyd George blamed Byng's defence of the Flesquières salient for the critical gap which opened between the Third and Fifth Armies: 'He was reluctant to give up the only bit of ground he had won in the bungled tank attack of Cambrai.'

The criticism was made in one of the later volumes of his memoirs. Byng died in 1935 without responding.

The March offensive showed once more that, despite the pre-eminence of cavalry generals, no real policy had been worked out for the mounted arm. The Corps was quickly formed into three small infantry divisions but these were broken up and went into action by brigades. On 26 March, with the enemy well into open country, horses were brought back though actual fighting was done on foot 'the horses being used to gallop from position to position where help was required.'[13]

The troopers brought timely relief on occasions, but scratch detachments of tanks, balloon units with Lewis guns, R.E. Special companies equipped as infantry, and the staffs and students of the various 'schools' also did valuable work. Supporters of the arme blanche later grumbled, 'If only there had been more cavalry,' but the days of charging lancers and hussars had gone for good. In 1918 the Life Guards formed a lorry-borne machine-gun unit.

The gloom engendered by the German offensives was accentuated in Paris by a series of mysterious explosions on 23 March. First thought to be caused by high-flying bombers they were quickly identified as the work of long-range artillery. In three days some 50 shells (8.26 inch) fell on the city and its suburbs. Then 'Big

Bertha' fell silent. Had she blown herself up as was hoped and rumoured?[14]

On Good Friday Comtesse Anne de Francqueville went with a young cousin to the old church of St Gervais in the Rue Miron to join a congregation of women and children praying for those who had fallen in battle recently and for those who were still fighting, including Comte Bernard. The priest had finished his address and les Petits Chanteurs à la Croix de Bois were watching the conductor's poised baton when, with a thunderous roar, the roof caved in. More than seventy-five people died, including Anne de Francqueville's cousin who had been standing alongside her when the shell, one of four fired that day, exploded[15].

In far-off Cambrai the civilian population was temporarily safe from shells but had other problems. Abbé Delval recorded:

'According to do some people sugar beet roasted in the oven for twelve hours tastes better than banana and as good as the best pear. But who ever would have thought that we would have to compete for rabbit food?'

The city's sombre mood deepened as the German successes continued. On 21 March Cambrai had been near enough to the battlefield to be affected by gas drifting back from shells, but by May the sound of guns had faded. Air attacks increased and thirty-three people died in raids during the summer.

The railway stations were always crowded – troops and munitions coming south, wounded going north. A procession of Red Cross trains steamed slowly towards the Fatherland as the fighting intensified. In mid-summer the attitude of the soldiery in the town changed. News filtered through that on 15 July the Germans had walked into a French trap in the Champagne and stormed deserted positions deliberately tainted with mustard gas. After three days, light Renault tanks had swarmed out of the woods. The French had scored a resounding success.

On 8 August British tanks led the Fourth Army in a massive surprise attack which drove the enemy from the approaches to Amiens, with the Australians and Canadians spearheading a drive towards Péronne. At the end of August the Third Army had cleared the old Somme battlefield. Bapaume fell.

By 3 September there were British sailors in Tadpole Copse, men of the Royal Naval Division. Marines probing Inchy and the neighbouring village of Moeuvres provoked a fierce reaction. New Zealand patrols entered Havrincourt Wood where a German battalion was reported to have panicked, shouting 'The English are coming'.[16]

Bourlon was in sight, Cambrai within striking distance.

Notices went up in the city announcing that the evacuation of civilians would begin on 6 September and last for three days. Arrangements broke down and crowds besieged the stations where only thirty cattle trucks had been provided for the elderly. The sick and infirm were taken by barge to Valenciennes but most citizens finally set off on foot pushing prams and wheelbarrows. Even the turbaned statuettes of Martin-Martine, which had been striking the hours at the Hotel de Ville for 400 years, joined the fugitives, brought down from their perch and despatched to Brussels. Only half a dozen very old people remained in the care of the Curé of St Druon, the Abbé Thuiliez. It was anyone's guess what might happen to them. Wickerwork trunk packed, Abbé Delval wrote: 'I doubt if I shall ever see my home again.'

CHAPTER TWENTY
Canadian Capers

The airmen had the best view of the war's return to the derelict acres south-east of Arras. Navigation was easy, landmarks plentiful – canals, dark woods, the lakes and pools of the flooded Sensée valley. In good visibility pilots could distinguish pygmy figures moving across a landscape spasmodically riven by volcanic eruptions which left dirty clouds drifting on the wind. German fliers reported khaki columns moving over the old Somme battlefields; the British noted constant railway traffic in Belgium.

Teenage soldiers marching up to take the place of lost legions stared thoughtfully at smashed guns, rusting tanks, airfields where canvas shreds flapped on empty hangar frames, signposts pointing the way to vanished headquarters and plundered depots.

It wasn't all gloom and doom. Divisional concert parties and entertainers did their bit. On 4 September Mr Harry Lauder[1] gave a little concert to Scots clearing the battlefield near Quéant.[2] Cavalrymen halted a column of prisoners to watch him give a rollicking rendering of 'Roamin' in the Gloamin'' and listen to his haunting refrain 'Keep right on to the end of the road'.

Another Scot, not noted for singing or joking, was determined to do just that – 'keep right on to the end'.

Haig's aim was to establish three of his five powerful armies within striking distance of what was left of the Hindenburg system and 'the general line St Quentin–Cambrai'.[3] East of the canal lay the railway network he had hoped to paralyse the previous November; west of it stood a stretch of the German 1917 position. The

FINAL CAPTURE OF BOURLON 27-8 SEPTEMBER 1918
MAIN MOVES OF ATTACKING DIVISIONS

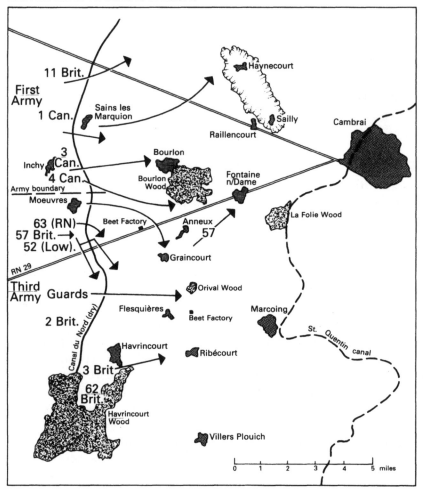

defensive expert General von Lossberg considered it too 'dilapidated' for prolonged resistance and proposed a withdrawal to a line from Antwerp to the Sambre at Charleroi and extending along the Meuse.[4] The 45-mile contraction of the front would free divisions for a reserve.

Ludendorff, concerned at the political effect of yielding so much French and Belgian territory, was opposed to a withdrawal. He blamed the 'troops and their leaders' for the unpleasant developments since 8 August and decided instead to fight in the old Hindenburg system while developing a new rear position (the Hermann–Hunding–Brunhilde line).

Towards the middle of September Byng's Third Army began clearing the unlucky ground previously fought over. Old maps were re-issued with familiar names – Metz-en-Couture, Gouzeaucourt, Revelon Farm, Gonnelieu. Familiar numbers appeared, 62 among them. The West Riding Division was no longer exclusively Yorkshire; after the reorganization of brigades into three instead of four battalions[5] some of the original units had been amalgamated, others incorporated. It had a new commander,[6] but he sent his troops into battle on the 12th with the order: 'The 62nd Division will recapture Havrincourt'. Hampshires and Durhams as well as Dukes were involved in the stiff fighting. A strongpoint south of the village which threatened to hold up the advance was eliminated by a young sergeant in the 5th KOYLI who wiped out two machine-gun detachments.[7]

The Guards were also on the scene, but without Feilding, transferred to London District at the beginning of the month. Was it coincidence that a short time previously he had clashed with the Corps Commander (Lieutenant-General Haldane) over machine-gun dispositions?

On the approaches to Bourlon itself was the 52nd (Lowland) Division[8] which had been hurried to the Western Front from Palestine in the spring. For a week it fought over the ruins of Moeuvres which changed hands several times. A handful of men of the 5th HLI, given up for lost, hung on to an isolated post for more than three days during which the British barrage 'crept' over their position twice and the German bombardment three times.[9]

If these were the preliminaries, the troops had every right to wonder what the final bout would be like.

Order from GHQ dated 22 September: 'The First Army will attack on Z-Day with a view to capturing the heights of Bourlon Wood in the first instance. It will then push forward and secure its left flank on the Sensée River and operate so as to protect the left of the Third Army.'[10]

First Army: 'The Canadian Corps will free the crossings of the Canal du Nord between E14 Central (map reference of the boundary with the Third Army) and Lock 3; attack and capture the Marquion Line, Bourlon village and wood; and secure the general line Fontaine Notre Dame – La Maison Neuve – Sauchicourt Farm – railway crossing over the Canal du Nord.'[11]

The choice of the Canadian Corps meant that the Higher Command had given the responsibility of tackling one of the toughest obstacles on the Western Front to an amateur, a 43-year-old professional insurance broker. Lieutenant-General Sir Arthur Currie from Strathroy, Ontario, had begun his working life as a teacher but quickly turned to commerce. Joining the militia before the turn of the century, he went to France as a brigadier and by 1917 was in command of the corps which secured Passchendaele. In April, 1918, General Horne told Haig that the Canadian was suffering from a 'swollen head'.[12] Currie had little to be modest about.

Sir Douglas and General Horne had been irritated because Currie had insisted on keeping the Canadian divisions together as a corps and obtained the backing of the Dominion government for his policy. As a result they were not actively engaged in the defensive battles of the spring but were fresh for the arduous role allotted to them in the summer offensive. They had seen severe fighting since 8 August. Bourlon would provide another test.

Tactical requirements had changed since the previous year when the German defences ran north-west from Havrincourt towards Arras – the so-called Drocourt–Quéant line – and the Third Army had attacked Bourlon Wood from the south and south-west. *Then* the 56th and 36th Divisions had been striking up the enemy system in a direction slightly west of north. In September, 1918, the 'D–Q' position had been overwhelmed and from Havrincourt the front ran more or less due north, embracing the Canal du Nord. An eight-mile stretch of the unfilled cutting was still an essential part of the enemy defences from Havrincourt to Marquion. German trenches, wire and outposts lay to the west of it; to the east was the Hindenburg support line with an offshoot running close to the canal and the 'Marquion Line' on the slopes of a more distant ridge. 'These . . . and the usual network of fortified villages and trenches . . . resulted in the . . . open slopes of the western side being swept by tiers of machine-guns.'[13] The infantry would have to cross this exposed area carrying light scaling ladders to help them in and out of the canal cutting, sappers hauling sections of pre-fabricated bridges.

The plan was ambitious. Nine divisions assisted by sixty-five tanks were to break into the enemy's line along a 13-mile front and five more were to 'go through' them in the central sector. Bourlon lay on the axis of the advance and the flanking formations were to swing right and left to widen the breach. Currie decided to strike due west, thrusting past each side of the massif while smothering the wood with smoke. Once his troops had reached the railway line where the HLI had been trapped the woodland could be cleared. No one knew what it might hide; the British had built strong wire entanglements during their brief occupation. Ludendorff was not expected to give it up easily. He had already relieved General von der Marwitz for losing Havrincourt.

If Bourlon was regarded as the hardest nut to crack, Lieutenant-General Sir Charles Fergusson's[14] XVII Corps on Third Army's left flank had a task which was almost as daunting and even more complicated.

Both the 52nd and 63rd Divisions were to turn south after forcing the canal at Moeuvres, the Lowlanders driving down the trenches on each side, the Naval Division at an angle of 45 degrees towards Graincourt. Both formations were to link up with VI Corps (Guards and the 2nd Divisions) and the 52nd would be 'squeezed' out. While this movement was being completed a brigade of the 57th Division was to push along the Cambrai road and take Fontaine Notre Dame. The scope for confusion was unlimited.

The cramped assembly area around Inchy worried Currie who warned his heavy artillery to be ready to neutralize any attempt to swamp the waiting troops with gas shells. German outposts west of the canal were to be ignored until zero hour in the hope that, initially, the enemy defensive barrage would fall well in front of them as the attack rolled east. Units were expected to show initiative. The 72nd Battalion (Seaforth Highlanders of Canada) were simply told that when they came up in support they would 'find their own way through or around Inchy-en-Artois and across the Canal du Nord'.[15] Initiative was something for which the Canadians were renowned, and not just in the military sphere. Earlier in the year, when it was decided to supplement rations with a little private farming, battalions reported that there were no ploughs to be found anywhere in the region. The day it was let slip that £2 would be paid for the first plough brought in to the transport lines seven had arrived by the afternoon and others were on their way. No one asked where they came from.[16]

The Canadians had been enjoying a brief respite from action when Haig decided on 27 September as Z-Day. They had played 'indoor baseball', trained, absorbed reinforcements and weeded out the unfit. On the 25th they shouldered their packs and began the approach march. On 'a beautiful clear moonlight night' some of them camped in old trenches on a site where every building had been 'completely razed'. Pierced tank hulks cast grotesque shadows. A simple notice-board said Bullecourt.[17]

Enemy planes flew overhead but left the arid ruins in peace. Good news from Palestine and Macedonia had a 'very cheering effect on the men' the next day. Soon Bourlon Wood could be 'plainly seen'.[18] In the 1st Canadian Division the Burials Officer checked over 'full supplies' including 500 ready-made crosses.[19]

Rain set in on the night of the 26th and burdened troops slithered and slipped along muddy roads jammed with transport. A politer-than-usual Canadian officer recorded that conditions were 'very disagreeable'.[20] Random salvoes of HE caught the scouts of the 47th (Western Ontario) Battalion laying tapes, killing a lance-corporal and stunning his comrades. A badly-shaken lieutenant saw the job through. Assembling companies received a rum ration (based on the scale of a gallon to every hundred soldiers) and were reported to be 'quite cheerful' despite the weather. Around 2 am the rain stopped and 90 minutes later word came that zero hour was to be 5.20 am.[21]

Over no-man's-land the flares lost their harshness in the moisture which muffled the shots of jumpy sentries. At 4.30 a violent shell storm burst over the Third Army front but died away.

It was still dark when the infantry went over and, as it grew lighter, Currie's men could see stretching into the distance 'nothing but long lines of leaping, billowing . . . dense white smoke, shot through at intervals with the flashes of bursting shrapnel, or the black smudge of high explosive'.[22] There was a gun for every seventeen yards on the Canadian front.

The 10th Brigade advanced across the canal under heavy fire from Germans at Lock 4 who had to be overcome. Quarry Wood also spouted a fiery greeting but a recently-joined private of the 50th (Calgary) Battalion[23], racing ahead of his platoon, opened rapid fire and drove the defenders into cover. When help arrived, 146 prisoners emerged from dug-outs.

Opposition varied. Some detachments of a dismounted cavalry division displayed 'rather poor morale'; others 'put up a stiff fight before giving in'. The last surviving company commander of four who had set out with the 50th on 8 August was killed.[24] A tank was blown up by a land mine after crossing the canal but seven others crawled on. Shortly before 8 am the 10th Brigade was on its objective. The 50th, 47th and 44th Battalions set up a joint headquarters in Quarry Wood and at 8.20 fresh waves moved past them.

The wood was to be encircled by two Ontario battalions of the 11th Brigade – the 102nd taking the southern edge while the 54th formed the northern pincer and the 12th Brigade attacked the village. Things did not go according to plan. A chance shell wounded the Colonel and Adjutant of the 102nd, killing the signals officer and three runners. The CO of the 75th Battalion[25] added the 102nd to his command. Shells continued to thump down and men watched with admiration as the RC padre searched for wounded amid smoking craters.

The 87th (Canadian Grenadier Guards) Battalion was straddled by 5.9s before zero hour and though the canal was crossed without difficulty more men were hit on the eastern bank where a joint HQ was formed with the 54th. In the next stage of the attack the sunken road which ran diagonally in front of Bourlon Wood was occupied without serious resistance and the Guardsmen began to clear the southern corner of the village. The 54th pushed on along the edge of the trees.

In the ensuing battle the 12th Brigade was pounded by 'friendly' batteries 'dropping short' and 'lost' its own barrage.[26] Troops attacking the village were raked by machine guns on the wooded ridge until these were hastily swung round to oppose the 54th Battalion. Intense fire from Anneux swept the 102nd Battalion advancing along the southern edge of the trees. By that time hundreds of automatic weapons were in action on both sides and a single battery of the 1st Canadian Machine Gun Battalion fired 6,500 rounds at 'targets in Bourlon Village', using two captured weapons as well as its own.[27] Observers could make little sense of the fortunes of the combatants until at 10.58 am a rocket soared above the drifting smoke and exploded in a shower of golden rain. The 54th were signalling: 'We have captured and hold the east side of Bourlon Wood.'[28] Enemy batteries increased their fire.

The success signal was a little premature. The Germans rallied on Maxims and mortars dug into the railway embankments and cuttings east of Bourlon. To the north, across the bare plateau, the 12th Brigade's 38th (Ottawa) Battalion had reached the line about 11 am and by 12.30, after 'hard fighting',[29] linked up with the Nova Scotia Highlanders.

Canadian Seaforths had rushed wildly through point-blank fire to take eight field guns in the pits, plus 115 prisoners. Some time later 'an organized bayonet charge accompanied by loud cheering . . . appeared to have a demoralizing effect on the enemy as their surrender was immediate'. Two hundred more prisoners were taken. Other Germans were more obstinate and continued to dispute Bourlon Wood. The 1st Division was under the impression that it was not captured until 2 pm[30] and even an hour later the 11th Brigade was pushing forward two companies to reinforce troops 'within 500 yards of the eastern edge of the wood'.[31]

The 102nd and the 54th linked up, but the enemy in Fontaine was showing fight and 'the failure of the Imperials (ie the British) on our right had left our flank exposed and been the cause of heavy casualties'.[32] Efforts were made at 4 pm 'to get the Imperials to advance' but after numerous warnings that the right flank was 'in the air' seven Canadian machine-guns were sited to cover it.

What had held up the 'Imperials'? The simple answer was heavy fighting all along the line. Some Third Army assault units ran into determined resistance almost immediately. The outbreak of shelling an hour before dawn had roused the occupants of a post hidden under the ruins of an iron bridge on the canal between Demicourt and Graincourt. Wide awake when the British barrage fell, they shot down an entire platoon of the 1st Coldstream before a handful of volunteers scrambled into the cutting and up the other side to silence two Maxims and take twelve prisoners.[33] Three tanks zig-zagging through the barbed wire helped a brigade of the 52nd Division to push down the trenches covering the approach to the canal. Though Prussian guardsmen entrenched in the spoil heaps had to be disposed of with bombs, the 6th and 7th HLI were in touch with VI Corps units within two hours. A second brigade advancing without tanks ran into dense entanglements hidden by weeds and tall grass before reaching the canal. The 4th Royal Scots and 7th Cameronians fought their way through, losing men to fire first from the higher eastern bank and later from positions on the western spur of Bourlon Wood. There the 4th Bedfords and 7th Royal Fusiliers of the Naval Division's all-Army brigade had run into trouble, but the supporting battalions left them to fight it out and charged over the ridge towards the Bapaume–Cambrai road. A few Anson men occupied the beet factory briefly before being driven out.

Marines made contact with Canadians on the edge of the wood and the Naval Division prepared to renew the attack. As this drama unfolded the Guards were advancing between Graincourt and Flesquières, shot at from both villages and by machine-guns in little Orival Wood which lay between them. The beet factory at Flesquières had been turned into another fortress but the defenders, disillusioned after being bombarded by their own artillery, surrendered to the Irish Guards about mid-day. The 2nd Grenadiers formed up in the shelter of the building and advanced to Orival. Fifteen guns and howitzers were captured on the way but the assault could go no further. The 1st Grenadiers also attacked from the vicinity of the factory but were held up by a strongly-held trench. Its occupants turned savagely on three tanks which appeared, knocking out two and damaging one. Lieutenant-Colonel Lord Gort took advantage of the diversion to send a platoon forward. Hands went up all along 'Beet Trench'. Hit soon afterwards, Gort tried to direct his men from a stretcher but was carried to the rear 'much against his will'.[34] The CO of the Welsh Guards, Lieutenant-Colonel Luxmoore Ball, later established a defensive position in depth – a prudent step in view of the uncertainty of developments elsewhere.

The Bapaume road beet factory, Anneux and Graincourt disappeared under pillars of smoke and brickdust at 2.15 pm as the heavy artillery prepared the way for a new assault. The objectives were taken – though the factory claimed the life of Chief Petty Officer George Prowse who had been awarded the VC barely a month earlier.[35] A brigade of the 57th (2nd West Lancashire) Division was brought up to advance south of Graincourt about 6 pm – behind another barrage – and the evening was spent in beating off counter-attacks.

Later the Canadians said the slow progress of XVII Corps (the

52nd, 63rd and 57th Divisions) meant 'the encircling movement which was to have given us Bourlon Wood could not be developed'. However, 'fully alive to the gravity of the situation which would be created . . . by the failure to capture and hold Bourlon Wood' the 11th Brigade had attacked from the north and captured the high ground'.[36] The 'high ground' was probably inside the wood where the situation remained confused. Enemy machine-guns were reported active there quite late in the day. An attempt by the 54th Canadians and a company of the 102nd to push into Fontaine ran into the enemy coming in the opposite direction and was halted. About 6 pm Germans were reported to be 'trickling' back into the Bois from Fontaine.

They were too late. The Canadians were determined to consolidate their gains and the 75th Battalion 'went over' about 7 pm and the 87th about 7.30, the Ontario men establishing themselves on the eastern outskirts of the wood, the Grenadiers on the railway line.[37]

In 1917 the enemy had been able to pick his lines of attack on the Bourlon salient. On 27 September, 1918, his options had vanished. The key to the position lay on the open ground to the north where the 1st Division had driven towards the Arras–Cambrai road. It had not been easy – the 2nd and 3rd Battalions had been reduced to cutting thick entanglements by hand – but they had reached their objectives. With the 4th Division in possession of the railway line and embankment east of the wood and the maligned 'Imperials' dug in south of it, any Germans left inside the wood were isolated. New masters occupied the Ferme de l'Abbaye where the CO of the Canadian Grenadiers had set up his HQ in the vaulted cellar next door to another containing Colonel Carry of the 54th. In the concrete bunker under the farm was a regimental aid post. There was no lack of decision. The last uncommitted company of the 75th Battalion was ordered to sweep the wood by morning and dutifully did so. 'They met no opposition as the enemy . . . retired during the night'. At dawn the 3rd Canadian Division filed up woodland paths to take over the front line and renew the battle. To the south the 57th Division completed its deployment through the 63rd. Later Canadians and Lancashiremen both claimed the capture of Fontaine.

Of the Canadian troops who fought in the wood, the 75th had the shortest casualty list – two officers and three other ranks killed and a total of thirty wounded.[38] The 102nd had the longest – six officers and forty-four men killed and 151 wounded. The 87th suffered a total of 150 casualties and the 54th had 109. Most were caused by machine-gun fire. The butcher's bill was heavy throughout the Corps as evinced by the 50th Battalion which lost an officer and thirty-seven men killed and 161 wounded crossing the canal. Waking the next morning in the sandpits on the edge of the Bois the officer charged with keeping the War Diary of the 102nd Battalion recorded that the 28th was 'as quiet as yesterday had been the opposite'. It did not last. German bombing planes appeared and inflicted heavy casualties on transport crowding into the area.

For the Naval Division's Hood Battalion hopes of a quiet life ended with orders in mid-afternoon to march via Anneux to La Folie Wood. They were met by machine-gun fire and sent in two companies to search out the enemy. Fighting could be heard throughout the night.

'Reports were to the effect that the considerable amount of bombing which was going on in the wood was gradually moving eastwards and that the machine-gun which had been firing from [map reference] F23.d.7.6. had suddenly ceased and not re-opened.'[39]

The Hood eventually reached the Scheldt canal – full, unlike the Canal du Nord. They spent the next day in La Folie using the massive bunkers to shelter from a rain of high explosive and Blue Cross gas shells. The battalion suffered ninety-three casualties (including ten dead), took thirty prisoners and reported the capture of three machine-guns . . . and a piano.[40] Did some musical sailor strike a few notes to remind the ghosts in the wrecked château of happier times?

Cambrai did not fall for some days, no allied bombardment being permitted. Finally it was outflanked and patrols of the 4th and 5th Canadian Mounted Rifles approached the city on 'a clear cool autumn night', the sky being lit by 'the reflections from the fires burning in Cambrai'.[41] Piles of inflammable material were found 'ready for the torch' (the Germans were destroying stores they could not remove) and Canadian sappers began fighting the fires and dealing with booby traps and mines. It was 9 October.

Lessons were to be learned from the 1918 Bourlon battle. When the after-action reports were written Lieutenant-Colonel Guy Kirkpatrick of the Canadian Seaforths criticized his riflemen for shooting standing at long-distance targets they had no hope of hitting. Lewis gunners had wasted drums on individuals and neglected to conceal their positions. From another report it is clear that the Burials Officer of the 1st Division had under-estimated the number of crosses required. He had filled 834 graves after impartially collecting dead 'Imperials' found in the area. Then there was the rum ration – 'always a bone of contention' according to the 1st Division. Authority to draw 100 gallons per division per day had at first been reduced to 60 but as a result of the GOC's representations the 100 gallon quota had been restored. It had since been reduced to 60 gallons again even for divisions on the line and:

'It is understood that there is an actual shortage of rum and that is now being supplemented by an issue of Pea Soup twice a week.'

Fortunately for the Canadians within a month the war was over. On 11 November Sir Douglas Haig passed by Bourlon Wood en route for Cambrai where he met his Army Commanders at 11 am.

A few weeks later Abbé Delval returned to the ruined city and noted that the house he had been born in was totally destroyed.

CHAPTER TWENTY-ONE

Boom Town

The events of 1918, followed by the Armistice, put paid to further delving into the reasons for wartime débâcles. The Bourlon saga was seen in its sorry perspective, just another convulsion during four years of carnage, but there was more to it than that. Relations between politicians and generals were never quite the same after December, 1917. Confidence in the good faith of the military was seriously eroded; just as their distrust of government ministers hardened.

During the Victorian and Edwardian eras, apart from automatically being assumed to be decent and upright, officers were expected to be honest when they made a hash of things, such as in the Crimean and the Boer Wars. Sir John French's ambiguous account of the use of reserves at Loos had cost him the command of the BEF in 1915. The soldiers themselves had seen to that.

After Cambrai, military integrity was again in question. The insistence that the Third Army had not been taken by surprise on 30 November had a hollow ring about it.

The supplementary questions asked suggested that the relevant commanders in France were being, to use a topical phrase, economical with the truth. But no one was guiltier of that than the Government spokesmen in the House of Commons. Generals who were asked in stern terms to explain themselves to ministers behind the scenes must have wondered at the devious face shown by the same people to MPs. The War Cabinet's public exoneration of the Higher Command is almost inexplicable unless it was part of a deal. The removal of Kiggell, Maxwell and Charteris left observers to speculate why Haig had put up with them for so long but their inefficiency could be attributed to overwork and war weariness. The posting home of Pulteney, Snow and Woollcombe might suggest to some people that Byng could not tell a good corps commander from a button stick, but the same explanation could serve.

What about Byng himself? Lloyd George writing in the 1930s stated that the original attack of 20 November had been 'badly muddled' by Byng and classified him, because of his role in March, 1918, as a bungler.[1]

As for the Hesdin Inquiry it was 'a sham'.[2] Byng had not been called. This was fair neither to the three generals nor to Byng. They faithfully carried out their terms of reference – to give their opinion – and Byng, who had already given a written explanation of his views, could hardly have been expected to appear before his juniors. There had been nothing, however, to prevent the attendance of Major-General Vaughan, his chief staff officer . . . unless Byng disapproved. And we may assume that he did. For, writing in the *Army Quarterly* of September 1935 (the year Byng died) Vaughan (who retired as a lieutenant-general), wrote:

'Byng himself never had any use for post-mortems. He considered controversy after the event to be valueless.'

(It is to be hoped Vaughan meant 'recriminations'. Controversy over the Somme and Passchendaele meant that attrition was not a strategy employed in the West in the Second World War.)

Vaughan on Byng: 'His sense of loyalty was so great that he himself never attributed blame to those who, in his opinion, had done their best, nor as far as it lay in his power to do so, would he allow others to impart blame.'

Had then Snow, Woollcombe and Pulteney failed to give of their best?

Vaughan: 'It may suffice to say that Byng's conception of the battle of Cambrai was brilliant, provided that it could have been put into execution at a suitable time with sufficient reserves to exploit success.'

If, as the man in charge (under Haig) on 20 November Byng must take credit for presiding over the tank's coming of age, he cannot escape his responsibilities for 30 November.

Jeffery Williams in his absorbing biography of Byng states that the 'false impression' that Byng had 'blamed the troops' was perpetuated by the Official Historian and by the 'calumny' in

Lloyd George's memoirs. Williams[3]: 'It is simply not a done thing in the Army for a commander to blame his men.' Yet some troops felt that they had been held responsible – the witnesses from the Machine Gun Corps who heard Byng's words read out to them at Hesdin. The history of the 7th Royal Sussex (edited by a committee of officers)[4] states in the account of 30 November: 'Even General Byng, our own Army Commander declared (to the disgust of all the fighting troops) "I attribute the reason etc . . ."'

After the war Byng continued to discourage 'controversy' and because of his known wishes (according to Vaughan in 1935) it was for this reason that the Third was the only one of Haig's armies of which 'no private history has been published'. Genuine modesty or plain arrogance? The Third Army had fought hard under Allenby before Byng took over. It was not his personal property.

Haig also talked of 'my soldiers' and 'my armies' but the evidence is that he had an acute awareness of a commander-in-chief's responsibility to the government of the day. If he did not like politicians he knew how to live with them. His knowledge of events and assessment of people off the battlefield seems to have been more profound at times than his professional judgment on it. Otherwise he might never have become obsessed with a wood called Bourlon.

What the 5.9s and 18-pounders had failed to destroy during the war a new breed of residents finished off during the Armistice. British pioneer companies, the Chinese labour corps, German prisoners, all had a hand in the final destruction of the château. Solid oak doors, delicate panelling, stout joists, window frames, roofing beams, staircases, all were consigned to the camp fires of the men 'clearing up' the battlefields. Comte Bernard, the first of the de Francqueville family to return, found himself heir to a tottering ruin which, on hearing of the state of things, his father refused to visit. The young comtesse could not recognize the mansion she had left in 1914. The couple camped out in what had been Comte Roger's study using an umbrella to keep off the rain dripping through the gaping roof. The driest place was the fine marble cheminée – chipped but with its fleur de lys motif undamaged. Later a hut became available.

The village was slow to recover. Not all those who survived the war wanted to return.[5] Others could not resist the lure of 'home'. When Edmonde Foulon rejoined her family in 1919 (she had been ill) they were living under corrugated iron sheets laid over the farm's broken walls. It was impossible to walk in the woods because of the 'appalling stench of corpses'.

Léonce Carrez found his parents in the cellars of the old brewery when he got back in 1919. He had been conscripted the moment he was liberated and sent off to join the army of occupation on the Rhine. Quite a number of older men who had spent the war on the wrong side of the line through no fault of their own were drafted into Territorial regiments though they were employed mainly on the land.

Even the boundaries of the fields had to be re-established at Bourlon. Tracing them was not too difficult – they had been marked by stones in mediaeval days – but danger lay below the surface. Emil Leclerc was killed by a shell; Monsieur Foulon wounded by a grenade. Buried barbed wire took days to clear. Only slowly with a borrowed plough did the land gradually become workable.

On a hot summer's day an ammunition dump at a spot known locally as the Malakoff blew up spontaneously showering the countryside with shells, though no one was hurt. Some battlefield scavengers were not so lucky on another occasion. Three Chinese graves were added to the cluster in the Canadian cemetery.

Things improved when reparations arrived. Six German mares were delivered to Bourlon in 1921, one of which went to Léonce . . . 'a horse with the character of a swine but she produced nine foals during her lifetime'.

Returning French prisoners, though remaining on the strength of their regiments, worked on construction projects. Dozens of huts were built by Germaine Laude's husband and the Coguillons at Moeuvres and Bourlon. Two large prefabricated Black Forest timber houses were erected at La Folie as substitutes for the destroyed châteaux. There was no point in trying to erect one at Bourlon. Madame de Francqueville had difficulty in furnishing them. What had not been destroyed had been stolen. Only the Gobelin tapestries were traced to a Belgian museum.

When permanent building began in 1921 Bourlon assumed the appearance of a boom town. The thrifty village women were quick to take advantage of commercial opportunities and liquor could be bought at fifty-two houses or huts. Some put up signs which gave their own or their family's name – Café Celine, Café Sylvie, or Café Humberts – but in the Rue de Marquion, where the Suffolks and East Surreys had fought, a mechanical piano tinkled out popular songs at the 'Chant des Oiseaux'. These early juke boxes were in great demand. Swarms of foreigners and labourers from the Midi, attracted by the high pay, cleared the cafes for dancing in the evenings. In the Rue de Cambrai, which had seen Falcon, Flirt and Firespite hammered by armour-piercing bullets, the 'Sunshine is Free' competed for customers with the 'Why Go Anywhere Else?'

Thirsty workmen made their way cautiously up the narrow footpath to the 'Ramblers' Rest', on the slopes behind the Ferme de l'Abbaye where the Germans had been cut down by the waiting Welsh. Beyond lay the Bois, its splintered beeches, oaks, elms and firs worthless; no timber merchant would risk putting a saw through the riddled trunks and gangs of Czechs and Poles worked haphazardly to clear the debris. Corpses frequently came to light. The military cemeteries expanded. British visitors to the area sometimes remarked on the rarity of graves dated November 1917 compared with 1918. Villagers hesitated to tell them the widely-held belief that the dead had been burned – just as the French had burned German corpses after the Marne, and the English had burned their own . . . after Agincourt.

After the bistros came the monuments. Wooden crosses were replaced by tombstones. A magnificent bronze Newfoundland caribou at Masnières marked the furthest advance of the 29th Division in 1917. At Havrincourt a white obelisk commemorated the 62nd Division, the pelican symbol cut into the stone balustrade. On the edge of Bourlon Wood a dignified memorial to the Canadians was unveiled on land given by the de Francquevilles. Veterans of the 40th Division, which had added an acorn and oak leaf device to its bantam cock insignia after Bourlon, paid for the new high altar in the church and returned to see it inaugurated, along with a plaque to commemorate fallen comrades. By the side of the track to Fontaine the parents of Lieutenant Windeler placed a cross in memory of the son whose body was never found.

When they visited the wood in the 20s the Windelers could hear Cambrai's restored bells ringing across the fields. It was a sound that always moved Abbé Delval. In 1922 his poem 'Voix des Cloches', written in 1914, won him an important literary prize.

CHAPTER TWENTY-TWO
Plus ça change . . .

If the village recovered Bourlon château did not. A new brick
building was eventually built at La Folie, some distance from the
original mosquito-plagued site, and Comte Roger spent some time
there each year. He may have visited the ruins of his old home
once – then never went back. The wreck was demolished, only the
study fireplace being preserved and re-erected, shrapnel scars and
all, in the new building at La Folie. The old man, whose wife had
died in 1918, spent much of the rest of his life in Paris. Had Comte
Roger been approachable his grandchildren, Pierre, Guy, René
and Bernadette, could have told him about the wood – of the
rusting tank at a fork in the paths, of the helmets near the
Carrefour Madame, of the detritus choking the crumbling trenches
and the undulating stretches of overgrown shell craters. He
remained aloof, maintaining a frigid dignity until his death in
1934. He was 82.

Another man who had coveted Bourlon had already vanished
from the scene. Haig died suddenly in 1928, aged 67. He had
devoted himself to ex-servicemen's welfare after the war. Viscount
Byng of Vimy, who had continued in public service, first as
Governor-General of Canada and later Chief Commissioner of the
Metropolitan Police, survived Comte Roger by a year.

In much better health was the former lord of Bourlon, Reserve
Lieutenant Mayer, who pulled up outside the Carrez farm in a big
car one summer. He and Frau Mayer were sight-seeing in the area
and sought a bed for the night. The farmers were polite but drew
the line at that.

During the Phoney War a British general asked permission to visit the wood. Pierre de Francqueville accompanied Harold Alexander to the spot where he had set up his headquarters for the ill-fated attack of 27 November. Veterans returning to the area in 1939 were astonished to find the dry stretch of the Canal du Nord still dry, still battered. It might have formed a fine anti-tank ditch but a few weeks later another general who had never made Bourlon's acquaintance simply bypassed it. Erwin Rommel's panzers thrust up the road from Le Cateau to Cambrai and roared on to Arras. By that time Comtesse Bernard de Francqueville, whose husband was once again in uniform, had left La Folie for Paris – the Luftwaffe having served notice by bombing Cambrai and its surrounding airfields. Canon Delval (as he had become) stayed put and opened a new diary.

For Léonce Carrez May, 1940, was a re-run of an old picture. He sat on a cart in the same field from which, in 1914, he had seen the French infantry staggering down the Bapaume–Cambrai road. This time it was refugees. Most of Bourlon's villagers joined them and Léonce drove his aged parents and family in a fine new 14 hp Ford to friends in Britanny. A labourer volunteered to look after the farm but it might have been better for Léonce if he had stayed. In Brittany he was mobilized and sent in charge of a squad of middle-aged reservists to help defend the Seine. It took him days to make his way back after the final collapse, during which he was lucky to survive the murderous bombing of Évreux.

The little farmer could not resist the call of his own fields and finally cycled back to Bourlon alone (the car he left with a village official in Britanny).[1] He found the corn ripe and the hay harvested. The farm-hand had managed to save a horse and three heifers but the Germans had taken the other draught animals and slaughtered the rest of the herd for meat. Once more he found himself face to face with an interpreter . . . who requisitioned some of the remaining furniture for an officer's billet.

'Plus ça change . . . plus c'est la meme chose!'

Once communities had returned, encouraged by the Germans who wanted to restore normal life, they found themselves subject to familiar harassment. Men had to work three days out of eight for the occupying forces. Gradually all horses were seized and in desperation farmers experimented with oxen from the Nièvre-Allier region. Saddlers had to learn to make yokes, smiths to fit special shoes.

Soldiers were billeted in the old tile factory and fighter pilots in Bourlon itself.

In April, 1941, the telephone lines connecting the village with the airfield at Epinoy were cut. Explanations were called for by the Kommandantur at Arras. The authorities agreed that as the line passed across open country anyone from three or four communes could have been guilty – so all would have to provide guards and woe betide them if anything went wrong. From then on villagers had to patrol the wire every night.

It is unlikely that any of the crews of the Flying Fortresses which roared towards Epinoy on 1 December, 1943 realized the day was dedicated to old St Éloi. They cannot have known that Albertine Fièvet, Jeanne Lamand, Vincent Lagon and Henri Hocquet with his donkey were gathering dead wood in the Bois. A few adjustments to the flight pattern and it was simply a matter of 'Bomb doors open . . . bombs gone'. The edge of the wood vanished under rolling clouds of smoke and soil. When they drifted away four tattered figures and a donkey emerged, all more frightened than hurt. St Éloi figured in heartfelt prayers that night.

As if to compensate for its total destruction in the first great conflict, Bourlon's buildings were spared in the second. A torrent of bombs meant for the airfield just missed the village at 3 o'clock one morning. An errant V-1 plunged into the fields not far away. But if Bourlon enjoyed good fortune its most distinguished son did not.

The essential impression left by Bernard de Francqueville is one of decency and simplicity. He had survived the May débâcle, escaped from the encircling French Army by fishing boat and was officially demobilized in the south. He was a patriot dedicated to his family and loyal to his friends and the people of Bourlon. In 1940, at 55, he might have been content to sit back in Paris and await developments. The Luftwaffe had requisitioned La Folie.[2] When the seeds of resistance ripened it was only natural that he was drawn in. In 1941 the family sheltered Scottish soldiers still hiding after escaping from St Valéry in June 1940. Young Pierre acted as an escort for a party which escaped into Vichy France.[3]

Prime mover in the affair was Bernard's nephew, Pierre d'Harcourt, who used the de Francqueville house in the Rue Elysée Récluse as a base, his own home being too risky for him.

Towards the end of 1941 he was arrested at a métro station and held in solitary confinement.

Even then it might have been possible for Bernard to take a discreet back seat but when, with the help of a German priest, a German male nursing orderly sneaked out a letter from d'Harcourt asking for money to be smuggled in to Fresnes, he acted swiftly. A brief case with a secret pocket was prepared. The Gestapo found it and the nursing orderly was shot. The priest, a resolute anti-Nazi called Stock, escaped detection but the hunt was on. Madame de Francqueville saved the family by her prompt warning when men in long raincoats emerged from a big car outside No. 14 Rue Elysée Récluse. The family left by a back entrance and escaped across the Champ de Mars.

After further adventures she and her husband reached Morocco but Comte Bernard was not prepared to sit out the war in the sun. He smuggled himself back to Paris – where Pierre had managed to survive – but was identified and arrested after being seen at his home. After a spell in Fresnes he travelled to Germany in the same train that carried Pierre d'Harcourt.[3] He was in a concentration camp when Bourlon Wood was again the scene of bloodshed and tragedy.

CHAPTER TWENTY-THREE
A Hand of Cards

Sunday, 11 June, 1944. In Normandy fighting rages round the invasion beaches; in Cambrésis the morning passes peacefully. Cléophas Cattraux and Josué Turpin, both 20, had decided to join a maquis that day. An embryo unit was camping in the Bois Boquet, an isolated copse just above the village and set apart from the main wood. Young maquisards, they wore blue dungarees and alpine berets. Cléophas and Josué walked down the track that separates one wood from the other and shouted, but got no reply. They left, intending to make some inquiries in the village, which the maquisards visited despite the presence of German anti-aircraft troops.[1]

Albert Lecat, caretaker of the de Francqueville estate, was struck by the unusual behaviour of the German officer billeted on him. So was his wife (Albert was married to Edmonde Foulon). They had a reasonable relationship with their lodger who was clearly on edge. Albert slipped out and told one of his helpers, old Mercier, to warn the Resistance leader to move out of the Bois Boquet into the main wood. Something odd was going on. Mercier was no luckier than the two would-be recruits and went on to the Café Hocquet, sole survivor of the honky-tonks of the Roaring Twenties, which the maquis chief sometimes frequented. He wasn't there. The old man must have missed him by minutes. That morning he had called to ask the patron if he would cook some beans for his men. Monsieur Hocquet was happy to oblige but his stove was not. The coal burned badly and it was late afternoon before the maquisards got their indifferent haricots.

They were still in the Bois Boquet at 5.30 pm, by which time a regular card school had assembled in the café.

There were about twenty of them, including Cléophas Cattraux. Eugène Decool, an invalid, arrived by motor-tricycle. Cards helped to pass the time. A game of belote was not going to change the course of a battle being waged hundreds of miles away. Madame Hocquet went off to visit her sister a few doors away and her daughters, Jeanne and Irene, prepared to serve their customers from the meagre stock. Their father was the first to notice two lorries full of Germans pulling up at the water tower some 500 yards from his café. Wearing his white summer cap, he raced across back gardens to the little wood. There was still time for the maquisards to flee but, in response to his warning, he received a quiet: 'We're going to fight. Get out of the way'.

By that time it was too late to take the most direct route back to the café. Mathieu Hocquet slithered over the edge of an old sandpit, hung for a moment and then plunged down a steep incline. He landed unhurt, scrambled up the other side and arrived panting at his sister-in-law's house. As he closed the door he heard a long burst from an automatic, followed by sporadic shooting which lasted for fifteen minutes.

In the café the crowd fell silent. Cléophas fished a photograph of General de Gaulle from his pocket and poked it into the stove where it charred slowly.

'Let's lie on the floor,' someone suggested.

'No. Let's go down to the cellar.'

'Stay where you are and keep quiet,' said the cripple.

The doors were thrown open and German soldiers burst in, ripping down curtains and demanding blankets for their casualties. Shortly afterwards the Frenchmen saw the troops bringing back a body in a blanket.

'One of the feldgendarmerie.'

Twice men tried to leave the café. Twice they were sent back by soldiers in the Rue Sablonièrre. An armed guard was posted on the door.

'Right! On your feet. Hands up!'

A German NCO entered, pistol in hand, followed by soldiers who used rifle butts to hasten laggards. Even the cripple was struck.

'Right! What are you doing here?'

Cléophas attempted to explain that they met for cards every Sunday.

'Better not try that story on me,' snapped the NCO. 'Do you take me for an imbecile?'

The group was pushed into line with their backs to a wall. A magazine clipped into an automatic. The Germans wanted to know the identity of a man in a white cap who had been seen running away from the wood. No one spoke. The NCO left but the card players remained against the wall, though they were able to exchange a few words. Cléophas even managed to slip his wallet to Jeanne Hocquet. It contained a *Service Travail Obligatoire* document – proof that he should have been working in Germany, that he was a *réfractaire*.

Tension eased when the guards changed about midnight. The newcomers were older men and promptly demanded coffee. While they drank it they asked if anyone present was employed repairing the bomb craters on the airfield. To a man the Bourloniens swore, *'Ich arbeit boum-boum Epinoy'*.

After some discussion they were allowed to leave, but Cléophas had no intention of risking a journey through the village and sought refuge in a house opposite. He spent the rest of the night helping Monsieur and Madame Godon destroy thousands of incriminating Allied propaganda leaflets collected as souvenirs by their young son. They were as reluctant to burn as General de Gaulle's photograph.

Most of the card players were arrested on their way home by a German patrol which was not impressed by the magic words *'Ich arbeit boum-boum Epinoy'*. Booted into the state school, they were taken one by one and interrogated before being released.

In the cellar of the Mairie, hands in air, stood twenty-two captured maquisards. Earlier, when the mayor and his secretary were seen hurrying up the street the Lecats' German lodger had become highly agitated.

'What happens, they must not identify anyone from Bourlon among the prisoners. Try to get word to them.'[2]

There was no time. In any case, Monsieur Dartois hardly needed telling.

'Anyone from the commune here?'

The mayor stared into frightened eyes, resigned eyes, defiant eyes. Not a spark of recognition. The two officials were allowed to leave but were called out about midnight and told to provide a vehicle and a party of villagers to collect bodies from the wood. There were eleven in all. Ten were found quickly; there was some trouble locating the last of them. Finally the grisly load was taken to an outbuilding of the Mairie. Each maquisard had been shot in the back of the neck. The Germans had simply finished off the wounded and made sure of any doubtful cases. One body was still warm.

Two live maquisards were found the next day. Cléophas Cattraux, still in the Godon house, watched them being dragged from a tiny tunnel formed by a pile of corrugated iron sheets. Three girl couriers were luckier. They were found by Madame Hocquet in the morning, hiding in her privy. At an appropriate moment they left the café and walked down the main street, joking with the young Germans on duty. They got clean away. Three men were later smuggled out of Bourlon in loads of straw.

If a lorry-load of Germans had not asked 'Fortuné' Lagon, a local character, the way to 'the château' there might have been no escapes at all. In all innocence he directed them to the site of the old château – not to the water tower, the *château d'eau*. They were late in closing the cordon and a handful of men escaped through the gap. A machine-gun set up by the Canadian memorial had covered the road between the little Bois Boquet and the big wood.

On Monday the dead were taken to the Salle des Catechismes near the presbytery and placed in coffins provided by the Germans for burial in the communal cemetery. Their comrades went by lorry to the citadel at Arras. Thirteen of them were taken to the execution ground below the ramparts and shot on 18 June. Eight were sent to concentration camps. The maquisards belonged to a unit of the Communist Franc Tireurs Partisans and came from the mining community of Annezin near Béthune. Bourlon had been the first stage of a journey to join a major maquis. Very few had weapons.

What might have happened had Cléophas Cattraux and Josué Turpin joined up that Sunday morning, or if any other Bourlonien had been identified, may be guessed. Only the day before the SS had wiped out the entire population of Oradour-sur-Glane because they believed an inhabitant had sheltered the killer of one of their officers.

Allied planes flew over Bourlon frequently in the summer of 1944, bombing the railway network Byng had hoped to sever with his cavalry. More than half of Cambrai's houses were wrecked and 250 citizens died in raids. On 2 September the Americans arrived and what was left of the 9th and 10th SS Panzer divisions retreated towards Belgium. Bourlon's inhabitants took to their cellars when the last enemy soldier left. US armoured cars sprayed the empty streets with their Brownings but received no reply. Only two prisoners were taken – Poles who had climbed into a hay loft and pulled up the ladder behind them. Léonce Carrez negotiated their surrender. In Cambrai Canon Delval heard the bells again.[3]

The war still had eight months to run. Young villagers went into the French army in which the de Francquevilles were already serving. Guy had been in an armoured unit since 1939. The diminutive Pierre was in the infantry. He was wounded during fighting in the Vosges, trying to clear a wood.

Comte Bernard never knew that both of his sons won decorations. He died in a concentration camp just before the final collapse of the Reich. In 1945 his wife returned alone to la Folie. It was undamaged but thoroughly looted. Only two armchairs and a sofa were ever found.

At Bourlon more poignant relics were recovered. Relatives of the young maquisards came from Annezin to reclaim their bodies. Nine were identified and taken away. Two *inconnus* remain side by side in the cemetery. A memorial to the others was raised in the wood not far from the Canadian monument.

CHAPTER TWENTY-FOUR
Rattle a Rib Cage

You can easily miss the signs to Bourlon on the busy roads converging on Cambrai. The wood itself is as discreet as ever. Drive up from Bapaume along the old RN 29, which has been translated into the RN 30 on new maps, and the fine lock and broad ribbon of the Canal du Nord catch the eye. The Bois keeps its distance. In the villages, mellowing seventy years after their restoration, each church wears its witch's hat again and looks suspiciously over fields which are deserted more often than not. The horses went long ago, not requisitioned to pull alien guns but made redundant by *les tracteurs*. Beet crops that used to take a month to lift are now gathered, topped and tailed in a twinkling, and left in incredible heaps by roaring, gluttonous machines. The ready-made forts where the harvest used to be processed have been closed or converted to other uses – even the drab old death trap on the Bapaume–Cambrai road. An aluminium chimney poking out of the haze across the fields towards Arras marks the site of a monster *sucrerie* which gulps down all it is offered and demands more. The Eurocrats will get round to dealing with another surplus problem some day.

The permanent army of occupation which shares the fields is unobtrusive in the growing season. On rare brilliant autumn days, with the beet gone, trim-walled rectangles of white headstones brighten the shorn landscape. They are less obvious during the grey Artois winter and, in any case, many well-ordered plots are tucked away in folds in the ground. Behind Havrincourt Wood the host of Yorkshiremen assembled at the end of the lane have few visitors. As if in compensation, the number of their division[1] is to be seen on car and bus registration plates everywhere. The Pas de Calais is 62nd in the list of French administrative departments. It makes up for the pamphlet issued by the tourist office in Cambrai in which the West Riding warriors are described as the '62 D.I. Highlanders'.

Alongside the rebuilt church at Graincourt is a wedge of masonry like a sentry-box, marking the entry to the underground shelters used by both sides. The key is in the Mairie but the steps lead only to a rubble-packed wall. The catacombs, as the British called them, are an ancient feature of Cambrésis. According to legend *'souterrains'* once connected all the villages and might run as much as four miles from one to another.

In August, 1944, a local architect surveyed the workings at Graincourt – potential shelters if battle rolled over the region again. He listed forty-one rooms and corridors providing a total space of 1,232 cubic metres. There were 'wells', vents and a chamber with an apse-like end which might have been a place of worship. At Moeuvres there are underground stables. Was either side aware in 1917 of the full extent of the ready-made defensive system under them? It is unlikely. Peasants kept such things secret – these were their traditional refuges in times of trouble, in the wars of religion and perhaps even earlier. They deserve a book to themselves. In 1939 an entrance was explored at Bourlon but the tunnel petered out after a few feet. All the same, one wonders.

Another interesting survey was carried out quite recently for the Department of Sport and Leisure, to produce an orienteering chart of the Bois. It is covered with neat saucer-shaped symbols indicating depressions that were once shell holes. They cluster thickest on the western end of the horseshoe ridge inside the wood. Bigger blobs show where the US bombs fell on the St Éloi's day raid. Traces of trenches are marked but they are hard to identify on the ground unless one has the benefit of the company of 'Monsieur Pierre'.

Probably every oak that survived the bombardments of 1917 and 1918 is known to him. He points out scars which cover the shrapnel wounds: 'Yes, that's one of the old ones.' The hollow trunks of the huge limes around the Canadian memorial are filled with cement and the branches held by metal rods and wired rope. The War Graves Commission is more successful in preserving the old than the new. An irate gardener spends ten minutes bemoaning the theft of decorative shrubs. Monsieur Pierre finds time to listen. It is not his concern but 'the fellow feels better for geting it off his chest'. If Monsieur de Francqueville has a problem it is Royan, a large shaggy dog of indeterminate breed who affects deafness from time to time and prefers to move at his own speed and along his own trails, though he is never far from his master.

The substantial foundations of the 'Chalet' evoke the past. Perhaps the body of Major Johnson VC was brought into that very corner. At the sandpits on the edge of the woods, where the Guards attacked, and where, as a boy, Monsieur Pierre saw tank hulks, a sour smell indicates a piggery; the slurry is seeping across the ground. It is not part of the estate and Monsieur de Francqueville does not approve. He indicates the cliff-like slopes running down to the lake of sludge.

'The British broke their teeth here. They can't have known.' A question arises. Why didn't the French lend Comte Bernard to the British? No one knew the Bois better.

'He always said he asked to be attached to the English,' explains Monsieur Pierre, 'but for some reason they turned down the idea.'

Deer burst through the brush and Royan pursues them noisily up the hillside which the Welsh brigade charged.

'Royan, Royan.'

The Comte shouts and the wood shouts back.

'Royan.'

Even on a fine, still day Bourlon has atmosphere, not brooding but vibrant, as if tremendous energy was compressed under its rugged contours. Comte Ludovic's indestructible paths and the mediaeval road wait patiently for travellers, but the action is in the fields. At dusk one evening Jérome, a bright-eyed boy, burst into the sitting room at the Ferme de l'Abbaye to tell his grandmother how he and Emmanuel had given chase to light-fingered motorists helping themselves to strawberries after the 'pick your own' plantation had closed. The villains had escaped down the road past the disused railway cutting where long ago some young Scots failed to make their getaway.

But it is the apple not soft fruit which rules in Bourlon village where Edmonde Lecat is among the locals packing Golden Delicious, Coxes and gleaming Jonagolds in modern warehouses. 'Pommartois' is more important than the timber these days, though the big poplars still go for cheese boxes. 'Camembert trees' the disrespectful call them.

There are orchards too down at La Folie where Comte Guy, a cheery, ex-cavalry colonel, drives a muddy Land-Rover full of grandchildren and dogs.

Deer lying between the rows of young trees look up as we bump across the fields to the sunken road from which the German machine-gunners took the Guards in the flank. It is deep and dark and overgrown with signs of old dug-outs, an ominous eerie place. By contrast La Folie wood, despite the low ground, is pleasant, with views of the lake. Sheep nibble the grass at the site of the old château. Did the Dragoon Guards with swords drawn really gallop up the drive over there? We turn under the trees and explore a group of reinforced concrete tombs cleared long ago of bodies and booty by impious grave robbers from the Royal Naval Division. Francqueville children cluster obediently at the entry to one blockhouse to lend perspective to a photograph. They are staying with their grandparents in the Black Forest houses which are still doing duty after all these years. In the brick château lives great-grandmother. At 96, the Comtesse Bernard has a lively mind, a fund of stories and an iron will. She manoeuvres herself round the ground floor, using a small tea trolley as a walking aid.

'It used to take us three hours to drive from here to Arras in 1919,' she says. 'The roads were nothing but shell holes.'

As for La Folie wood:

'Oh, you couldn't move for shells out there,' she gestures. 'They were lying all over the place.'

And Bourlon . . . the château?

'There were Indian soldiers ripping out the timber when I got there. They burned everything.'

Madame de Francqueville likes the heat herself. Each autumn she leaves Cambrai to its mists and returns to her flat in Paris. She wonders why she hasn't the sense to live in the Midi. Truly formidable, the women of her generation.

Of course, you might say that brave old ladies have no place in military history, any more than fruit packers, hungry priests, farmers who dig up barbed wire and young miners who don't have the sense to run while they have the chance. But there are ploughboys from every part of the old British Empire buried in Cambrésis; and town and country men who liked a good apple; and pit lads who thought they were escaping from tyranny by joining the army . . . and they all had grandmothers.

Again, you might say that one should let sleeping generals and politicians lie and not rattle their rib cages with a walking stick.

Why not?
As long as the noise makes us sit up and think.

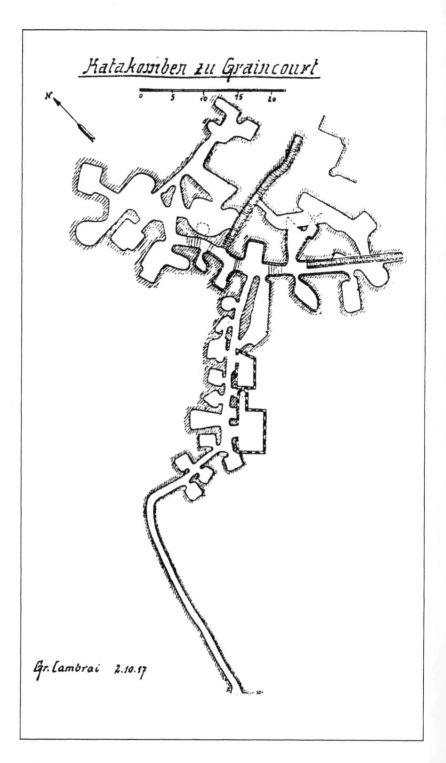

Katakomben zu Graincourt

Gr. Cambrai 2.10.17

APPENDIX A

'The Catacombs'

The part played in the 1917 Battle of Cambrai by what the British called the 'Catacombs' and the Germans equally *'Katakomben'* is unclear.

It is unlikely that either side was aware of the full extent of the ready-made shell-proof fortresses they were sitting on.

Many villages in Cambrésis were located over, or gave access to, 30 to 40 feet-deep warrens, ventilated and proof against the heaviest artillery.

French antiquarians are not entirely in agreement about their origins.

I have been fortunate in obtaining the guidance of Monsieur Jean-Luc Gibot, of Gouzeaucourt, and Comte Jacques de Francqueville, of Tirancourt near Arras.

Monsieur Gibot has sent me a copy of a pamphlet he compiled with the help of the pupils of the École Publique at Gouzeaucourt. It was from him that the map of the neighbouring village of Graincourt came.

He makes the point that despite theories as to the purpose of the workings, the most practical would appear to be to provide foundations for the Gallo-Roman villas in Cambrésis (there are eighteen around Gouzeaucourt itself and eight of them lie within the boundaries of the commune).

Crockery fragments of a later settlement point to the occupation of a hutted village away from the workings in the 7th and 10th centuries.

At that time the *'souterrains'* did not have any compelling requirement as a refuge or quarry.

The boom in the construction of abbeys, châteaux and houses in the Middle Ages brought back the commercial/industrial value of the quarries (the stone being hauled up from wells – *'puits d'extraction'* – rather like shaft-mined coal).

Were these natural refuges used during the Hundred Years' War? Opinions are divided.

Monsieur Gibot points out that coins found indicate that they were most probably used for short periods to hide inhabitants, animals and foodstuffs during the Wars of Religion from the end of the 15th century.

Why, one may ask, was Gouzeaucourt built on a veritable 'gruyère'? Simply because the builders in the later ages did not know what was beneath them.

Monsieur de Francqueville has kindly drawn my attention to the research of the Abbé Danicourt (1846–1912), whose thorough exploration of the underground Cité de Naours has made it a place of classic interest and a great tourist attraction.

This is indeed an old underground city, its occupants during the Great War being British and Canadians, who left their souvenirs on walls which had been engraved by refugees hundreds of years earlier. Coins found included pieces going back to Philippe le Bel (1285–1314).

In 1941 the Germans used the underground workings as a munitions depot. Two years later extensive works in concrete were completed and the place was clearly to have been a headquarters of some importance. Rommel and Hitler were reported to have inspected the site during the building of the Atlantic Wall.

Clearly the existence of such sheltered works at Gonnelieu, Villers Plouich, Graincourt, Gouzeaucourt, Villers Guislain, Moeuvres and seemingly almost every Cambrésian village, could have altered the approach of both sides to the battles of 1917 (and 1918), had they known the full extent of them.

APPENDIX B

Extracts freely translated from the *Dictionnaire historique et archéologique de Pas du Calais, Arondissement D'Arras, Tome II* (pp 141, 142) *et de Ternas; la Chatellerie d'Oisy* (pp 6, 7).

The estate of Bourlon belonged for many years to a family of that name.

In 1560 it was owned by Georges de Montigny, knight, Lord of Noyelles.

From him it seems it passed to Henry IV, who sold it to Robert de Barbaise, Lord of Hainville, in April 1603.

On 19 February, 1727, the Demoiselle de Cazier, widow of Louis de Scairal, sold the property to Jean Baptiste de Francqueville, Councillor and Secretary to the King.

The estate which had been sold for 20,000 livres in 1603, brought in, as rent and other emoluments in 1769, a total of 10,000 livres a year – to Jacques-Ladislas de Francqueville, knight, Lord of Bourlon and Elimont, councillor in the Parlement of Flanders, showing how much the value of property had increased in 166 years.

Notes and References

Chapter One 'Malbrouk s'en va . . .'

1 Allies – Austrians, British, Danes, Dutch, German, Prussians.
2 Facsimile produced in W. S. Churchill's *Life of Marlborough*, Harrap 1947 edn vol. II, p. 626.
3 *Ibid.*, p. 839.
4 Duc Claude-Louis-Hector de Villars (1653–1734), Marshal of France.
5 A geological phenomenon still active.
6 Tradition in the de Francqueville family.
7 Units of the French Army of the North.
8 France mobilized on 1 August; Britain declared war on 4 August, 1914.
9 Formed from mercenary bands in Picardy in the 16th century. Became the Picardy Regiment and then 1st Infantry of the Line.
10 Abbé Delval was later a canon. His diary *Sous Leur Griffe* (Under Their Heel) was published in the 1920s.

Chapter Two Secret Tumbrils

1 Recollections recorded by Monsieur de Francqueville.
2 They were later released.
3 Recorded by Monsieur de Francqueville.
4 Metal rods were part of the statue's framework.
5 E. Junger, *Storm of Steel*, Chatto, 1929, p. 163.

Chapter Three   Dinner Guests

1 W. Miles (ed.), *Military Operations France and Belgium, 1917* (Cambrai), p. 8. Future references will be given as 'O.H. Cambrai' plus any further information, page etc.

2 John Humphrey Davidson (1876–1954). Became major-general. Knighted 1919. Joined 60th Rifles 1896. Retired 1922 and became MP. According to his obituary notice in *The Times* he opposed the Cambrai operation.

3 British military terminology in both world wars: G = Operations; A = Administration and discipline; Q = Supplies and quartering.

4 Dublin-born leader of the Ulster Unionists; distinguished lawyer; became Lord Carson (1854–1935).

5 R. Blake (ed.), *The Private Papers of Douglas Haig 1914–1919*; Eyre and Spottiswoode, 1952, second edition p. 255.

6 Herbert Henry Asquith (1852–1928), scholar and Liberal leader. Became Earl of Oxford and Asquith. David Lloyd George (1863–1945), solicitor and Liberal politician. Became Earl Lloyd George of Dwyfor. Both men had sons serving in France.

7 Blake, *op. cit.*, p. 145.

8 Sir James Edmonds (ed.), *Military Operations France and Belgium 1917*, vol. II, fn p. 101. Future references under 'O.H. (3rd Ypres)'.

9 Nivelle (1856–1924) commanded on the Western Front. French overseas operations (e.g. Salonika) were not his responsibility.

10 O.H. (3rd Ypres), p. 107.

11 Edward George Villiers Stanley (1865–1948), 17th Earl, was War Secretary from December, 1916, to April, 1918. Ex-Grenadier Guards; private secretary to Lord Roberts in the Boer War.

12 Joined 65th Foot in 1876. It became the 1st York and Lancaster Regiment (1881). Later Field-Marshal Viscount Plumer of Messines (1857–1932).

13 Joined 16th Lancers 1889. Retired as General Sir Hubert de la Poer Gough (1870–1963).

14 O.H. (3rd Ypres), p. 296.

15 E. Blunden, *Undertones of War*, London, 1930, p. 241.

16 O.H. (3rd Ypres), p. 296.

17 Kiggell (1862–1954) was Chief of the General Staff of the British Expeditionary Force. The term 'Chief of Staff' did not appear in the British Army until much later.

18 Blake, *op. cit.*, p. 256.

19 O.H. (3rd Ypres), p. 297.

20 G. le Q. Martel in article in *Encyclopaedia Britannica*, 1927. Sterling cited as at 1917 value.

21 Mustard gas, lay term for dichlorethylsulphide, a vesicant (blister agent).
22 D. Jerrold, *The Royal Naval Division*, Hutchinson, 1923, p. 252. The Division was formed of surplus naval personnel in 1914 and served at Antwerp. Later numbered 63rd.
23 Blake, *op. cit.*, p. 257.
24 O.H. (3rd Ypres), p. 328.
25 *Ibid.*, p. 300.
26 H. Gough, *The Fifth Army*, Hodder, 1931, p. 218.
27 C. Harington, *Plumer of Messines*, Murray, 1935.
28 Mustard gas shells were marked with a yellow Lorraine cross.
29 Drinking water was scarce at Ypres. Wells sunk in the clay filled with polluted surface water.
30 R. S. H. Moody, *Historical Records of the Buffs*, Medici Society, 1922.
31 Gough, *op. cit.*, p. 213.
32 O.H. (Cambrai), p. 9.
33 Reginald Baliol Brett, second Viscount Esher (1852–1930), was a link between the Crown and Government most of his life.
34 E. Wyrall, *The History of the Duke of Cornwall's Light Infantry, 1914–1919*, Methuen, 1932.
35 Blue Cross (from the shell marking) contained an arsenical compound: diphenylchlorarsine.
36 Alongside the French First Army.
37 Major-General Sir Charles Knox (1846–1938).
38 Cousin of Queen Victoria. Served in cavalry and commanded Guards Division in the Crimea for a time. Commander-in-Chief 1856–1895. Died 1904 aged 85.
39 The Corps was sent from France to the Middle East.
40 D. Lloyd George, *War Memoirs*, Odhams edn, p. 1425.
41 J. H. Thomas, Labour politician and Cabinet minister (1874–1949).

Chapter Four   A Malicious Dwarf

1 The Hon. Sir Frederick William Stopford (1854–1929), son of the Earl of Courtown (Irish peerage). Brought from retirement to be C-in-C First Home Army 1914. Joined Grenadier Guards 1871. Buller's Military Secretary in Boer War.
2 General Sir Ian Standish Monteith Hamilton (1853–1947), regarded as one of the best brains of the Edwardian army.
3 Harington, *op. cit.*, p. 77
4 An objective of 1 July, 1916.
5 J. Williams, *Byng of Vimy*, Cooper, 1983, p. 162.
6 For example Second Army at Cassel.
7 E. Fayolle, *Cahiers Secrets de la Grande Guerre*, Paris, 1964.

8 O.H. (3rd Ypres), p. 296.
9 Liddell Hart, *History of the First World War*, Pan ed., p. 301.
10 'Hindenburg' to the Allies; 'Siegfried' to the Germans.
11 Jerrold, *op. cit.*, p. 187.
12 C. Falls, *History of the 36th Division*, Belfast, p. 127.
13 *Ibid.*, p. 134.
14 Comment by ed. of Fayolle's Cahiers, *op. cit.*
15 R. Seth, *Caporetto, The Scapegoat Battle*, Macdonald, 1965.
16 Robertson (1860–1933) enlisted in the 16th Lancers in 1877; commissioned into the 3rd Dragoon Guards 1888; later Commandant at Staff College and Director of Military Training, War Office; Field-Marshal 1920.
17 Quoted in Lloyd-George, *op. cit.*, p. 1278.
18 *Ibid.*, p. 1318.
19 Gough, *op. cit.*, p. 155.
20 *Ibid.*

Chapter Five   Enter 'Uncle' Harper

1 G. H. Hill joined 7th Royal Sussex, June, 1917.
2 Regular officer, Royal Sussex (DSO and bar).
3 O. Rutter (ed.), *The History of the Seventh (Service) Battalion, The Royal Sussex Regiment 1914–1919*, Times Publishing Co., 1934.
4 Falls, *op. cit.*, p. 135.
5 *Ibid.*
6 Initials used by politer soldiers to describe themselves – Poor Bloody Infantry.
7 Falls, *op. cit.*
8 *Ibid.*
9 O.H. (Cambrai), p. 5.
10 John Frederic Charles Fuller (1878–1966). Commissioned into Ox. and Bucks LI 1898. Played important role in embarkation of BEF in 1914. Set up various officers' schools in France. Became major-general in 1930 but conflict with the military hierarchy led to retirement in 1933. Nickname: 'Boney' (Bonaparte).
11 Sir Hugh Jamieson Elles (1880–1945). Joined RE in 1899. Inspiring Tank Corps leader in Great War. Ineffective postwar. General 1938. Civil Defence Commissioner for South-West 1939–45.
12 See Liddell Hart, *op. cit.*, p. 340, and O.H. (Cambrai), p. 6.
13 His father had been Surveyor General of India.
14 Sir Charles Louis Woollcombe (1857–1934). Parson's son. Joined Army 1876; 25th Foot/King's Own Scottish Borderers. Extensive service on North-West Frontier. GOC Highland (Territorial)

Division pre-1914. GOC 11th (Northern) Division on Somme. Retired 1920.

15 The Military Service Act received the Royal Assent on 25 May. All men between 18 and 21 had to register.

16 A lighter standard machine gun, the Erfurt, was introduced during the war.

17 Scott and Brumwell, *The History of the 12th (Eastern) Division*, London, 1923, p. 133.

18 See para. 16 of *Third Army Training Note* issued on 30 October, 1917, and reproduced in O.H. (Cambrai).

19 As per the 'flash' or 'patch' on Royal Armoured Corps vehicles today.

20 Joined RE in 1884. Lieutenant-general in 1918. Died in car crash 1922 while GOC-in-C Southern Command.

21 E. L. Spears, *Prelude to Victory*, Cape, 1939.

22 O.H. (Cambrai), p. 35.

23 Spears, *op. cit.*

24 See Liddell Hart, *op. cit.*

25 *Ibid.*

26 Wyrall, *The History of the 62nd (West Riding) Division*, vol. 1, Bodley Head.

Chapter Six   Low Fliers from Down Under

1 N. M. Parnell, article in *Aviation Historical Society of Australia Journal*, January–February 1972. R. L. Howard MC was killed in March 1918; Harry Taylor MC, MM, in an accident in August.

2 H. A. Jones, *The War in the Air*, vol. IV, O.U.P., 1934.

3 Falls, *op. cit.*, p. 141.

4 Wyrall, *op. cit.* (62nd Div.), p. 74.

5 At HQ IV Corps, Villers-au-Flos.

6 Later Sir Joseph Austen Chamberlain (1863–1937), half-brother to Neville and son of the Victorian statesman Joe.

7 Blake, *op. cit.*, p. 268.

8 F. Maurice, *The Franco-German War*, Allen and Unwin, 1900.

9 M. Durand, *The Thirteenth Hussars in the Great War*, Blackwoods, 1921, p. 285.

10 Anon, *The Second-Seconds in France*, Ballantyne, 1920.

11 *Ibid.*

12 Major-General H. D. De Pree (1870–1943), *Royal Artillery Journal*, vol. LV No. 2, July, 1928. He became Commandant of the RMA Woolwich ('The Shop') in 1926.

13 General Debeney says four divisions were offered, all infantry – *La Guerre et Les Hommes*, Plon, 1937.

14 O.H. (Cambrai), p. 23.

15 Pulteney (1861–1941) had commanded III Corps since 1914. A parson's son, he had joined the Scots Guards in 1881. Retired as a lieutenant-general and became Black Rod, House of Lords, 1920.

16 General Joseph Degoutte (1866–1938). Later commanded French Sixth Army. Became Chief of Staff to the King of Belgians (1918). Infantryman: 4th Zouaves.

17 Snow (1858–1940) joined the 13th Foot (Somerset Light Infantry) 1879. Later served in R. Inniskilling Fusiliers and the Northamptonshires. Divisional commander at Le Cateau 1914, Ypres 1915.

18 W. Moore, *See How They Ran*, Cooper, 1970.

19 O.H. (Cambrai), p. 46.

20 Anderson, *War Services of the 62nd Divisional Artillery*.

21 That is, the use of the phone was forbidden.

22 A. E. Sheppard, *The Ninth The Queen's Royal Lancers 1715–1936*, Aldershot, 1939.

Chapter Seven   Frustration at Flesquières

1 O.H. (Cambrai), p. 384.

2 Early marks of 9.2-inch howitzer fired 290-lb shells; 8-inch fired 200-lb shells.

3 Rutter, *op. cit.*, p. 153.

4 *Ibid.*

5 A. S. G. Lee, *46 Squadron RFC*, quoted in Jones, *op. cit.*, p. 237.

6 C. Prigg (ed.), *The War Despatches – Sir Philip Gibbs*, London, 1964, p. 296.

7 Now the colours of the Royal Tank Regiment symbolizing 'through mud and blood to the green fields beyond', green being the uppermost stripe.

8 'Male' tanks carried two six-pounder low velocity cannon in addition to their Lewis guns; 'females' had machine guns only.

9 Neumann, *In der Luft unbesiegt*, Berlin, p. 96.

10 Died of wounds 27 November.

11 Of *46 Squadron RFC*. See Jones, *op. cit.*, p. 237.

12 *Guide Bleu*, Hachette, Paris.

13 O.H. (Cambrai), p. 59, and David Chandler's article in Purnell part work, p. 2420.

14 DH 5s of 64 Squadron RFC.

15 Macbeath was awarded the VC. Born Kinlochbervie, Lairg, Sutherland, 1897. Died Vancouver, Canada, 1922.

16 O.H. (Cambrai), p. 57.

17 Fuller, *Tanks in the Great War*, p. 149.

18 Wyrall, *op. cit.* (62nd Div.).

19 2nd/4th and 2nd/5th Battalions.

20 Falls, *op. cit.*, p. 149.

21 *Ibid.*

22 Wyrall, *op. cit.* (62nd Div.).

23 Rutter, *op. cit.*

24 S. Gillon, *The Story of the 29th Division*, London, 1925.

25 Joined RE 1893. Commanded East Anglian TA division after the war. Retired 1935. Died 1960.

26 Major-General Sir Louis Ridley Vaughan (1875–1942). Entered army 1895. Captain Indian Army 1905. Commanded division in Afghan War 1919.

27 Quoted in O.H. (Cambrai), p. 279.

28 Later Sir Walter Pipon Braithwaite (1865–1945), Infantryman: Somerset Light Infantry 1886. Though a Yorkshireman, his grandfather was Seigneur of Noirmont, Jersey, CI, hence 'Pipon'. Sir Walter had been Chief Staff Officer to Sir Ian Hamilton, Gallipoli.

29 O.H. (Cambrai), p. 86.

30 Later Sir Thomas Owen Marden (1866–1951). Joined 22nd (Cheshire) Regiment 1886; CO 1st Welch Regiment 1912. GOC 53rd Welsh (Territorial) Division after the war.

31 O.H. (Cambrai), as note 29

Chapter Eight   Sabres Flash at La Folie

1 See *History of the Sixth Tank Battalion*.

2 Prigg; *op. cit.*

3 De Pree, *op. cit.*

4 Sheppard, *op. cit.*, p. 287

5 *Ibid.*

6 Gillon, *op. cit.*, p. 153.

7 *Ibid.*

8 Major-General Walter Howorth Greenly (1876–1955). Joined 12th Lancers 1895. Took over 14th Infantry Division in March, 1918. Later member of British Mission to Rumania.

9 John Edward Bernard Seely, first Baron Mottistone (1868–1947). Lawyer and politician. Major-General 1918–19.

10 Curragh Incident – threat by British officers (mainly cavalry) to resign en masse if ordered against Ulster unionists.

11 O.H. (Cambrai), p. 70.

12 *Ibid.*, p. 282.

13 Rutter, *op. cit.*

14 O.H. (Cambrai), p. 96.

15 *Ibid.*, p. 18

16 Wyrall, *op. cit.* (62 Div.), p. 72.

17 H. Essame, *US Military Review*, May 1964.

18 His brother, Lieut-Commander George N. Bradford, RN, also won the VC, at Zeebrugge, April, 1918.

19 See Moore, *History of the DLI*, Cooper, 1975.

20 Quoted in Wyrall, *op. cit.* (62nd Div.).

21 De Pree, *op. cit.*, p. 220, and Cooper, *The Ironclads of Cambrai*, p. 123.

22 Wyrall, *op. cit.* (62nd Div.).

23 Falls, *op. cit.*, p. 154.

24 Wyrall, *op. cit.* (62nd Div.), p. 93.

25 O.H. (Cambrai), p. 92.

26 See J. Foley, *Armour in Profile*, London, 1967.

27 O.H. *Medical Diseases of the War*, London, 1923, p. 527.

28 O.H. (Cambrai), p. 343.

29 Born at Bo'ness (Borrowstouness), West Lothian, 1889. Commanded Edmonton Fusiliers in World War II.

Chapter Nine   Brandenburg Cigars

1 Brigadier-General Cuthbert Henry Lucas (1879–1958) 87th Bde. Staff College graduate and machine-gun expert. Joined Royal Berkshire Regiment 1898.

2 Gillon, *op. cit.*, p. 157.

3 Wyrall, *op. cit.* (62nd Div.).

4 C. T. Atkinson, *The History of the South Wales Borderers in the Great War*, Medici Society, 1931.

5 Probably a machine later photographed by the Germans abandoned in the main street of Rumilly.

6 Gillon, *op. cit.*

7 O.H. (Cambrai), p. 90

8 Wyrall, *op. cit.* (62nd Div.), p. 98.

9 *Ibid.*

10 De Pree, *op. cit.*, p. 226.

11 Public Record Office ref. WO158/54 – copy of Haig's report, classified secret, dated 23 December, 1917.

12 O.H. (Cambrai), p. 117.

13 Ludendorff, *Memoirs*, Hodder, London 1920.

14 *Ibid.*, p. 494.

15 Wyrall, *op. cit.* (62nd Div.).

16 Jones, *op. cit.*, vol. IV p. 243, quoting article by Grosskreutz in *Die Luftwacht*, July, 1928.

17 O.H. (Cambrai), p. 118.

18 The Germans are said to have concentrated behind the spoil heaps still being contested near the canal – Wyrall in *The West Yorkshire Regiment in the Great War*, Bodley Head.

19 *Narrative of Operations 51st Division*, PRO WO 158/390.

20 Falls, *op. cit.*, p. 159.

21 De Pree, *op. cit.*, p. 227.

22 16th County of London Regiment.

23 5th City of London Regiment.

Chapter Ten   Etonians and Mongrels

1 F. E. Whitton, *The History of the 40th Division*, Gale and Polden, 1926.

2 H. C. Wylly, *The Green Howards 1914–1919*, Richmond, 1926.

3 Whitton, *op. cit.*, p. 85.

4 Atkinson, *op. cit.*

5 Ponsonby (1866–1952), was later knighted. Joined Coldstream Guards 1887. Commanded 5th Division in 1918; 7th Cumberland Home Guard 1940–1.

6 Three out of the five corps commanders in the Third Army were Old Etonians. Snow (VIIth) was the oldest, Pulteney (IIIrd) was a contemporary of Byng; Fergusson, whose XVIIth had not been heavily engaged, was the youngest. Jeudwine, GOC 55th Division, was also a contemporary of Byng.

7 Lieutenant-Colonel (later General Sir) Bertie Drew Fisher (1877–1972) who became guardian of Haig's son. Came out of retirement and was GOC-in-C Southern Command, 1940.

8 Blake, *op. cit.*

9 O.H. (Cambrai), p. 123.

10 Falls, *op. cit.*, p. 163

11 Wylly, *op. cit.*, p. 370.

12 *Ibid.*

13 Whitton, *op. cit.*

14 Falls, *op. cit.*, p. 163

15 O.H. (Cambrai).

16 *Ibid.*, p. 129.

17 Moody, *op. cit.*, p. 265.

18 Wyrall, *op. cit.* (62nd Div.), p. 103.

19 Wylly, *op. cit.*, p. 371, quoting Lieutenant-Colonel Bernard Granville Baker (1870–1957), CO 13th Green Howards. Educated at Dresden Military College; Commissioned into cavalry; attached 9th Prussian Hussars 1894–1900. Accomplished author and artist.

20 Whitton, *op. cit.*, pp. 97/98.
21 *Ibid.*
22 *Ibid.*, p. 95.
23 As per map attached to *Narrative of Ops of 51 Division*, PRO/WO 158/390.
24 Wylly, *op. cit.*
25 Whitton, *op. cit.*, p. 104.
26 *Ibid.*
27 Wylly, *op. cit.*, p. 372, quoting Lieutenant-Colonel Baker (see note 19 above).
28 De Pree, *op. cit.*, p. 233.
29 Falls, *op. cit.*, p. 164.
30 De Pree, as per note 28.
31 Accounts taken from operational reports of tank commanders.
32 De Pree, *op. cit.*, p. 229.
33 O.H. (Cambrai), p. 126.
34 *Ibid.*
35 See Fuller, *Decisive Battles of the Western World*, Paladin paperback edn, p. 368.
36 Relics still discernable.

Chapter Eleven   Ordeal of the HLI

1 Later Major-General Sir Geoffrey Percy Thynne Feilding (1866–1932). Joined army 1888: Coldstream Guards.
2 C. Headlam, *The Guards Division in the Great War*, Murray, 1924.
3 War Diary, 2nd Grenadier Guards.
4 Whitton, *op. cit.*, p. 101.
5 The 9th Colberg Grenadier (Von Gneisenau) Regiment led the counter-attack; they were formerly the 2nd Pomeranian Regiment.
6 Parnell, *op. cit.*
7 An announcement in the 'In Memoriam' column of *The Times* shortly afterwards read: 'To an UNKNOWN AIRMAN, shot down on 23rd November, 1917, whilst attacking a German strong-point south-west of Bourlon Wood, in the effort to help out a company of the Royal Irish Rifles, when other help had failed.'
8 Jones, *op. cit.*, p. 247.
9 O.H. (Cambrai), p. 134.
10 Parnell, *op. cit.*
11 De Pree, *op. cit.*, p. 229.
12 A Regular officer from the Scottish Rifles, possibly the Benzie referred to by Lord Reith in his account of service in France in 1915 – *Wearing Spurs*, Hutchinson, 1966.

13 Whitton, *op. cit.*, p. 111.
14 De Pree, *op. cit.*, p. 236.
15 Atkinson, *op. cit.*, p. 362.
16 *Ibid.*
17 Crozier (d. 1937) in a newspaper article in the 1930s. See also ref. in Moore, *The Thin Yellow Line*, Cooper, 1974.
18 De Pree, *op. cit.*, p. 236.
19 See Falls, *op. cit.*, and O.H. (Cambrai), p. 136.
20 Source; RHQ Royal Highland Fusiliers.
21 Whitton, *op. cit.*
22 De Pree, *op. cit.*, p. 237.
23 O.H. (Cambrai), p. 138.
24 *Ibid.*, p. 141.
25 Headlam, *op. cit.*, p. 301.
26 *Ibid.*
27 From Cahiers for 1916 (on the Somme) – '*Les troisièmes jours de batailles ne valent jamais rien*'.
28 Herbert Lawton Warden, partner in Hagart and Burn-Murdoch. Director of Pensions, Scotland, 1919.
29 Whitton, *op. cit.*
30 O.H. (Cambrai), p. 139.
31 Headlam, *op. cit.*, p. 303.

Chapter Twelve   Toll for the Brave

1 Wyrall, *op. cit.* (62nd Div.).
2 Atkinson, *op. cit.*
3 Wyrall *op. cit.* (62nd Div.).
4 From correspondence with the Central Council of Church Bellringers.
5 Williams, *op. cit.*
6 O.H. (Cambrai), p. 148.
7 See Haig's Official Despatches.
8 Headlam, *op. cit.*, vol. I, p. 295.
9 *Ibid.*, p. 53.
10 *Ibid.*, p. 307.
11 See Wyrall, *op. cit.* (62nd Div.).
12 Headlam, *op. cit.*, vol. I, pp. 308–9.
13 Wyrall, *op. cit.* (62nd Div.).
14 See Whitton, *op. cit.*
15 *Ibid.*, p. 143.
16 Falls, *op. cit.*, p. 167.

Chapter Thirteen   Greenhouse in a Hailstorm

1 See *History of the Sixth Tank Battalion*.
2 Wyrall, *op. cit.* (West Yorks Regt), p. 170.
3 *Ibid*.
4 R. Kipling, *The Irish Guards in the Great War*, vol. II, p. 178.
5 P. Verney, *The Micks*, London, 1970.
6 Headlam, *op. cit.*, vol. I, p. 313.
7 De Pree, *op. cit.*, p. 240.
8 Headlam, *op. cit.*, vol. I, p. 314.
9 De Pree, *op. cit.*
10 *Ibid*.
11 *Ibid.*, p. 241.
12 Headlam, *op. cit.*, vol. I, p. 320.
13 Frederick Henry Johnson (b. 1890), won his VC at Hill 70 in September, 1915. He came from Streatham, London.
14 Blake, *op. cit.*, p. 269.
15 O.H. (Cambrai), p. 372.
16 *Ibid*.
17 Jones, *op. cit.*, p. 248.
18 George William Clare born St Ives, Huntingdonshire, 1889, and brought up at Chatteris, Cambridgeshire.
19 O.H. (Cambrai), p. 175
20 See note 31, Chapter 3.
21 Later a lieutenant-general (1867–1945). Joined RE 1888. ADC to Kitchener in the Boer War. Severely wounded in Mesopotamia 1916.
22 Falls, *op. cit.*, p. 138.
23 Gillon, *op. cit.*, pp. 160–1.

Chapter Fourteen   Twenty-Two Ravine

1 Rutter, *op. cit.*
2 Later General Sir Beauvoir de Lisle (1864–1955). Served 20 years with DLI before transferring to the Royal Dragoons. Cavalry brigadier in 1914. Corps Commander 1918. Celebrated polo player and pony breeder.
3 Gillon, *op. cit.*, p. 169.
4 *Ibid*.
5 Parnell, *op. cit.*
6 Ludendorff, *op. cit.*, vol. II, p. 496.
7 See *The Gunner*, August 1919, p. 166.
8 Reduced from six to four guns by previous enemy action.

9 'Section' – two guns.
10 *The Gunner*, August 1919.
11 Gillon, *op. cit.*, p. 168.
12 Scott-Brumwell, *op. cit.*
13 He had served as an official observer with the Japanese in the war in Manchuria in 1904. Later knighted.
14 Scott-Brumwell, *op. cit.*, p. 148.
15 De Pree, *op. cit.*, p. 246.
16 *Ibid.*
17 Wyrall, *op. cit.* (DCLI), p. 309.
18 N. Lytton, *The Press and the General Staff*, London, 1921, pp. 131–2.
19 De Pree, *op. cit.*
20 See account in O'Neill, *The Royal Fusiliers in the Great War*, Heinemann, 1922.
21 Wyrall, *op. cit.* (DCLI), pp. 309–10.
22 1st/19th County of London (St Pancras) battalion. Served as RA in World War II.
23 1st/6th were the City of London Rifles; 1st/15th County of London, the Civil Service Rifles.
24 Prisoners taken from the German 55th Res. Inf. Regt stated later that there had been 'practically no resistance' at Lateau Wood. See intelligence reports attached to GHQ File OAD 731 in PRO Cambrai Enquiry file.
25 Gee (1876–1960), retired as a captain. Became Unionist MP for East Woolwich and later for Bosworth, Leics. Died in Australia.
26 See Atkinson, *op. cit.*
27 PRO WO 158/54.
28 Headlam, *op. cit.*, vol. II p. 6.
29 100th Siege Battery – see O.H. (Cambrai), p. 190.
30 Falls, *op. cit.*, p. 170.
31 Blake, *op. cit.*, p. 270.
32 According to the Brigade Narrative of Operations – 26 of the Liverpool Scottish, 94 of the 1st/5th King's Own and 26 of the 1st/5th Loyals.

Chapter Fifteen 'Draw swords . . . gallop!'

1 O.H. (Cambrai), p. 238.
2 Captain George Henry Tatham Paton, aged 22, was awarded the VC. He already had the MC. Born in Inellan, Argyllshire. Buried at Metz-en-Couture. See Headlam, *op. cit.*, vol. I, p. 273.
3 O.H. (Cambrai), p. 232.

4 *Ibid.*
5 Lance Dafadar Gobind Singh, 28th Cavalry, was awarded the VC.
6 O.H. (Cambrai), p. 237.
7 Gillon, *op. cit.*, p. 174.
8 Cheape (1881–1957), a Scot, had served four yers as a midshipman RN before joining the army. Retired to the Isle of Mull, 1919.
9 Gillon, *op. cit.*
10 O.H. (Cambrai), p. 245.
11 At 58 Fanshawe was two years younger than Woollcombe. Joined RA in 1878. Brigadier-General Gerald Boyd, his Chief Staff Officer, was 40.
12 O.H. (Cambrai), p. 305.
13 Atkinson, *op. cit.*, p. 368.
14 Captain Arthur Moore Lascelles (b. London 1880) was awarded the VC. He died in France a few days before the armistice. His family were connected with Penmaen Dyfi, Mon.
15 O.H. (Cambrai), p. 376.
16 Various, *The 23rd London Regiment 1914–1919*, Times Publishing 1936, p. 54.
17 *The Gunner*, August 1919.
18,19 ref. as per note 16 above.
20 Lieut. James Samuel Emerson, who came from Collon, Co. Drogheda, was awarded the VC posthumously. See Falls, *op. cit.*
21 Prigg, *op. cit.*
22 Whitton, *op. cit.*, p. 149.
23 Ludendorff, *op. cit.*
24 Headlam, *op. cit.*, vol. II, p. 14.
25 Falls, *op. cit.*
26 Jerrold, *op. cit.* p. 265.
27 Neither was in fact 'sent home'.

Chapter Sixteen Questions in the House

1 Blake, *op. cit.*, p. 270.
2 Lloyd George, *op. cit.*, p. 1338.
3 Prigg, *op. cit.*, pp. 308–10.
4 Quoted in Blake, *op. cit.*
5 Blake, *op. cit.*, p. 270.
6 Lloyd George, *op. cit.*, p. 1337.
7 Dillon (1851–1927), was a surgeon by profession.
8 Parliamentary Debates, Commons, 1917, vol. C.
9 Perhaps counting the Fontaine thrust as separate from the Bourlon and Banteux attacks.

10 Blake, *op. cit.*, p. 273.

11 Falls, *op. cit.*, p. 177.

12 Parliamentary Debates, Commons, Vol. C., p. 1623.

13 PRO WO/158/54 – copy of Third Army GS 56/244 of 18–12–17.

14 Joined Leinster Regiment 1901. Later Field-Marshal Sir John Dill (1881–1944). CIGS in 1940. Then to USA.

15 PRO WO 158/54.

16 Parliamentary Debates, Commons, Vol. C (20 December, 1917). Wedgwood directed machine guns from the bridge of the *River Clyde* during the Dardanelles landings.

17 PRO WO 158/54.

18 See 29th Division's Narrative of Operations.

19 OAD 731/3 in PRO WO 158/54.

20 As per Liddell Hart in *History of the First World War.*

21 In same PRO file as serials 15, 17 and 19, under 'Report Summarizing the operations between November 20th and December 7th, 1917', classified secret.

22 Jerrold, *op. cit.*, p. 270.

23 Major-General Sir Charles Edward Callwell (1859–1928). Joined RA 1878. Called from retirement to be Director of Military Operations, War Office, 1914. Assumed special duties in spring, 1917.

24 Special 'operations priority' telegram OAD 731/5 to Third Army, in PRO 158/54.

25 Retired as Lieutenant-General Sir Richard Hart Keatinge Butler (1870–1935). Joined Dorsetshire Regiment in 1890.

26 Copy on file in PRO WO 158/54.

27 Major-General Sir Arthur Binny Scott retired in 1920. Died 1944.

28 Copy of letter dated 20 December, 1917 on Cambrai Enquiry file in PRO. Hugh Sandham Jeudwine (1862–1942) joined RA 1882. In 1913 he was an instructor at the Staff College.

29 General Sir John Burnett-Stuart (1875–1958). Joined Rifle Brigade 1895. GOC in C Southern Command (1934–8).

30 The message went to the Chief of Staff, Major-General Vaughan.

31 Parliamentary Debates, Commons, vol. 101, 1918.

Chapter Seventeen   A Shell Hole in Glass Street

1 O.H. (Cambrai), p. 297.

2 PRO WO 158/53

3 Lieutenant-General Sir A. Hamilton Gordon (1859–1939). Ret. 1920.

4 Heneker Diary entry for 7 June 1917.

5 Later General Sir Ivor Maxse (1862–1958). Joined Royal Fusiliers 1882; transferred Coldstream Guards 1891.

6 Major-General (later Sir) Reginald John Pinney (1863–1943).

7 Record of evidence in PRO WO 158/53.

8 No battalions of the Devonshire Regiment were engaged at Cambrai in 1917.

9 Lord Derby, War Secretary, had a special interest in the 55th Division having been chairman of the West Lancashire Territorial Association since its formation in 1908.

10 Copy in PRO WO 158/54.

11 Lieut. J. Neil, 7th Argyll and Sutherland Highlanders.

12 Major Caddick-Adams.

13 Lieut. E. W. Pither, MC.

14 A belt contained 200 rounds.

15 From contemporary intelligence reports. The 6th Res. Inf. Regt attacked in the 20th Division's sector; the 109th in the 12th's.

16 David Davies (1880–1944). CO 14th Royal Welsh Fusiliers 1914–16.

17 Such as internal police disciplinary inquiries.

18 Referred to in *Hansard* as 'Mr' but presumably Lieutenant-Commander Henry Douglas King DSO (1877–1930), who had commanded the Drake Battalion of the Royal Naval Division at Gallipoli and in France. A new Member of the Commons in 1918 (North Norfolk), he was then serving directly under the Admiralty. This may have made it easier for him to criticize Haig. The same possibly applied to Wedgwood and Pemberton-Billing who were no longer inhibited by being attached to the Army.

19 Kennedy-Jones (1865–1921), Scottish journalist, was also co-founder of the *Daily Mirror*.

20 James Ian Macpherson (1880–1937), seems to have specialized in occupying unpleasant posts. He was Chief Secretary for Ireland 1919–20 and Pensions Minister 1920–22. Knighted in 1933 when Recorder of Southend. Baron Strathcarron 1936.

Chapter Eighteen   A Grumbling Appendix

1 Captain Tong, acting Brigade-Major, 166th Inf. Bde.

2 Captain J. Faulkner.

3 O.H. (Cambrai), p. 298.

4 Recorded in Cambrai Enquiry file.

5 John Frederick Andrew Higgins (1875–1948). Joined RA 1895. Air Officer Commanding India 1939–40.

6 See PRO WO 154/53.

7 O.H. (Cambrai) also refers to men who escaped after being taken prisoner.

8 Attached to copy of report in the PRO file.

9 Also attached.
10 AG memorandum to CGS – AG/940/PS on Cambrai file.
11 Mr A. A. Lynch on 30 January.
12 He became C-in-C Home Forces in June, being followed at Eastern Command by Woollcombe.
13 Jeudwine did not serve under Byng's command after the 55th left Third Army. The Division earned a glowing tribute from Haig for its defence of Givenchy in April, 1918. Jeudwine became a Lieutenant-General, was knighted and served as Director General of the TA 1923-7.
14 Noel Pemberton-Billing (1880–1948), Ind. East Herts, had served in the Boer War. With Royal Naval Air Service, 1914–16. Journalist and son of a Midlands industrialist.
15 Blake, *op. cit.*, p. 270.
16 VII Corps Narrative of Operations.
17 Rutter, *op. cit.*
18 In author's possession.
19 Gillon, *op. cit.*
20 O.H. (Cambrai), p. 297.
21 De Pree, *op. cit.*, quotes General Moser as saying the Caudry and Busigny groups were to advance with 'about 12 divisions' from the line Rumilly–Vendhuille, while his own Arras group struck towards Graincourt – 'most was expected from the southern attack'.

Chapter Nineteen Flesquières Again

1 The Second was renumbered Fourth when Plumer went to Italy and was replaced temporarily by Rawlinson. It became the Second again in mid-March on Plumer's return.
2 O.H. 1918, vol. I, p. 94.
3 Jerrold, *op. cit.*
4 *Ibid.*
5 J. H. Foulkes, *Gas! The Story of the Special Brigade*, Blackwoods 1934, p. 264
6 O.H. 1918, vol . I, p. 303.
7 O'Neill, *op. cit.*, p. 409.
8 *Ibid.*, p. 239.
9 Jerrold, *op. cit.*, p. 279.
10 O'Neill, *op. cit.*, p. 239.
11 Jerrold, *op. cit.*, p. 280.
12 Gough, *op. cit.*, p. 280.
13 O.H. 1918, vol. 1, p. 499.
14 The breech of one of two guns 'blew out' on 25 March. See O.H. 1918, vol. I, p. 327.

15 Mme de Francqueville's memories were still vivid in 1986.
16 Prince Rupprecht quoted in O.H. 1918, vol. IV, p. 467.

Chapter Twenty   Canadian Capers

1 Knighted in 1919. Sir Harry Lauder (1870–1950) had been 'an indefatigable recruiter'. Wrote *A Minstrel in France 1918*.
2 R. R. Thompson. *The 52nd Lowland Division 1914–1918*. Maclehose, 1923, p. 547.
3 O.H. 1918, vol. IV, p. 474.
4 *Ibid.*, p. 468.
5 In February 1918, though the change did not apply to Australian and Canadian divisions or the British divisions in Italy.
6 Braithwaite had been promoted to command a corps vice Hamilton Gordon (in ill health).
7 Sergeant Laurence Calvert, MM, was awarded the VC. He bayoneted three and shot four of the Germans manning the guns at the Boggart Hole (see Chapter 7). Born Hunslet, Leeds, 1892; died Dagenham, Essex, 1964.
8 The 52nd has lost heavily in Gallipoli and Palestine.
9 Corporal David Hunter, the section commander, was awarded the VC and all his men were decorated. Hunter was born at Kingseat, Dunfermline, 1891, and died in Dunfermline 1965.
10 See O.H. 1918, vol. V, p. 14.
11 *Ibid.*
12 Blake, *op. cit.*, p. 303.
13 Thompson, *op. cit.*, p. 550.
14 Father of Brigadier Sir Bernard Fergusson of World War II fame.
15 War Diary of 72nd Can. Inf. Bn – PRO WO 95/3908.
16 War Diary 11th Can. Inf. Bde – PRO WO 95/3900.
17 War Diary 75th Can. Inf. Bn – PRO WO 95/3903.
18 *Ibid.*
19 Report on the Operations of the 1st Canadian Division 1918, typescript in Imperial War Museum.
20 As 17 above.
21 War Diary 47th Can. Inf. Bn
22 *The First Canadian Division in the Battles of 1918*, London 1919. (IWM).
23 Pte Richard Bloor.
24 War Diary of 50th Can. Inf. Bn
25 Lieutenant-Colonel Thompson of the 124th Can. Pioneer Bn was in temporary command of the 75th.
26 O.H. 1918, vol. V.

27 See serial 22 above.

28 In words of the War Diary: 'golden spray shot.' 'Shot': ie fired.

29 War Diary 12th Can. Inf. Bde.

30 As per 19 above.

31 As per 17 above.

32 War Diary 102nd Can. Inf. Bn – PRO WO 95/3903.

33 Headlam, *op. cit.*, vol. II. Two VCs were awarded. One to Lance-Corporal Thomas Norman Jackson, who was killed the same day. The other went to Captain Cyril Frisby, who came from New Barnet, Herts, and died in 1961, aged 76.

34 He was awarded the VC. As Field-Marshal Lord Gort he commanded the BEF in 1940.

35 Prowse was born in Newton Abbot, Devon, 1895. Brought up at Gorseinon, Carmarthenshire, and Swansea.

36 Report of the Ministry – Overseas Military Forces of Canada 1918, HMSO, p. 159.

37 Unit war diaries.

38 The 75th's luck did not hold. In an attack on a sunken road near Haynecourt on the 30th their losses were: killed, seven officers and eighteen other ranks; wounded, seventeen officers and 270 other ranks; missing 67 all ranks.

39 Narrative of Operations 189 Inf. Bde.

40 War Diary Hood Bn.

41 Article in *Canadian Army Journal*, October, 1935 (Held by IWM).

Chapter Twenty-one   Boom Town.

1 Memoirs, *op. cit.*

2 *Ibid.*

3 Lieutenant-Colonel Williams saw active service in Europe in World War II and later in Korea.

4 Rutter, *op. cit.*

5 Even today Bourlon has only half the 1914 population of 2,000.

Chapter Twenty-two   Plus ça change

1 The car was recovered in excellent condition in autumn, 1944. It needed only a new battery.

2 A Luftwaffe police unit.

3 He had recovered from wounds received when he resisted arrest.

Chapter Twenty-three   Hand of Cards

1 Facts supplied by Monsieur Cattraux to Monsieur de Francqueville.

2 Facts supplied by Madame Lecat.

3 He died in December, 1945.

Chapter Twenty-four Rattle a Rib Cage

1 The senior West Riding division was the 49th.
2 See Appendix A.

Index

191, 209

Gouzeaucourt, crisis at, 147–8; recapture of, 152–3

Graincourt, capture of, 79; 'catacombs' riddle of, 234

Havrincourt, use of wood as hiding place, 56, 58, 61; bottleneck at, 82, 88, 98, 102; N.Z. troops enter, 205; fights for Boggart Hole, 70, 219; mentioned, 5, 7, 203

Hermies, 38

Hobart Trench, 106

Holzminden (prison camp), 14

Inchy-en-Artois, 211

Kildare Post, 157

Knoll, The, 78, 174

Kut-el-Amara, mentioned, 57

Lateau Wood, captured 72; lost, 151

Les Rues Vertes/Masnières, reached Nov. 1917, 74–6; crisis at, 150–1, 158

Limerick Post, defence of, 154

Louverval, 58

Lucheux, 96, 101

Marcoing, cavalry decision at, 76

Marquion, 78, 210–11

Masnières (see Les Rues Vertes) Metz-en-Couture, importance of, 145; also 153, 209

Moeuvres, Irish fight for in 1917, 89, 93, 105; Scots fight for in 1918, 209

Montreuil, 2, 19

Noyelles, 76; tactical importance of, 129

Ostrich Avenue Trench, 160

Ostrich Lane, 176

Oradour-sur-Glane, ref. to, 231

Paris, shelled by long-range guns, 204–5

Pelican Trench, 145

Péronne, as assembly point, 57, 138

Pézière-Épehy, cavalry action at, 155–7

Quarry Wood, 105–6, 118, 135, 213

Rat's Tail Trench, 149

Ravines

Banteux (Twenty-Two), 146–7, 150; Pigeon, 146, 154, 157; Quail, 146;

Targelle, 146, 157

Revelon Farm/Ridge, 148, 209

Ribécourt, 68, 72, 75

Round Trench, 106–7

Rue des Vignes, 151

Rumilly, assault on, 86; importance of, 129, 195; mentioned, 5

Sailly, bombardment of, 63

St Quentin, 6, 47, 53

St Quentin Canal, 38

Somain, bombing of, 113

Tadpole Copse, 93, 199

Thiepval, mentioned, 33

Trescault, 97

Vacqueriesha, 72, 161, 170, 197

Valenciennes, 5, 206

Villers-au-Flos, 128

Villers Guislain, Byng's description of, 170; Snow's warning about, 178; mentioned at Hesdin inquiry, 182–5; see also 146, 191, 195

Vimy Ridge, 16, 33, 70

Welsh Ridge, 160, 165, 176

Woking, Surrey, 40th Div. embark at, 96

GENERAL

A-A guns in anti-tank role, 101

Cambrai Despatch pub., 196

Casualties at Bourlon 1917, 163

Cathedrals ring victory peals, (St Paul's, Salisbury, Southwark), 126

'Catacombs', origins of, 239–40

Defence of the Realm Act (re bells), 125

Hesdin Inquiry, 181–5, 190–5; 'a sham', 220

Hindenburg Line, withdrawal to, 36–7; mentioned 65, 98, 207

Loos, Battle of, referred to, 46, 140–1, 219

Malplaquet, Battle of, ref. to, 1–2

Messines, Battle of, ref. to, 22

Mons, Battle of, ref. to, 8

Rum ration, 218

Shows mentioned, *Aladdin*, 177; *Chu Chin*